Paper F8

AUDIT AND ASSURANCE

EXAM KIT

PUBLISHING

British Library Cataloguing-in-Publication Data

A catalogue record for this book is available from the British Library.

Published by:

Kaplan Publishing UK

Unit 2 The Business Centre

Molly Millar's Lane

Wokingham

Berkshire

RG41 2QZ

ISBN: 978-1-78415-697-8

Acknowledgements

The past ACCA examination questions are the copyright of the Association of Chartered Certified Accountants. The original answers to the questions from June 1994 onwards were produced by the examiners themselves and have been adapted by Kaplan Publishing.

We are grateful to the Chartered Institute of Management Accountants and the Institute of Chartered Accountants in England and Wales for permission to reproduce past examination questions. The answers have been prepared by Kaplan Publishing.

CONTENTS

Section

Features in this edition

In addition to providing a wide ranging bank of real past exam questions, we have also included in this edition:

- An analysis of all of the recent new syllabus examination papers.

- Paper specific information and advice on exam technique.

- Our recommended approach to make your revision for this particular subject as effective as possible.

  This includes step by step guidance on how best to use our Kaplan material (Complete text, pocket notes and exam kit) at this stage in your studies.

- Enhanced tutorial answers packed with specific key answer tips, technical tutorial notes and exam technique tips from our experienced tutors.

- Complementary online resources including full tutor debriefs and question assistance to point you in the right direction when you get stuck.

You will find a wealth of other resources to help you with your studies on the following sites:

www.MyKaplan.co.uk

www.accaglobal.com/students/

Quality and accuracy are of the utmost importance to us so if you spot an error in any of our products, please send an email to mykaplanreporting@kaplan.com with full details.

Our Quality Co-ordinator will work with our technical team to verify the error and take action to ensure it is corrected in future editions.

INDEX TO QUESTIONS AND ANSWERS

INTRODUCTION

The majority of the questions within the kit are past ACCA exam questions, the more recent questions are labelled as such in the index. Where changes have been made to the syllabus, the old ACCA questions within this kit have been adapted to reflect the new style of paper and the new guidance. If changed in any way from the original version, this is indicated in the end column of the index below with the mark *(A)*.

Note that

The specimen paper is included at the end of the kit.

KEY TO THE INDEX

PAPER ENHANCEMENTS

We have added the following enhancements to the answers in this exam kit:

Key answer tips

All answers include key answer tips to help your understanding of each question.

Tutorial note

All answers include more tutorial notes to explain some of the technical points in more detail.

Top tutor tips

For selected questions, we walk through the answer giving guidance on how to approach the questions with helpful 'tips from a top tutor', together with technical tutor notes.

These answers are indicated with the 'footsteps' icon in the index.

ONLINE ENHANCEMENTS

 Timed question with Online tutor debrief

For selected questions, we recommend that they are to be completed under full exam conditions (i.e. properly timed in a closed book environment).

In addition to the examiner's technical answer, enhanced with key answer tips and tutorial notes in this exam kit, you can find an answer debrief online by a top tutor that:

- works through the question in full
- discusses how to approach the question
- discusses how to ensure that the easy marks are obtained as quickly as possible
- emphasises how to tackle exam questions and exam technique.

These questions are indicated with the 'clock' icon in the index.

SECTION A-TYPE QUESTIONS

SECTION B-TYPE QUESTIONS

Planning and risk assessment

Internal controls and audit evidence

KAPLAN PUBLISHING

ANALYSIS OF PAST PAPERS

The table below summarises the key topics that have been tested in the new syllabus examinations to date.

	Specimen	June 13	Dec 13	June 14	Dec 14	June 15	Sept/Dec 15
Audit Framework							
Audit vs. assurance engagements						✓	
Statutory audits							
Benefits/limitations of an audit							
The regulatory environment							
Corporate governance				✓			
Audit committee					✓		
Ethics	✓	✓	✓			✓	✓
Acceptance			✓				
Engagement letter							✓
Limited assurance engagements	✓					✓	
Internal Audit							
Scope/limitations	✓	✓					
Contrast with external audit	✓						
Outsourcing internal audit				✓			
Value for money				✓			
Planning and risk assessment							
Audit risk	✓	✓	✓	✓	✓	✓	✓
Analytical procedures	✓	✓					
Understanding the entity							✓
Materiality		✓					
Fraud & error					✓	✓	
Laws & regulations							
Audit strategy & plan	✓		✓				
Interim & final	✓			✓			
Audit documentation				✓			

	Specimen	June 13	Dec 13	June 14	Dec 14	June 15	Sept/Dec 15
Internal control							
Components						✓	
ICQs	✓						
Systems/tests of controls:							
– Revenue system	✓		✓		✓		
– Purchases system	✓	✓				✓	
– Payroll system				✓			✓
– Capital system	✓					✓	
– Inventory system							✓
– Cash system							
Systems documentation			✓				
IT controls	✓	✓					
Audit Evidence							
Definitions: tests of controls and substantive	✓		✓				
ISA 500 Audit procedures		✓					
Assertions	✓					✓	
Audit sampling				✓			
Sufficient appropriate evidence	✓	✓	✓				✓
Use of experts	✓		✓		✓		
Use of internal audit							
Estimates							
CAATs							
The audit of specific items:							
– Revenue					✓	✓	
– Purchases							
– Payroll				✓			✓
– Non-current assets	✓	✓	✓		✓		
– Trade receivables	✓		✓			✓	
– Inventory			✓	✓	✓		✓
– Bank		✓				✓	
– Trade payables						✓	
– Provisions	✓						

	Specimen	June 13	Dec 13	June 14	Dec 14	June 15	Sept/Dec 15
Completion & reporting							
Misstatements	✓			✓			
Final review			✓				
Subsequent events	✓	✓			✓		
Going concern	✓	✓		✓			✓
Written representations							
Audit reports/opinions	✓	✓	✓	✓	✓	✓	✓
Reporting to those charged with governance		✓					

EXAM TECHNIQUE

- At the beginning of the exam:
  - read the questions and examination requirements carefully, and
  - begin planning your answers.

- **Divide the time** you spend on questions in proportion to the marks on offer:
  - there are 1.95 minutes available per mark in the examination
  - within that, try to allow time at the end of each question to review your answer and address any obvious issues

  Whatever happens, always keep your eye on the clock and **do not over run on any part of any question.**

- **Objective test case questions:**
  - Don't leave any questions unanswered. If in doubt, guess.
  - Try and identify the correct answer.
  - If you can't identify the correct answer, try and rule out the wrong answers.

- Spend the last **five minutes** of the examination:
  - reading through your answers, and
  - **making any additions or corrections.**

- If you **get completely stuck** with a question leave space in your answer book, and **return to it later.**

- Stick to the question and **tailor your answer** to what you are asked.
  - pay particular attention to the verbs in the question.

- If you do not understand what a question is asking, **state your assumptions.**

  Even if you do not answer in precisely the way the examiner hoped, you may be given some credit, if your assumptions are reasonable.

- You should do everything you can to make things easy for the marker.

  The marker will find it easier to identify the points you have made if your **answers are legible.**

- **Written questions:**

  Your answer should:
  - Have a clear structure
  - Be concise: get to the point!
  - Address a broad range of points: it is usually better to write a little about a lot of different points than a great deal about one or two points.

- **Reports, memos and other documents:**

  Some questions ask you to present your answer in the form of a report, a memo, a letter or other document.

  Make sure that you use the correct format – there could be easy marks to gain here.

PAPER SPECIFIC INFORMATION

THE EXAM

FORMAT OF THE F8 EXAM

		Number of marks
Section A:	3 objective test case questions	
	5 questions worth 2 marks per case	30
Section B:	2 × 20 mark questions (mainly scenario based)	40
	1 × 30 mark question (mainly scenario based)	30
		100

Total time allowed: 3 hours and 15 minutes.

KAPLAN GUIDANCE

* F8 may be sat as a paper based exam or a computer based exam.

* All questions are compulsory.

* Any part of the syllabus can be tested in any section.

* Section A objective test questions will be based around a short scenario and you will have to choose the correct answer(s) from the options given.

* Section B will contain some knowledge based written questions. Requirements are typically 'list and explain', where you pick up ½ for listing the point and ½ for explaining it. Knowledge of ISAs is usually required in this question.

* The scenario based questions in Section B will require application of knowledge to the scenario provided. It is important you relate your answers to the scenario rather than just regurgitate rote-learned knowledge.

* For the scenario based questions it is important to read the information carefully and only use this information to generate your answers. There are unlikely to be any marks awarded to students creating their own scenario and generating answers from that.

Paper based exams

* **Skim through the whole paper**, assessing the level of difficulty of each question.

* **Write down** on the question paper next to the mark allocation **the amount of time you should spend on each part.** Do this for each part of every question.

* **Decide the order** in which you think you will attempt each question:

   This is a personal choice and you have time on the revision phase to try out different approaches, for example, if you sit mock exams.

   A common approach is to tackle the question you think is the easiest and you are most comfortable with first.

Others may prefer to tackle the longer questions first.

It is usual, however, that students tackle their least favourite topic and/or the most difficult question last.

Whatever your approach, you must make sure that you leave enough time to attempt all questions fully and be very strict with yourself in timing each question.

- **For each question** in turn, read the requirements and then the detail of the question carefully.

  Always read the requirement first as this enables you to **focus on the detail of the question with the specific task in mind**.

  For written questions:

  Take notice of the format required (e.g. letter, memo, notes) and identify the recipient of the answer . You need to do this to judge the level of sophistication required in your answer and whether the use of a formal reply or informal bullet points would be satisfactory.

  With F8, whilst there are occasions when you are requested to write a formal document, there are many times when you can use tables to present your answer. This is the case when you are asked to link answers together. Pay attention to the format of the answers in this text to help identify when such layouts are appropriate.

  Spot the easy marks to be gained in a question. Make sure that you do these parts first when you tackle the question.

- With your plan of attack in mind, **start answering your chosen question** with your plan to hand.

Computer based exams

- **Do not leave any questions unanswered**. Start by looking for the correct answer. If you are not sure which answer is correct, try working out which answers are incorrect so you are left with the correct answer. Otherwise – guess.

- **Highlight questions for review if you are not sure and want to check your answers before you end your exam.**

 Always keep your eye on the clock and do not over run on any part of any question!

PASS MARK

The pass mark for all ACCA Qualification examination papers is 50%.

DETAILED SYLLABUS

The detailed syllabus and study guide written by the ACCA can be found at:

www.accaglobal.com/students/

KAPLAN'S RECOMMENDED REVISION APPROACH

QUESTION PRACTICE IS THE KEY TO SUCCESS

Success in professional examinations relies upon you acquiring a firm grasp of the required knowledge at the tuition phase. In order to be able to do the questions, knowledge is essential.

However, the difference between success and failure often hinges on your exam technique on the day and making the most of the revision phase of your studies.

The **Kaplan complete text** is the starting point, designed to provide the underpinning knowledge to tackle all questions. However, in the revision phase, pouring over text books is not the answer.

Kaplan Online progress tests help you consolidate your knowledge and understanding and are a useful tool to check whether you can remember key topic areas.

Kaplan pocket notes are designed to help you quickly revise a topic area, however you then need to practice questions. There is a need to progress to full exam standard questions as soon as possible, and to tie your exam technique and technical knowledge together.

The importance of question practice cannot be over-emphasised.

The recommended approach below is designed by expert tutors in the field, in conjunction with their knowledge of the examiner and their recent real exams.

The approach taken for the fundamental papers is to revise by topic area. However, with the professional stage papers, a multi topic approach is required to answer the scenario based questions.

You need to practice as many questions as possible in the time you have left.

OUR AIM

Our aim is to get you to the stage where you can attempt exam standard questions confidently, to time, in a closed book environment, with no supplementary help (i.e. to simulate the real examination experience).

Practising your exam technique on real past examination questions, in timed conditions, is also vitally important for you to assess your progress and identify areas of weakness that may need more attention in the final run up to the examination.

In order to achieve this we recognise that initially you may feel the need to practice some questions with open book help and exceed the required time.

The approach below shows you which questions you should use to build up to coping with exam standard question practice, and references to the sources of information available should you need to revisit a topic area in more detail.

Remember that in the real examination, all you have to do is:

- attempt all questions required by the exam

- only spend the allotted time on each question, and

- get them at least 50% right!

Try and practice this approach on every question you attempt from now to the real exam.

EXAMINER COMMENTS

We have included the examiners comments to the specific new syllabus examination questions in this kit for you to see the main pitfalls that students fall into with regard to technical content.

However, too many times in the general section of the report, the examiner comments that students had failed due to:

- 'misallocation of time'

- 'running out of time' and

- showing signs of 'spending too much time on an earlier questions and clearly rushing the answer to a subsequent question'.

Good exam technique is vital.

THE KAPLAN PAPER F8 REVISION PLAN

Stage 1: Assess areas of strengths and weaknesses

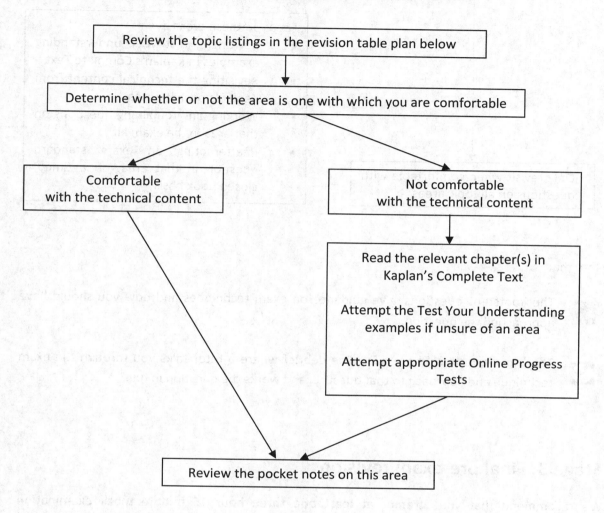

Review the topic listings in the revision table plan below

Determine whether or not the area is one with which you are comfortable

Comfortable with the technical content

Not comfortable with the technical content

Read the relevant chapter(s) in Kaplan's Complete Text

Attempt the Test Your Understanding examples if unsure of an area

Attempt appropriate Online Progress Tests

Review the pocket notes on this area

Stage 2: Practice questions

Follow the order of revision of topics as recommended in the revision table plan below and attempt the questions in the order suggested.

Try to avoid referring to text books and notes and the model answer until you have completed your attempt.

Try to answer the question in the allotted time.

Review your attempt with the model answer and assess how much of the answer you achieved in the allocated exam time.

Fill in the self-assessment box below and decide on your best course of action.

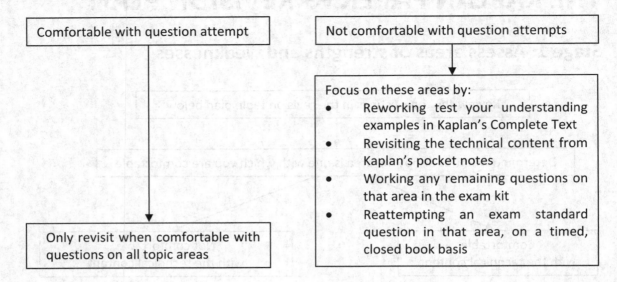

Comfortable with question attempt	Not comfortable with question attempts
	Focus on these areas by: • Reworking test your understanding examples in Kaplan's Complete Text • Revisiting the technical content from Kaplan's pocket notes • Working any remaining questions on that area in the exam kit • Reattempting an exam standard question in that area, on a timed, closed book basis
Only revisit when comfortable with questions on all topic areas	

Note that :

 The 'footsteps questions' give guidance on exam techniques and how you should have approached the question.

 The 'clock questions' have an online debrief where a tutor talks you through the exam technique and approach to that question and works the question in full.

Stage 3: Final pre-exam revision

We recommend that you **attempt at least one three hour 15 minute mock examination** containing a set of previously unseen exam standard questions.

It is important that you get a feel for the breadth of coverage of a real exam without advanced knowledge of the topic areas covered – just as you will expect to see on the real exam day.

Ideally this mock should be sat in timed, closed book, real exam conditions and could be:

• a mock examination offered by your tuition provider, and/or

• the specimen paper in the back of this exam kit, and/or

• the last real examination paper (available shortly afterwards on MyKaplan).

KAPLAN'S DETAILED REVISION PLAN

Topics	Complete Text (and Pocket Note) Chapter	Questions to attempt	Tutor guidance	Date attempted	Self-assessment
1 Audit framework and regulation	1, 2, 3, 11, 12	165 167 169	You must also be able to discuss the purpose of assurance and the levels of assurance offered by accountants. Make sure that you can define the elements of the Code of Ethics and that you practice applying the concepts to specific scenarios. Internal audit questions tend to focus on: differences between internal and external auditors; how internal and external auditors interact; considerations before establishing an internal audit department; and advantages and disadvantages of outsourcing internal audit. You need to be able to identify and explain the main requirements of corporate governance regulations (e.g. UK Corporate Governance Code) and be able to identify when a company is not compliant with best practise.		
2 Planning and risk assessment	4 & 5	142 144 146 148	Audit risk is a vital concept. You need to be able to: discuss what it is, including materiality; perform risk assessment for a client; and discuss its impact on audit strategy.		

KAPLAN PUBLISHING

3	Internal controls	7	149 150 153 154	You need to know how a simple financial control system (e.g. sales, purchases, payroll etc.) operates. You may be asked to identify deficiencies in control systems and provide recommendations. You need to be able to state how those systems and controls should be tested, including CAATs.	
4	Audit evidence	6 & 8	159 160 161	It is vital that you are able to identify **specifically** what procedures are required (e.g. tests of control, analytical procedures) and what assertions are being tested (e.g. completeness, existence, accuracy) for a particular balance or issue given.	
5	Review and reporting	9 & 10	170 171 172 173	There are a wide range of issues that need to be considered at the completion phase of an audit. Typical examples include: subsequent events, going concern, written representations and evaluation of misstatements. It is important that you are able to assess a scenario and identify how it might impact upon your audit report and opinion. You also need to be able to discuss the content and purpose of the sections of an audit report. You also need to be able to identify matters which should be reported to those charged with governance.	

You should practise a selection of OT case questions from Section A of the exam kit.

Section 1

OBJECTIVE TEST CASE QUESTIONS

AUDIT FRAMEWORK

The following scenario relates to questions 1 – 5

Hummingbird Co (Hummingbird) is a retail company planning to list on a stock exchange within the next six months, and management has been advised by the company's auditors about the need for compliance with corporate governance provisions. The finance director has two potential non-executive directors whom he is considering approaching to join the board of Hummingbird. Andrew Finch is currently an executive sales director of a listed multi-national banking company; he sits on an audit committee of another company as a non-executive director and is agreeable to being paid a fixed fee which is not related to profits. Jack Macaw is currently a finance director of a small retail company, which does not compete with Hummingbird; he has expressed an interest in a fixed seven year contract and he is the brother of Hummingbird's chief executive. Hummingbird is aware that it will need to establish an audit committee to comply with corporate governance best practice.

1   Which of the following best describes the aim of corporate governance?

   A   To ensure companies are well run in the interests of their shareholders and the wider community

   B   To ensure company directors cannot commit fraud

   C   To ensure the wealth of companies contributes to the health of the economies where their shares are traded

   D   To ensure companies have a positive impact on the local community and environment   **(2 marks)**

2   Which other committees other than an audit committee are required to comply with the UK Corporate Governance Code?

   A   Controls, Remuneration and Nomination committees

   B   Risk and Financial Reporting committees

   C   Nomination and Risk committees

   D   Nomination and Remuneration committees   **(2 marks)**

3 Which of the follow are advantages of appointing Andrew Finch as a NED of Hummingbird?

(1) Andrew is independent of Hummingbird

(2) Andrew's experience in banking will complement the experience of the Hummingbird board

(3) Andrew is prepared to accept a fixed fee

(4) Andrew is not demanding a fixed term contract

A 1, 2 and 3 only

B 2 and 4 only

C 1, 3 and 4 only

D All of them **(2 marks)**

4 Which of the follow are advantages of appointing Jack Macaw as a NED of Hummingbird?

(1) Jack has close links to Hummingbird's chief executive

(2) Jack's experience in retail will help him understand issues faced by the Hummingbird

(3) Jack's financial experience will be useful if he serves on the audit committee

(4) Jack wishes to commit to a seven year contract

A 1, 3 and 4 only

B 2 and 3 only

C 1, 2 and 4 only

D All of them **(2 marks)**

5 Which of the following are roles of an audit committee?

(1) To prepare the financial statements to ensure they give a true and fair view

(2) To develop a policy on the engagement and remuneration of external auditors

(3) To implement effective financial reporting internal controls

(4) To monitor and review the effectiveness of the internal audit function

A 1 and 2 only

B 1, 2 and 4

C 2 and 3

D 2 and 4 only **(2 marks)**

The following scenario relates to questions 6 – 10

Nicholas Harvey Co operates a chain of 18 department stores located across the country selling quality goods. In the past year, senior management have noticed an increased level of cash discrepancies and inventory discrepancies, and they suspect that some employees have been stealing cash and goods from the company. Senior management are considering whether an internal audit department should be established. They would like the internal audit department to have as broad a role as possible, as this will make the decision to establish an internal audit department more cost effective. The board has received a proposal from the finance director to establish an internal audit department. There are two options to consider – firstly an in-house function and secondly to outsource the function to a large accountancy and assurance firm.

6   Which of the following statements, if any, is/are correct?

(1)   Internal auditors should report to the finance director as they understand internal controls and are best placed to implement any recommendations in a timely manner

(2)   Companies are not required to establish and maintain an internal audit function

A   1 only

B   2 only

C   Both 1 and 2

D   Neither 1 nor 2

(2 marks)

7   Which of the following is NOT a function that an internal audit department at Nicholas Harvey Co could undertake?

A   Implementation of changes to financial control system deficiencies recommended by the internal auditor

B   Mystery shopper reviews to assess customer satisfaction levels

C   Value for money assessments in areas such as procurement

D   Testing of regulatory compliance including health and safety, food hygiene and fire prevention

(2 marks)

8   Which of the following are advantages of outsourcing the internal audit function?

(1)   The outsourced firm will have a greater awareness of the client's business risks

(2)   It improves independence

(3)   The risk of staff turnover is passed to the outsourcing firm

(4)   Greater flexibility and availability of the internal audit staff

A   2 and 4

B   1 and 2

C   2 and 3

D   3 and 4

(2 marks)

9   Which of the following is NOT a way in which the new internal audit department of Nicholas Harvey Co could assist the directors in respect of fraud and error?

    A   When fraud is detected the internal auditor could lead the subsequent investigation

    B   The internal audit team will instigate disciplinary proceedings against suspected fraudsters

    C   The internal audit team will have a deterrent effect around the business

    D   The internal auditor could perform random cash counts and inventory counts across the company's stores   **(2 marks)**

10   Which of these are limitations of establishing an internal audit function at Nicholas Harvey Co?

    (1)   As the scope of the internal audit work is determined by senior management there is a risk that management divert attention away from areas of the business known to contain deficiencies

    (2)   There is no requirement for internal auditors to be professionally qualified

    (3)   There may be resistance from employees of the company

    (4)   The costs of establishing the function may outweigh the benefits gained

    A   1, 2 and 3 only

    B   2 and 3 only

    C   2, 3 and 4 only

    D   All of them   **(2 marks)**

The following scenario relates to questions 11 – 15

You are an audit senior of Bark & Co and have been allocated to the audit of Foliage Co (Foliage), a listed company which has been an audit client for eight years and specialises in manufacturing musical instruments. Jane Leaf was the audit engagement partner for Foliage and as she had completed seven years as the audit engagement partner, she has recently been rotated off the audit engagement. The current audit partner has suggested that in order to maintain a close relationship with Foliage, Jane Leaf should undertake the role of independent review partner this year. The total fees received by Bark & Co for last year amounted to 16% of the firm's total fee income. The current year's total fee income for audit, non-audit and tax services is expected to be greater than last year. The audit manager for Foliage has just announced that he is leaving Bark & Co to join Foliage as the financial controller.

11   Which of the following best describes a conceptual framework approach to ethics?

    A   A set of laws for the auditor to follow

    B   A set of rules which must be strictly applied

    C   A set of guidelines which the auditor can choose to apply at their own discretion

    D   A set of guidelines with which the auditor uses judgment to apply to specific circumstances   **(2 marks)**

12 **Which TWO of the following are fundamental principles as stated in the ACCA's Code of Ethics and Conduct?**

(1)   Objectivity

(2)   Independence

(3)   Confidentiality

(4)   Professional scepticism

A   1 and 3

B   3 and 4

C   1 and 2

D   2 and 4   **(2 marks)**

13 **What is the most appropriate response to the suggestion that Jane Leaf takes on the role of independent review partner?**

A   Jane Leaf could take the review role immediately

B   Jane Leaf could take the review role immediately but additional safeguards will be required

C   Jane Leaf should not serve as the independent review partner for a period of at least two years

D   Bark & Co will need to consider resigning as auditors of Foliage   **(2 marks)**

14 **Which is the LEAST appropriate response with regard to fee income received by Bark & Co from Foliage?**

A   Bark & Co should assess whether audit and non-audit fees would represent more than 15% of gross practice income for two consecutive years.

B   If the recurring fees are likely to exceed 15% of annual practice income this year Bark will need to resign as auditors of Foliage.

C   If the recurring fees are likely to exceed 15% of annual practice income this year, additional consideration should be given as to whether the taxation and non-audit assignments should be undertaken by the firm.

D   If the fees do exceed 15% then this should be disclosed to those charged with governance at Foliage.   **(2 marks)**

15 **Which ethical threat/threats will be created as a result of the audit manager leaving to join the client?**

(1)   Self-Interest

(2)   Familiarity

(3)   Confidentiality

(4)   Self-review

A   2 only

B   1 and 4

C   2 and 3

D   4 only   **(2 marks)**

The following scenario relates to questions 16 – 20

You are the audit manager of Miranda & Co and you are planning the audit of Milberry Co, which has been an audit client for four years and specialises in manufacturing luxury handbags. The audit senior has recently resigned and is now employed as financial controller of Milberry. During the planning stage of the audit you have obtained the following information. The employees of Milberry Co are entitled to purchase handbags at a discount of 40%. The audit team has been offered the same level of staff discount. From a review of the correspondence file you note that the partner and the finance director have known each other socially for many years and in fact went on holiday together last summer with their families. As a result of this friendship the partner has not yet spoken to the client about the fee for last year's audit, 20% of which is still outstanding.

16 **Which of the following threats to objectivity does the resignation of the audit senior and subsequent employment with Milberry create?**

(1)   Familiarity

(2)   Self-review

A   1 only

B   2 only

C   Both 1 and 2

D   Neither 1 nor 2   **(2 marks)**

17 **Which of the following threats to objectivity does the offer of the discount create?**

(1)   Self-interest

(2)   Self-review

(3)   Advocacy

A   1 only

B   2 and 3 only

C   1 and 2 only

D   All of them   **(2 marks)**

18 Which is the MOST appropriate response with respect to the discount by the audit team?

A   The discount may be accepted as it is the same as that offered to the client's employees

B   The discount should be rejected as it is not a modest monetary amount

C   The discount should be rejected as gifts or hospitality are not acceptable per the ACCA Code of Ethics

D   Audit manager approval must be obtained before the discount is accepted

(2 marks)

19 Which of the following threats to objectivity does the review of the correspondence file identify?

(1)   Self-interest

(2)   Intimidation

(3)   Advocacy

(4)   Familiarity

A   1, 2 and 3

B   1, 3 and 4

C   1, 2 and 4

D   All of them

(2 marks)

20 Which is the most appropriate response to the outstanding fees?

A   The auditor should resign from the client

B   The auditor should report the client to the ACCA

C   The auditor can continue working for the client but should ensure that the audit firm's credit control department are informed of the outstanding fees

D   No work should be performed until either payment is made or a repayment plan agreed

(2 marks)

The following scenario relates to questions 21 – 25

This objective test case question contains question types which will only appear in a computer-based exam, but this question provides valuable practice for all students whichever version of the exam they are taking

You are an audit manager in Tigger & Co, a large audit firm which specialises in the audit of car manufacturers. The firm currently audits Winnie Co but Winnie's main competitor, Piglet Co, has approached the audit firm to act as auditor. Both companies are highly competitive and Winnie is concerned that if Tigger & Co audits both companies then confidential information could be given to Piglet. The audit engagement partner for Winnie Co has been in place for approximately six years. Winnie Co has approached Tigger & Co to provide internal audit services as well as the external audit. They have suggested that the external audit fee should be renegotiated with at least 20% of the fee being based on the profit after tax of the company as they feel that this will align the interests of Tigger & Co and Winnie Co.

21   Which of the following is true in respect of confidential information?

A   Confidential information is any information about a company which is not publicly available

B   Confidential information is any information contained within the accounting records or financial statements of a client

C   A member of the audit team of Winnie Co may discuss matters with other employees of the audit firm provided they are not involved with the audit of Piglet Co

D   The primary reason of an accountancy firm maintaining confidentiality is to prevent being sued   **(2 marks)**

22   Which of the following is NOT an action that your firm should take to manage the conflict of interest?

A   Regular monitoring of safeguards by an independent review partner

B   Require every employee of Tigger & Co to sign a confidentiality agreement

C   Use separate engagement teams with different engagement partners

D   Operate secure data filing of all audit information   **(2 marks)**

23   Are the following statements true or false?

A familiarity threat arises where an engagement partner is associated with a client for a long period of time.	True	False
Contingent audit fees are acceptable if appropriate safeguards are implemented.	True	False
Being appointed internal as well as external auditors will create a confidentiality threat.	True	False

(2 marks)

24 Which TWO of the following statements relating to internal and external auditors are correct?

A   Internal auditors are required to be members of a professional body

B   The internal auditors' scope of work should be determined by those charged with governance

C   External auditors address their audit report to those charged with governance

D   Internal auditors can never be independent of the company

E   Internal auditors should implement any changes to internal controls that the recommend

F   External auditors will assess the effectiveness of a client's internal controls as part of the audit process

(2 marks)

25 For which TWO of the following situations should an auditor make VOLUNTARY disclosure of confidential information?

A   If an auditor knows or suspects his client is engaged in money laundering

B   Where disclosure is made to non-governmental bodies

C   Where it is in the public interest to disclose

D   If an auditor suspects his client has committed terrorist offences

(2 marks)

The following scenario relates to questions 26 – 30

This objective test case question contains question types which will only appear in a computer-based exam, but this question provides valuable practice for all students whichever version of the exam they are taking

Cameron Co (Cameron) has recently become a listed company. Cameron is required to comply with corporate governance principles in order to maintain its listed status; hence the finance director has undertaken a review of compliance with corporate governance regulations. Mr Osbourne is the chairman of Cameron and is also the chief executive. Cameron's board of directors comprises of six members, two of which are independent non-executive directors. Mr Osbourne is considering appointing one of his close friends as a non-executive director. The remuneration of each director is decided by Mr Osbourne.

---

26 Corporate governance is the system by which companies are directed and controlled. Boards of directors are responsible for the governance of their companies. The role of the _____ in governance is to appoint the directors and the auditors and to satisfy themselves that an appropriate governance structure is in place. The responsibilities of the _____ include setting the company's strategies, providing the leadership to put those strategies into effect and supervising the management of the business.

Select the appropriate word to complete the sentence above.

A   Chairman

B   Shareholders

C   Stakeholders

D   Board

E   Non-executives

F   Executives

(2 marks)

27 Which **FOUR** of the following statements are benefits to Cameron of forming an audit committee?

A If the finance director chairs the committee, this will ensure detailed knowledge of the finance department is available, increasing its effectiveness

B Quality of financial reporting should be improved

C Liaison with the external audit firm will ensure its independence

D Internal control awareness will be enhanced within Cameron

E Internal audit function effectiveness will increase through independent reporting lines

F External risks faced by the business will be reduced **(2 marks)**

28 For each of the following issues decide whether the matter is a corporate governance strength or weakness?

	Strength	Deficiency
Mr Osbourne is the chairman and chief executive of Cameron		
All of the current NEDs are independent		
The finance director will head the newly formed audit committee		
The remuneration of each director is decided by Mr Osbourne		

(2 marks)

29 For each of the following issues match the appropriate response.

Issue		Response	
1	The board is not balanced	A	An audit committee should be set up immediately
2	Mr Osbourne is considering appointing his friend as a non-executive director	B	Remuneration of executive directors should be performance related
		C	Appointment of non-executives should be based on experience
		D	Appoint two more non-executive directors
		E	Reduce the number of executive directors on the board

(2 marks)

30 **Which TWO of the following are NOT principles of the UK Corporate Governance Code?**

A There should be a rigorous and transparent procedure for the appointment of new directors to the board.

B The board should use the AGM to communicate with shareholders.

C A risk committee must be established to ensure effective risk management systems are established.

D The non-executive chairman should decide on the remuneration of executive directors.

E All directors should receive induction training on joining the board.

F All directors should receive regular training to ensure they maintain their skills and knowledge. **(2 marks)**

The following scenario relates to questions 31 – 35

This objective test case question contains question types which will only appear in a computer-based exam, but this question provides valuable practice for all students whichever version of the exam they are taking

Paramore Co has recently approached your firm to request an audit. This is the first year they have met the size threshold for audit requirement. The directors are unsure of the audit process and regulations governing an audit and have asked for some information.

---

31 **Select whether the following statements are true or false.**

	True	False
An audit must be performed in accordance with International Standards on Auditing		
International Standards on Auditing are legal requirements		
Where there is a difference between the requirements of an ISA and local law, local law should be followed		
Before an ISA is issued an Exposure Draft must first have been published		

(2 marks)

32 **For each of the following, state whether they are benefits or limitations of having an audit.**

	Benefit	Limitation
An audit may highlight deficiencies in internal controls which will be communicated to management		
An audit provides management with assurance that they have prepared their financial statements in accordance with the appropriate financial reporting framework		
Sampling will be used		
Evidence is persuasive rather than conclusive		

(2 marks)

33 Choose whether the following are rights of the auditor, duties of the auditor or neither.

	Right	Duty	Neither
Attend board meetings of the company			
Access to all books and records of the company			
Provide an opinion on the financial statements			
Receive notice of general meetings of the company			

(2 marks)

34 Which of the following is NOT a reason for following International Standards of Auditing?

A   To provide guidance to auditors

B   To enable consistency of audits across different firms and countries

C   To ensure all audit opinions issued are correct

D   To provide assurance to users that the audit has been performed to a required standard **(2 marks)**

35 Which of the following statements is NOT true in respect of who may act as auditor?

A   An auditor must be a member of a recognised supervisory body

B   A director or employee of the company cannot act as auditor

C   An auditor must have ten years' post qualification experience before being allowed to sign an audit report

D   Auditors must consider if there are any ethical reasons that would prohibit them acting as auditor to a company **(2 marks)**

PLANNING AND RISK ASSESSMENT

The following scenario relates to questions 36 – 40

You are planning the audit of Veryan Co. This is the first year your firm has audited Veryan Co.

At the first planning meeting you confirm that Veryan Co provides outsourced finance services for companies operating in the oil & gas exploration industry. It has been in existence for 10 years and has grown its revenue at an average of 12% per annum.

---

36   Which of the following would an auditor not obtain an understanding of at the planning stage?

A   Laws and regulations applicable to the entity

B   Events after the reporting period/subsequent events

C   Financing structure of the entity

D   Accounting policies used by the entity   **(2 marks)**

37   Which of the following is an appropriate auditor's response during the planning stage to the lack of cumulative audit knowledge and experience?

A   Extended controls testing should be performed.

B   More time and resource will need to be allocated to the audit in order to obtain an understanding of Veryan Co.

C   Reduce reliance on tests of controls.

D   Consideration should be given to relying on an independent expert   **(2 marks)**

During your planning meeting you were informed that the forecasted profit for this financial year was $8.4m based on revenues of $124m.

38   Which of the following would NOT be a possible materiality level for the audit of Veryan Co?

A $110,000

B $450,000

C $750,000

D $1m   **(2 marks)**

39   Which TWO of the following should be included in an audit engagement letter?

(1)   Objective and scope of the audit

(2)   Results of previous audits

(3)   Management's responsibilities

(4)   The need to maintain professional scepticism

A   1 and 2

B   2 and 4

C   3 and 4

D   1 and 3   **(2 marks)**

---

40 Which is of the following DOES NOT explain the term 'professional scepticism'?

    A   Assuming there is fraud or error unless evidence proves otherwise

    B   An open and questioning mind

    C   A critical evaluation of the evidence

    D   Being alert to conditions which indicate fraud   **(2 marks)**

The following scenario relates to questions 41 – 45

Flute Co (Flute) is a large mobile phone company which operates a network of stores in countries across Europe. The company's year end is 30 June. Flute is a new audit client and you are currently planning the audit in accordance with International Standards on Auditing (ISAs). You have been provided with planning notes from the audit partner following his meeting with the finance director:

During the year the company introduced a bonus based on sales for its sales persons. The bonus target was based on increasing the number of customers signing up for 24-month phone line contracts. This has been successful and revenue has increased by 15%, especially in the last few months of the year. The level of receivables is considerably higher than last year and there are concerns about the creditworthiness of some customers.

You are to undertake a preliminary analytical review of the draft financial statements and have been provided with the following information:

Revenue	$1,267,000
Cost of sales	$1,013,000
Receivables	$121,000
Payables	$87,500
Inventory	$60,000
Cash	$123,000

41 Which of the following statements relating to International Standards on Auditing (ISAs), if any, is/are correct?

    (1)   International Standards on Auditing (ISAs) are issued by the International Accounting Standards Board (IASB) and provide guidance on the performance and conduct of an audit

    (2)   In the event that ISAs differ from local legislation in a specific country, auditors must comply with the requirements of the ISAs

    A   Neither 1 nor 2

    B   Both 1 and 2

    C   1 only

    D   2 only   **(2 marks)**

42   Which of the following is an appropriate explanation of the audit risk relating to the bonus for its sales persons?

A   There is an increased risk of a reduction in profit for the company as a result of irrecoverable debts

B   There is an increased risk of inappropriate cut-off of revenue

C   There is an increased risk of understatement of revenue

D   There is an increased risk of non-response from customers following direct confirmation audit testing   **(2 marks)**

43   Which TWO of the following statements regarding the use of analytical procedures during the planning stage of the audit are correct?

(1)   Analytical procedures are useful when forming an overall conclusion as to whether the financial statements are consistent with the auditor's understanding of the company

(2)   Analytical procedures can be used to obtain relevant and reliable audit evidence

(3)   Analytical procedures can assist in identifying the risks of material misstatement

(4)   Analytical procedures can assist in identifying unusual transactions and events

A   1 and 2

B   2 and 3

C   3 and 4

D   1 and 4   **(2 marks)**

44   Which of the following is NOT an appropriate audit response to the increased risk of irrecoverable debts?

A   Extend cut-off testing

B   Review controls over the collection of debts to assess the effectiveness of the credit control function

C   Discuss receivable balances over 90 days old with the finance director to assess the adequacy of allowance for receivables

D   Extend post year-end cash receipts testing   **(2 marks)**

45   Using the figures provided, calculate the following ratios to one decimal place.

Receivables days	
Payables days	
Inventory days	
Quick ratio	

(2 marks)

The following scenario relates to questions 46 – 50

You are a manager in Spring & Co. You are reviewing the audit file of Autumn Co which is nearing completion. You have noted several issues during your review. Several working papers have not been signed as reviewed. You are aware that a review has taken place but it is not documented on the audit file. One audit working paper states that a sample of 30 purchase invoices should be tested but the results of the test show that only 25 invoices were tested. Several other areas document that samples sizes were reduced in order to save time. In the subsequent events review section of the file, the audit senior has documented that they have enquired of management whether there have been any subsequent events and were told that there have not been any. No further work was considered necessary as a result.

46   Which of the following is NOT a reason for having quality standards such as ISQC 1 and ISA 220 which auditors must follow?

     A   To reduce the risk of issuing an inappropriate audit opinion

     B   To maintain confidence in the audit process and audit profession

     C   To increase the amount of regulation for auditors to follow

     D   To protect the firm's reputation and minimises the risk of lawsuits brought against the audit firm   **(2 marks)**

47   Which of the following statements are true in respect of review of audit working papers?

     A   All team members' work should be reviewed by someone of manager level or above

     B   All team members' work should be reviewed by the audit partner

     C   All team members' work should be reviewed by someone other than the preparer

     D   All team members' work should be reviewed by someone more senior   **(2 marks)**

48   Which of the following statements are true in respect of the reduction in samples sizes?

     (1)   The audit plan has not been followed

     (2)   Sufficient appropriate evidence may not have been obtained

     (3)   Material misstatements may go undetected

     (4)   Those sections will need to be reviewed by a manager and the manager will form a conclusion on the balances.

     A   1, 2 and 3 only

     B   2 and 4 only

     C   1, 3 and 4 only

     D   All of the above   **(2 marks)**

49 **Which of the following statements is true in respect of the audit of subsequent events for Autumn Co?**

(1)   Enquiry does not provide sufficient appropriate evidence on its own

(2)   The auditor has demonstrated a lack of professional scepticism

(3)   A written representation should have been obtained from management confirming that they have disclosed all subsequent events to the auditor

(4)   The auditor only needs to perform procedures if they are made aware of any subsequent events

A   1 and 2 only

B   1, 2 and 3 only

C   3 and 4 only

D   All of the above

(2 marks)

50 **As a result of the quality control issues encountered during the audit of Autumn Co, which of the following actions should now be taken?**

(1)   The offending members of staff have demonstrated a lack of competence and due care therefore the firm should report them to the ACCA to be disciplined for failing to comply with the Code of Ethics

(2)   More frequent quality control reviews may need to take place

(3)   Further training may be provided to staff

(4)   The firm's policies and procedures may need to be updated

A   1 and 2 only

B   1 and 3 only

C   2, 3 and 4 only

D   All of the above

(2 marks)

The following scenario relates to questions 51 – 55

This objective test case question contains question types which will only appear in a computer-based exam, but this question provides valuable practice for all students whichever version of the exam they are taking

You are the audit senior planning the audit of Epica Co (Epica) for the year ended 31 March 20X3. Your audit manager has held a planning meeting with the finance director and has provided you with the following notes of his meeting and financial statement extracts:

Epica have experienced difficult trading conditions this year which has resulted in sales prices being reduced. Despite this, revenue has continued to fall. In an attempt to improve profit, Epica has switched to a cheaper supplier which has resulted in lower quality goods being purchased and a corresponding increase in returns from customers. During the year the directors have increased the useful life of tangible non-current assets which has resulted in a lower depreciation charge for the year.

Financial statement extracts for year ended 31 March

	DRAFT 20X3 $m	ACTUAL 20X2 $m
Revenue	12.5	15.0
Cost of sales	(7.0)	(8.0)
Gross profit	5.5	7.0
Operating expenses	(5.0)	(5.1)
Profit before interest and taxation	0.5	1.9
Inventory	1.9	1.4
Receivables	3.1	2.0
Cash	0.8	1.9
Trade payables	1.6	1.2
Loan	1.0	–

51 Using the financial information calculate the following ratios to 1 decimal place for both financial periods. Enter the answer into the relevant box.

	20X3	20X2
Gross margin		
Operating margin		

(2 marks)

52 Using the financial information calculate the following ratios for both financial periods. Enter the answer into the relevant box in round days (no decimal places).

	20X3	20X2
Receivables days		
Payables days		

(2 marks)

53 Which THREE of the following describe audit risks that should be addressed during the audit of Epica?

A   Inventory may be overstated if sales prices have fallen below cost

B   Provisions for the return of goods may be understated

C   Epica have experienced difficult trading conditions causing revenue to fall

D   Sales prices have been reduced which will impact profitability

E   Lower quality goods have been purchased resulting in complaints from customers

F   Inventory may be misstated if returned goods have not been recorded back into inventory   **(2 marks)**

54 Which TWO of the following describe an appropriate audit response to the audit risk related to the increase in the useful economic life of tangible non-current assets?

A   There is a risk that tangible non-current assets are overvalued if the change in useful economic life is not appropriate.

B   Discuss with the directors the reason for the change in useful life.

C   Compare the actual useful life of tangible non-current assets recently disposed of to the new depreciation policy to assess whether this reflects the actual useful economic life.

D   Compare the fixtures and fittings depreciation rate this year to last year.   **(2 marks)**

55 State whether the following explanations of the terms 'risk of material misstatement' and 'performance materiality' are true or false?

	True	False
Risk of material misstatement The risk that the financial statements are materially misstated prior to audit. This consists of two components – inherent risk and control risk		
Performance materiality The amount set by the auditor at less than materiality for the financial statements as a whole to reduce to an appropriately low level the probability that the aggregate of uncorrected and undetected misstatements exceeds materiality for the financial statements as a whole		

(2 marks)

INTERNAL CONTROLS

The following scenario relates to questions 56 – 60

You are the audit senior for the audit of Coastal Co. The internal control systems are currently being tested. You are reviewing the audit junior's documentation of the purchases and payroll cycle. The audit junior has used narrative notes and an internal control questionnaire to document the system.

56 **Which of the following components of an internal control system is not correctly explained?**

A **Control environment:** The control environment includes the governance and management functions and the attitudes, awareness, and actions of those charged with governance and management concerning the entity's internal control and its importance in the entity.

B **Control activities:** Control activities are the policies and procedures that help ensure that management directives are carried out.

C **Risk assessment:** Risk assessment is the engagement of independent third party experts to assess the risk management processes and procedures in place in an organisation and to provide a written report on system deficiencies with appropriate recommendations.

D **Information system:** The information system relevant to financial reporting objectives, which includes the accounting system, consists of the procedures and records designed and established to initiate, record, process, and report entity transactions (as well as events and conditions) and to maintain accountability for the related assets, liabilities, and equity. **(2 marks)**

57 **Which of the following is NOT an advantage of using narrative notes?**

A Simple to record

B Can be cumbersome for complex systems

C No specific expertise needed to prepare

D Easy to understand **(2 marks)**

58 **Which of the following is a disadvantage of using an internal control questionnaire?**

A It is easy for clients to overstate the actual level of controls in operation

B Quick to prepare and cost effective for the auditor

C Missing controls can be quickly identified

D Simple to complete **(2 marks)**

59 **Which of the following two features of the purchase cycle, if any, are a deficiency in the internal control system of Coastal Co?**

(1) Goods are counted and agreed to the supplier's delivery note before signing the delivery note to accept the goods.

(2) The purchase invoice is matched to and filed with the relevant goods received note and purchase order, by the purchase ledger team in the finance department.

A   1 only

B   2 only

C   Both 1 and 2

D   Neither 2 nor 2

(2 marks)

60 **Which of the following two features of the payroll cycle described, if any, are a deficiency in the internal control system of Coastal Co?**

(1) Standing data files are sent to departmental managers on a quarterly basis for review.

(2) Hours worked are entered onto a pre-printed payroll sheet by the wages clerk.

A   1 only

B   2 only

C   Both 1 and 2

D   Neither 1 nor 2

(2 marks)

The following scenario relates to questions 61 – 62

This objective test case question contains question types which will only appear in a computer-based exam, but this question provides valuable practice for all students whichever version of the exam they are taking

You are a member of the recently formed internal audit department of Halestorm Co (Halestorm). The company manufactures snacks such as potato chips which are supplied to large and small food retailers. Management and those charged with governance of Halestorm have concerns about the effectiveness of their sales and despatch system and have asked the internal audit function to document and review the system. The following deficiencies have been identified:

(i)   Availability of inventory is not checked at the time of ordering

(ii)   Telephone orders are not recorded immediately

(iii)   Order forms are not sequentially numbered

(iv)   The online ordering system allows customers to go over their credit limit

61   In respect of narrative notes choose whether the following statements are true or false?

Narrative notes	True	False
Simple to record		
Facilitates understanding by junior team members		
Can be cumbersome		
Usually very easy to identify missing controls		

(2 marks)

62   In respect of internal control questionnaires choose whether the following statements are true or false?

Internal control questionnaires	True	False
A timely method of systems documentation		
Does not consider all likely controls in a system		
Overstatement of controls present unlikely to occur		
Unusual controls may be missed		

(2 marks)

63   Match the control deficiencies to an appropriate explanation of the issue.

Deficiency		Explanation	
1	Availability of inventory is not checked at the time of ordering	A	Risk of incorrect orders being despatched
2	Telephone orders are not recorded immediately	B	Risk of irrecoverable debts
3	Order forms are not sequentially numbered	C	Risk of orders not being fulfilled on a timely basis
4	The online ordering system allows customers to go over their credit limit	D	Orders may go missing leading to unfulfilled orders

(2 marks)

64 Which TWO of the following are appropriate responses for the credit limit system deficiency?

A Credit limits should be reviewed by a responsible official on a regular basis and amended as appropriate

B Sales order clerks should be allowed to use discretion to raise credit limits

C Credit limits should be able to be breached by only 5%

D The online ordering system should be amended to not allow any orders that would breach an existing credit limit **(2 marks)**

65 Which TWO of the following are NOT objectives of a sales and despatch system?

A To ensure that orders are only accepted if goods are available to be processed for customers

B To ensure that all orders are recorded completely and accurately

C To ensure sales discounts are only provided to valid customers

D To ensure all requisitions are authorised before orders are placed

E To ensure discounts received are accounted for completely and accurately

F To ensure that all goods despatched are correctly invoiced **(2 marks)**

The following scenario relates to questions 66 – 70

This objective test case question contains question types which will only appear in a computer-based exam, but this question provides valuable practice for all students whichever version of the exam they are taking

Primrose Co has recently upgraded its computer system to enable greater automation of transaction processing. The new system has integrated the sales, inventory and purchasing systems resulting in minimal manual entry. Sales orders are entered into the system manually. The inventory system is automatically updated to reflect that the inventory has been sold. The system will flag if there is insufficient inventory to fulfil the order. The inventory system is linked to the purchasing system so that when inventory falls to a minimum level a purchase order is automatically created and sent to the purchasing manager for authorisation. Once the manager clicks 'authorised' the order is automatically sent electronically to the approved supplier for that item. The system is backed up daily to ensure minimal loss of data in the event of a system failure. Primrose's internal auditors were present during the implementation of the new system and performed tests during the process to ensure the information transferred into the new system was free from error. The internal audit plan of work has been updated to include regular tests of the system throughout the year to ensure it is working effectively. The external auditor of Primrose is planning to use test data during the audit for the first time this year as a result of the new system and is also planning on using the work of Primrose's internal audit department if possible.

---

66 State whether the following are general or application controls.

	General	Application
Daily back up of the system		
Authorisation of purchase orders		
Minimum order quantities		
Automatic updating of inventory once goods are sold		

(2 marks)

---

67 **Which of the following best describes the purpose of test data?**

A   Scrutinising large volumes of transactions to increase the efficiency of the audit

B   Testing the inputs and outputs of the client's systems

C   Testing the computerised controls operating within the client's systems

D   Scrutinising the source code of the system for errors in programming   **(2 marks)**

68 **Which of the following is NOT an advantage of using computer assisted audit techniques?**

A   CAATs are usually inexpensive to set up

B   Greater volumes can be tested

C   Aspects of a system which are not able to be tested by other means can be tested

D   Time-consuming tasks can be performed more quickly by a computer   **(2 marks)**

69 **Which of the following is NOT a test of control in respect of Primrose's system?**

A   Trace a sample of purchase orders through to the approved supplier list to ensure the supplier used is approved

B   Trace a sales order through to the inventory system and into the sales day book to ensure it is recorded

C   Enter a sales order for goods which there are insufficient quantities to fulfil the order to ensure the system flags this

D   Inspect copies of the back-ups taken to ensure these are taken on a daily basis
    (2 marks)

70 **Which of the following statements is NOT true in respect of using the work of Primrose's internal audit department?**

A   The external auditor must assess the internal audit function and the internal audit work before reliance can be placed on their work

B   The external auditor may rely on the work the internal auditor has performed during the year if it is relevant to the external audit and is considered reliable

C   The external auditor can use the work performed by the internal auditor without checking it if the company has an audit committee in place responsible for overseeing the internal audit function

D   The external auditor must re-perform some of the procedures performed by the internal auditor to ensure they reach the same conclusion   **(2 marks)**

AUDIT EVIDENCE

The following scenario relates to questions 71 – 75

You are the audit supervisor of Seagull & Co and are currently planning the audit of your existing client, Eagle Heating Co (Eagle), for the year ending 31 December. Eagle manufactures and sells heating and plumbing equipment to a number of home improvement stores across the country.

Eagle has experienced increased competition and as a result, in order to maintain its current levels of sales, it has decreased the selling price of its products significantly. The finance director has informed the audit manager that he expects increased inventory levels at the year end. You plan to attend the year-end inventory count of Eagle.

The finance director of Eagle has notified your manager that one of Eagle's key customers has been experiencing financial difficulties. Eagle has agreed that the customer can take a six-month payment break, after which payments will resume. The finance director does not believe that any allowance is required against this receivable. Your review of industry journals has identified several articles that suggest the key customer may soon stop trading.

71 **Which of the following financial statement assertions is LEAST relevant to the audit of inventory?**

A   Completeness

B   Existence

C   Occurrence

D   Classification   **(2 marks)**

72 **Which of the following procedures are tests of control an auditor should perform whilst attending the inventory count?**

(1)   Observe the client's staff to ensure they are following the inventory count instructions

(2)   Inspect the inventory for evidence of damage or obsolescence

(3)   Obtain a sample of the last goods received notes and goods despatched notes and follow through to the inventory records to ensure inclusion in the correct accounting period

(4)   Inspect and review management's inventory count instructions

A   2 and 3

B   1 and 4

C   1 and 2

D   3 and 4   **(2 marks)**

73 **Which of the following substantive procedures could be used to verify the valuation of inventory?**

A   Trace the items recorded on the count sheets to the final inventory listing

B   Trace the goods received immediately prior to the year-end to year-end inventory and payables balances

C   Inspect the ageing of inventory items to identify older/slow-moving amounts that may require allowance and discuss these with management

D   At the inventory count perform two-way test counts: select a sample of items from the inventory count sheets and physically inspect the items in the warehouse and select a sample of physical items from the warehouse and trace them to the inventory count sheets   **(2 marks)**

74 **Which TWO of the following substantive procedures provide evidence over the existence of trade receivables?**

(1)   Agree a sample of goods despatched notes to sales invoices and to the sales ledger

(2)   Perform a receivables circularisation

(3)   Review post year-end cash receipts, if these relate to year-end receivables follow through to the sales ledger

(4)   Recalculate the allowance for irrecoverable receivables

A   1 and 3

B   2 and 4

C   2 and 3

D   1 and 4   **(2 marks)**

75 **Which of the following substantive procedures would provide evidence as to the recoverability of the outstanding balance from the key customer?**

A   A direct confirmation letter to the key customer

B   A comparison of the current outstanding balance from the customer to the prior year

C   A review of the aged receivable listing of the key customer

D   A review of post year end cash receipts from the key customer   **(2 marks)**

The following scenario relates to questions 76 – 80

You the audit senior for the audit of Hawk Co. Hawk manufactures kites which it sells via its website directly to customers. Hawk has a year-end of 31 December and you are currently planning the audit.

The following notes were taken by the audit manager during a planning meeting with the finance director of Hawk.

In October the financial controller of Hawk was dismissed. He had been employed by the company for over 20 years, and he has threatened to sue the company for unfair dismissal. The role of financial controller has not yet been filled and so his tasks have been shared between the existing finance department team. In addition, the purchase ledger supervisor left in August and a replacement has only been appointed in the last week. However, for this period no supplier statement reconciliations or purchase ledger control account reconciliations were performed.

As part of the planning process you intend to perform an analytical review of the year to date financial statements.

76   **Which of the following statements, if any, are correct?**

(1)   Analytical procedures are required at the planning stage, but not as a substantive procedure.

(2)   Auditors are required to perform risk assessment procedures consisting of enquiries, analytical procedures, observation and inspection.

A   Both 1 and 2

B   1 only

C   2 only

D   Neither 1 nor 2   **(2 marks)**

77   **Which of the following are analytical procedures?**

(1)   Comparisons with a company in a similar industry

(2)   Comparisons of current and prior year balances

(3)   Proof in total calculations

(4)   Trend analysis

A   1 and 2 only

B   1, 2 and 4 only

C   3 and 4 only

D   All of them   **(2 marks)**

78 Which of the following is NOT true in relation to supplier statements and supplier statement reconciliations?

A   All suppliers will issue supplier statements therefore this procedure can be used for every client

B   There is an increased risk of overstatement in trade payables if supplier statement reconciliations are not performed

C   Misstatements in the purchase accrual balance may go undetected if supplier statement reconciliations are not performed

D   Supplier statements provide third party evidence which is more reliable than the client's payables ledger   **(2 marks)**

79 Which of the following are appropriate audit responses to the increased audit risks created by the finance team being allocated the work of the financial controller?

(1)   The audit team should be fully briefed and be alert throughout the audit for additional errors

(2)   The auditor would need to appoint an expert to properly assess the risks of misstatement

(3)   The finance director should be requested to provide the audit team with assistance for matters that cannot be addressed by the remaining finance function

(4)   The auditor should consider resigning from the engagement as audit risk cannot be managed to an acceptable level

A   1, 2 and 3

B   2, 3 and 4

C   1 and 3 only

D   1 and 4   **(2 marks)**

80 You have been made aware that a claim has been filed against the company by the former financial controller for unfair dismissal. Which of the following would be appropriate sources of evidence to enable the auditor to assess the appropriate accounting treatment of the claim in the financial statements?

(1)   Correspondence between the financial controller and the company

(2)   Board meeting minutes

(3)   Correspondence between the company and its solicitors

(4)   A telephone conversation with the financial controller and the auditor

A   1 and 2 only

B   1, 2 and 3 only

C   1, 3 and 4 only

D   All of them   **(2 marks)**

The following scenario relates to questions 81 – 85

You are the audit senior in charge of the audit of Swandive Co (Swandive), and are in the process of planning the final audit. You have been informed by your audit manager that during the year a fraud occurred at the client. A payroll clerk set up fictitious employees and the wages were paid into the clerk's own bank account. This clerk has subsequently left the company, but the audit manager is concerned that additional frauds have taken place in the wages department.

81   Which of the following is NOT a purpose of planning an audit?

 A   To facilitate an effective review of audit files

 B   To organise and manage the audit so that it is performed in an effective and efficient manner

 C   To ensure that the client obtains added value from the audit to increase the chances of retaining the audit next year

 D   To reduce the risk of giving an appropriate opinion to an acceptable level   **(2 marks)**

82   Which of the following would NOT appear in an audit strategy?

 (1)   Risk assessment and materiality

 (2)   Results of substantive analytical audit procedures

 (3)   Consideration of quality control procedures such as supervision and review

 (4)   Details of audit scope, direction and timing

 A   2 only

 B   1 and 3 only

 C   1, 3 and 4

 D   2 and 4   **(2 marks)**

83   Which of the following procedures would assist in the detection of further frauds of this type at Swandive?

 (1)   Recalculate the size of the detected fraud and assess whether it is material

 (2)   Discuss with management whether they are aware of further frauds at Swandive

 (3)   Analyse the bank details of all employees to identify duplicate bank accounts

 (4)   Report the fraud to the police to deter other employees from committing a similar fraud

 A   1 and 2 only

 B   2 and 3 only

 C   1, 2 and 3

 D   1 and 4   **(2 marks)**

84 **With respect to fraud and error which of these statements is NOT correct?**

A   Fraud can be split into two main types – fraudulent financial reporting and misappropriation of assets

B   The auditor's role is to determine whether there is a material misstatement in the financial statements as a result of fraud or error

C   As part of their audit procedures the engagement team should discuss the audit client's susceptibility to fraud

D   Fraud is an intentional act and therefore generally easier to identify than error

(2 marks)

85 **Which TWO of the following are substantive procedures that could be performed at the final audit to confirm the completeness and accuracy of Swandive's payroll expense?**

(1)   For a sample of employees recalculate the gross and net pay and agree to the payroll records

(2)   Perform a proof in total of wages and salaries and compare the expected total to actual wages and salaries in draft financial statements

(3)   Select a sample of hourly paid employees and verify hours worked have been authorised by their line manager

(4)   Ensure that the payroll report is authorised by the financial director before any payments are made to employees

A   1 and 2

B   2 and 3

C   3 and 4

D   1 and 4

(2 marks)

The following scenario relates to questions 86 – 90

You are an audit senior in Staple and Co and you are commencing the planning of the audit of Smoothbrush Paints Co for the year ending 31 August 20X0. Smoothbrush Paints Co is a paint manufacturer and has been trading for over 50 years, it operates from one central site, which includes the production facility, warehouse and administration offices. To avoid the disruption of a year-end inventory count, Smoothbrush has this year introduced a continuous/perpetual inventory counting system. A timetable of inventory counts is to be maintained and regularly reviewed. The warehouse has been divided into 12 areas and the counting team will always include a member of the internal audit department and a warehouse staff member.

The following inventory counting processes have been implemented by Smoothbrush Paints:

(1)   The team prints the inventory quantities and descriptions from the system and these records are then compared to the inventory physically present.

(2)   Any discrepancies in relation to quantities are noted on the inventory sheets, including any items not listed on the sheets but present in the warehouse area.

(3)   Any damaged or old items are noted and they are removed from the inventory sheets.

(4)   The sheets are then passed to the finance department for adjustments to be made to the records when the count has finished.

(5)   During the counts there will continue to be inventory movements with goods arriving and leaving the warehouse. No controls have been put in place to deal with any movements.

86   **Where a client uses a continuous inventory counting system which of the following statements is correct?**

(1)   The auditor must attend at least one count to ensure adequate controls are applied

(2)   If no count is carried out at the year-end, cut off testing need not be performed

(3)   All lines of inventory must be counted at least twice during the year

(4)   The auditor should visit the client's premises at least once a year to demand an instant inventory count

A   1 only

B   2 and 3 only

C   2, 3 and 4

D   1 and 4   **(2 marks)**

87   **Which of the following are deficiencies within the inventory count processes?**

A   1, 2, 3 and 4 only

B   1, 3, 4 and 5 only

C   2, 4 and 5 only

D   All of them   **(2 marks)**

88   What is the primary reason for maintaining an inventory count timetable?

A   To ensure obsolete inventory is identified on a timely basis

B   To ensure the warehouse staff are not stealing inventory

C   To ensure all areas are counted at least once a year

D   To ensure damaged inventory is identified on a timely basis   **(2 marks)**

89   During the inventory count the auditor will perform test counts agreeing inventory quantities on the client's count sheets to that physically present in the warehouse. This procedure addresses which financial statement assertion?

A   Existence

B   Rights and obligations

C   Completeness

D   Accuracy, valuation and allocation   **(2 marks)**

90   Which of the following audit procedures would provide the MOST reliable evidence to verify the net realisable value of finished goods in inventory at the year end?

A   Inspect bank statements post year end and verify a sample of payments to suppliers

B   Obtain a written representation from management verifying the net realisable value of a sample of inventory items

C   Inspect year-end selling price lists for a sample of inventory items

D   Inspect post year end sales invoices for a sample of inventory items   **(2 marks)**

The following scenario relates to questions 91 – 95

You are performing the audit of Dory Co. Testing is currently being performed over receivables and property, plant and equipment. An audit junior has been assigned to these sections and you are responsible for reviewing their work. Receivables circularisation letters have been sent out to a sample of 15 customers. 11 responses have been received which confirm the balance on the client's receivables ledger. Two responses have been received which contain differences between the customer's ledger and Dory. Two responses have not been received.

91   What is the most appropriate initial response in respect of the circularisation letters for which no response has been received?

A   Document the non-response and continue with other audit work

B   Send a follow up circularisation request

C   Perform other receivable substantive procedures on the balance

D   Request a written representation from management   **(2 marks)**

92 Which of the following are NOT appropriate substantive procedures for the responses where differences are identified?

(1) Discuss with management the reason for the difference

(2) Agree differences due to timing, such as cash in transit to post year-end cash receipts

(3) Consider the need for a modified audit report for all differences identified

(4) Request a written representation from management to confirm all differences noted are not material

A   1 and 2 only

B   1, 2 and 3

C   2 and 3 only

D   3 and 4   **(2 marks)**

93 Which of the following substantive audit procedures would provide the best evidence over completeness of additions to property, plant and equipment?

A   Obtain a breakdown of additions; cast the list and agree the total to the non-current asset register

B   Review the list of additions and confirm they are assets rather than repairs and maintenance

C   Inspect title deeds for property additions to ensure they are in the name of the client

D   Select a sample of additions and agree the cost to supplier invoices   **(2 marks)**

94 The audit junior has obtained the following evidence in respect of property, plant and equipment:

(1) Asset register reconciliation carried out by client management

(2) Valuation report from an independent Chartered Surveyor

(3) Depreciation proof in total carried out by the audit junior

(4) Verbal confirmation from the directors that they plan to dispose of one of the buildings

Rank the order of reliability of the audit evidence starting with the most reliable first?

A   4, 2, 1 and 3

B   2, 1, 4 and 3

C   2, 3, 1 and 4

D   4, 3, 2 and 1   **(2 marks)**

95 For the following procedures state which type of procedure is being used as given in ISA 500 *Audit Evidence*?

1	Casting the non-current asset register	
2	Physical verification of the existence of assets	
3	Checking the reconciliation of the asset register to the nominal ledger	
4	Discussing with management the basis for the depreciation rate used	

A   Inspection

B   Enquiry

C   Recalculation

D   Re-performance

E   External confirmation   **(2 marks)**

The following scenario relates to questions 96 – 100

You are the audit junior assigned to the audit of Hemsworth Co. You are ready to commence the audit of payables and receivables. The following procedures are listed in the audit plan:

Payables

Trace a sample of invoices listed in the payables ledger back to the purchase invoice to ensure they have been recorded at the correct amount in the ledger. Start at a random point and test every $200th.

Receivables

Identify all receivables balances over $200 and for those customers, inspect after date cash receipts to identify whether payment has been received post year end.

---

96 In respect of the payables testing, which of the following sampling methods is described?

A   Monetary unit sampling

B   Random sampling

C   Systematic sampling

D   Haphazard sampling   **(2 marks)**

97 In respect of the payables testing, if the sampling method stated to test every 20th item, which sampling method would be described?

A   Monetary unit sampling

B   Random sampling

C   Systematic sampling

D   Block sampling   **(2 marks)**

98   **In respect of the receivables testing, which of the following statements is true?**

A   Testing balances over $200 will ensure a sufficiently large sample size is tested

B   Testing all invoices over $200 represents statistical sampling

C   This method demonstrates the use of stratified sampling

D   This method is a form of selection   **(2 marks)**

99   **Which of the following would be the most appropriate initial response if misstatements were found during these tests?**

A   Report the matter to the client

B   Extend the sample

C   Suggest the audit opinion is modified as a result of material misstatement

D   Discuss the issue with the audit senior or audit manager   **(2 marks)**

100   **When deciding whether to use sampling which of the following should be considered?**

(1)   Completeness of the population

(2)   Appropriateness of the population

(3)   The size of the population

(4)   The time the auditor has available to perform the procedures

A   1, 2 and 3 only

B   2, 3 and 4 only

C   1 and 4 only

D   All of them   **(2 marks)**

The following scenario relates to questions 101 – 105

Delphic Co is a wholesaler of furniture (such as chairs, tables and cupboards). Delphic buys the furniture from six major manufacturers and sells them to over 600 different customers ranging from large retail chain stores to smaller owner-controlled businesses.

All information is stored on Delphic's computer systems although previous audits have tended to adopt an 'audit around the computer' approach. You are the audit senior in charge of the audit of the receivables balance. For the first time at this client, you have decided to use audit software to assist with the audit of the receivables balance.

Computer staff at Delphic are happy to help the auditor, although they cannot confirm completeness of systems documentation, and warn that the systems have very old operating systems in place, limiting file compatibility with more modern programs. As the system is old the auditor will be provided with copy files and not be allowed any direct access to Delphic's computer system.

101   Which of the following is NOT a substantive test for trade receivables?

A   Cast the aged receivables listing

B   Agree invoices included within the year end receivables listing to goods despatch notes

C   Inspect credit reports obtained for new customers to ensure credit checks have been performed prior to accepting the customer

D   Inspect board minutes for any evidence of disputes with customers   **(2 marks)**

102   Which of the following is an advantage of using CAATs?

A   Greater volumes can be tested

B   Audit software can be used to test the programmed controls within a system

C   CAATs are usually inexpensive to set up

D   Specialist expertise may be required   **(2 marks)**

103   Which of the following are procedures that could be carried out using audit software on the receivables balance at Delphic Co?

(1)   Cast the receivables ledger to ensure it is arithmetically correct

(2)   Compare the balance on each receivable account with its credit limit to ensure this has not been exceeded

(3)   Stratify the receivables balances to show all material items and select an appropriate sample for testing

(4)   Produce an aged receivables analysis to assist with the identification of irrecoverable receivables

A   1 and 2 only

B   1, 3 and 4 only

C   2, 3 and 4 only

D   All of them   **(2 marks)**

104   Which of the following is NOT a limitation of using CAATs at Delphic?

A   There may be substantial setup costs to use the software, especially where the computer systems of the client have not been fully documented

B   The computer audit department at Delphic cannot confirm that all system documentation is available, especially for the older 'legacy' systems currently in use

C   There are over 600 customers on the system making the use of audit software inappropriate at Delphic

D   The use of copy files means that the auditor will not be certain that these are the actual files being used within Delphic's computer systems   **(2 marks)**

105   The term 'auditing around the computer' means that the internal software of the computer is not audited but that the inputs to the computer are agreed to the expected outputs from the computer. Which of these is a valid explanation why audit risk increases when auditing 'around the computer'?

(1)   The actual computer files and programs are not tested; therefore the auditor has no direct evidence that the programs are working as expected

(2)   Where errors are found in reconciling inputs to outputs, it may be difficult or even impossible to determine why those errors occurred

A   Neither 1 nor 2

B   Both 1 and 2

C   1 only

D   2 only   **(2 marks)**

The following scenario relates to questions 106 – 110

You are the audit manager of Hightown Local Government (Hightown), a public sector organisation. You have assigned a new junior to your team to help complete the audit work for this client. This is the first time this member of staff has audited a Not-For-Profit (NFP) organisation and is unsure of the differences between an audit of a profit making company and a NFP.

---

106   Which of the following is a reason why an audit of a not-for-profit organisation can differ from an audit of a profit making company?

A   Management of NFPs have no financial qualifications therefore greater risk of material misstatement.

B   NFPs do not have shareholders therefore an audit is voluntary whereas an audit is a statutory requirement for a company of a certain size.

C   There are fewer auditing standards applicable to audits of NFPs.

D   An NFP has differing objectives to a profit making company and the financial statements will be used by different groups with different needs to those of a company.   **(2 marks)**

107 **Which of the following risks require specific consideration for an audit of a not-for-profit organisation?**

(1) Less segregation of duties due to fewer paid staff

(2) Increased risk over going concern due to uncertainty of income

(3) Complexity of taxation rules

(4) Competence of volunteer staff

A 1, 2 and 3 only

B 1, 3 and 4 only

C All of the above

D 1 and 4 only **(2 marks)**

108 **Which of the following elements of an audit engagement will be different for a not-for-profit organisation as compared with that for a company?**

A Responsible party

B Practitioner

C Sufficient appropriate evidence

D Intended user **(2 marks)**

109 **Which of the following statements is true in relation to NFPs?**

A As the organisation is not profit making the risk of manipulation of the financial statements is lower

B An audit will be required for local governments such as Hightown as they are funded by taxpayers

C The audit report of a NFP is not publicly available

D The audit of a NFP such as Hightown will take longer than the audit of a company due to the extra regulations applicable to NFPs. **(2 marks)**

110 **Hightown has been notified by central government of a significant cut in its funding for the following financial year. Which of the following statements is NOT true?**

A Audit risk will increase due to the threat to the going concern status of the organisation

B The auditor will need to review plans and forecasts to assess how the organisation will ensure it has sufficient funds to continue

C An audit report for a local government department will never need to refer to going concern uncertainties

D The auditor should review any plans Hightown has to reduce costs in the future to assess whether this could realistically be achieved and therefore indicate the organisation has sufficient funds to pay its liabilities when they fall due **(2 marks)**

REVIEW AND REPORTING

The following scenario relates to questions 111 – 115

You are the manager responsible for the audit of Mississippi Co (Mississippi) and you are completing the audit of the financial statements. The draft financial statements report revenue of $18m (Prior year – $17m). The draft chairman's statement, to be included in the annual report, was received yesterday. The chairman comments on the performance of the company, stating that he is pleased that revenue has increased by 20% in the year.

111   Which of the following statements is true in respect of the Chairman's statement?

A   The Chairman's statement forms part of the audited financial statements

B   The Chairman's statement forms part of the other information published with the financial statements

C   The auditor gives a separate opinion on the Chairman's statement

D   The Chairman's statement is only of concern to the auditor if it contains financial information   **(2 marks)**

112   How should 'Other information' be dealt with in the audit report?

A   The auditor should modify the audit opinion as the Chairman's statement is inconsistent with the financial statements

B   The auditor should draw attention to the inconsistency using an Emphasis of Matter paragraph

C   The auditor should explain their responsibilities in respect of the other information, such as the Chairman's statement, in the auditor's responsibility section of the audit report

D   The auditor should include an 'Other Information' section in the audit report and describe the inconsistency between the Chairman's statement and the financial statements   **(2 marks)**

113   Which of the following best describes why the auditor must refer to the other information in the audit report?

(1)   Users may be misled if the other information contains incorrect information or information which contradicts the financial statements

(2)   Users may believe the auditor has not audited the financial statements properly if there are inconsistencies which are not highlighted

(3)   The auditor must expose management's incompetence

(4)   Inconsistencies may undermine the credibility of the audit report if not highlighted

A   2 and 3 only

B   1, 3, and 4

C   1, 2 and 4 only

D   All of them   **(2 marks)**

114   Which of the following would NOT be considered 'Other information'?

A   Director's report

B   Corporate social responsibility report

C   Notes to the financial statements

D   Operating review   (2 marks)

115   Which of the following statements best describes the auditor's responsibilities in respect of other information?

A   The auditor provides limited assurance over the other information

B   The auditor must read the other information to ensure it is consistent with the financial statements and their knowledge of the entity obtained during the audit

C   The auditor must audit the other information and obtain sufficient appropriate evidence that the other information is true and fair

D   Other information only needs to be considered if it is available at the start of the audit with the draft financial statements   (2 marks)

The following scenario relates to questions 116 – 120

You are completing the audit of Pacific Co and the audit report is to be signed shortly. Revenue for the year is $2.6 million and profit before tax is $1.4 million. A key customer, with a receivables balance at the year-end of $65,000, has just notified Pacific that they are unable to pay the balance on their account due to cash flow problems. The finance director has notified the auditor that he will write this balance off as an irrecoverable debt in the following year's financial statements.

116   Which of the following are elements of an unmodified audit report as given in ISA 700 (Revised) *Forming an Opinion and Reporting on Financial Statements*?

(1)   Addressee

(2)   Basis for opinion

(3)   Auditor's address

(4)   Emphasis of matter paragraph

A   1, 2 and 3 only

B   2, 3, and 4 only

C   1 and 3 only

D   All of them   (2 marks)

117   Which TWO of the following are reasons why an auditor would need to modify the audit opinion?

(1)   They conclude that there is a material inconsistency between the audited financial statements and the other information contained in the annual report

(2)   They wish to draw attention to a matter that is fundamental to the users' understanding of the financial statements

(3)   They conclude that the financial statements as a whole are not free from material misstatement

(4)   They have been unable to obtain sufficient appropriate evidence to conclude that the financial statements as a whole are free from material misstatement

A   1 and 2

B   3 and 4

C   1 and 3

D   2 and 4   (2 marks)

118   Which of the following statements is correct regarding the materiality of the matter?

A   The matter is not material as the debt is less than 10% of profit

B   The matter is not material as the debt is less than 10% of profit and 5% of revenue

C   The matter is likely to be material as it is just under 5% of profit

D   The matter is likely to be material as it is over 1% of revenue   (2 marks)

119   Which of the following procedures would NOT be performed to allow the auditor to form a conclusion as the level of adjustment required to the receivables balance?

A   Review correspondence with the customer to assess whether there is any likelihood of payment.

B   Discuss with management why they feel an adjustment is not required in the financial statements being audited.

C   Perform a direct confirmation of the balance outstanding at the year end.

D   Review post year-end bank statements to identify any payments received from the customer.   (2 marks)

120   Assuming the matter is considered material and Pacific's directors have refused to adjust the financial statements, what would be the appropriate audit opinion to be issued?

A   Qualified due to material misstatement within financial statements

B   Qualified due to an inability to obtain sufficient appropriate audit evidence

C   Adverse

D   Disclaimer   (2 marks)

The following scenario relates to questions 121 – 125

Magical Mystery Tour (MMT) is a travel agency which has been trading for over five years. The company arranges holidays and hotel bookings to individual customers and corporate clients. The company is funded partly through overdrafts and loans and also by several large shareholders. The year end is 30 April. In the current year a new competitor, Pure Shores Co has entered the market and through competitive pricing has gained considerable market share from MMT. One of MMT's larger corporate clients has moved its business to Pure Shores. In addition, a number of MMT's agents have left the company and joined Pure Shores. MMT has found it difficult to replace these employees due to the level of skills and knowledge of remote overseas locations required. The directors have produced a cash flow forecast which shows a significantly worsening position over the coming 12 months. The auditors have been informed that MMT's bankers will not make a decision on the renewal of the overdraft facility until after the audit report is completed. The directors have agreed to include some going concern disclosures.

121 Which of the following procedures provide evidence regarding the going concern status of MMT?

(1) Inspect correspondence with the bank to identify any disputes which may indicate the overdraft facility will not be renewed

(2) Calculate key ratios to identify possible financial problems

(3) Inspect board minutes for discussions of management as to how they plan to improve the financial position of MMT

(4) Enquire with management whether any new clients have been obtained and if so, inspect contracts to ascertain the level of income to be generated

A   1, 3 and 4 only

B   2 and 4 only

C   1, 2 and 3 only

D   All of them   **(2 marks)**

122 Which of the following indicators of going concern issues are correctly explained?

(1) *New competitor:* There is a risk that if MMT continues to lose market share this will impact on future cash flows. In addition, there may be pressure to drop their prices in order to compete, which will impact profits and cash flows

(2) *Loss of key client:* This could result in a significant loss of future revenues and profit, and unless this customer can be replaced, there will be a decrease in future cash flows

(3) *Specialist agents left company:* The loss of staff will mean customers have to wait longer to speak to someone about their holiday

A   All three

B   1 and 2 only

C   2 and 3 only

D   1 and 3 only   **(2 marks)**

123 **What would be the impact on the audit report of MMT if the auditors believe the disclosures made by the directors are adequate?**

  A Unmodified opinion

  B Qualified opinion

  C Unmodified opinion with a section included in the audit report with the heading Material Uncertainty related to Going Concern

  D Unmodified opinion with an emphasis of matter paragraph **(2 marks)**

124 **What would be the impact on the audit report of MMT if the auditors believe the basis of preparation of the financial statements is incorrect?**

  A Unmodified opinion

  B Unmodified opinion with an emphasis of matter paragraph

  C Qualified opinion

  D Adverse opinion **(2 marks)**

125 **In which of the following circumstances would a 'Basis for opinion' paragraph be included in the audit report?**

  A All modified audit reports

  B Unmodified audit reports only

  C Audit reports with a modified audit opinion

  D All audit reports **(2 marks)**

The following scenario relates to questions 126 – 130

This objective test case question contains question types which will only appear in a computer-based exam, but this question provides valuable practice for all students whichever version of the exam they are taking

You are an audit manager in Bond & Co and you are nearing completion of the audit of Paddington Co (Paddington). You are now resolving the last few issues before deciding on the appropriate audit opinion. Paddington's profit before tax is $29m. During the year being audited Paddington's' main competitor filed a lawsuit for $3m alleging a breach of copyright. This case is on-going and will not be resolved prior to the audit report being signed. Paddington's lawyers believe the claim is only possible to succeed. Paddington has sufficient cash to make the settlement if they lose the case.

126 **Which TWO of the following issues, individually would lead the auditor to give an adverse opinion on Paddington's financial statements?**

    A   A provision amounting to $25m has not been recognised in the financial statements

    B   Depreciation of $1m has not been recorded in the financial statements

    C   Intangible assets have been overstated in the financial statements by $12m

    D   Paddington has prepared the financial statements on the going concern basis when they are not a going concern   **(2 marks)**

127 **Match the following audit report sections to the appropriate explanation of its purpose.**

Element		Purpose	
1	Title	A	Provides a description of the professional standards applied during the audit to provide confidence to users that the report can be relied upon
2	Addressee	B	Identifies the intended user of the report
3	Basis for opinion	C	Identifies the person responsible for the audit opinion in case of any queries
4	Key audit matters	D	Clearly identifies the report as an Independent Auditor's Report
5	Name of engagement partner	E	Draws attention to any other significant matters of which the users should be aware

(2 marks)

128 **Which of the following statements is true in respect of the lawsuit and its impact on the financial statements and audit report thereon?**

    A   A provision should be recognised in the financial statements of $3m

    B   A contingent liability should be disclosed in the notes to the financial statements

    C   The matter is not material as it represents 10.3 % of profit before tax.

    D   The lawsuit does not need to be referred to in the financial statements as the case is not settled at the year-end date   **(2 marks)**

129 Assuming that the lawsuit of $3m is correctly treated in the financial statements and all other issues have been resolved, choose the appropriate audit opinion to be issued for Paddington and choose an appropriate explanation.

Opinion		Explanation	
1	Unmodified	A	As there is a lack of evidence regarding the outcome of the claim
2	Unmodified with emphasis of matter paragraph	B	As $3m is a significant amount of money and therefore pervasive
3	Adverse	C	As the claim is material but unlikely to have a pervasive effect on the company
4	Qualified – material misstatement	D	As the matter should be brought to the attention of the shareholders
5	Qualified – inability to obtain sufficient appropriate evidence	E	As the matter is correctly treated in the financial statements and there is no significant uncertainty facing Paddington
6	Disclaimer	F	As there is a lack of evidence regarding the outcome of the claim and the matter is pervasive

(2 marks)

130 Match the following audit opinions to the corresponding wording for that opinion.

Opinion		Wording	
1	Unmodified	A	Except for.................the financial statements give a true and fair view
2	Disclaimer	B	The financial statements give a true and fair view
3	Adverse	C	We do not express an opinion
4	Qualified	D	The financial statements do not give a true and fair view

(2 marks)

The following scenario relates to questions 131 – 135

This objective test case question contains question types which will only appear in a computer-based exam, but this question provides valuable practice for all students whichever version of the exam they are taking

Humphries Co operates a chain of food wholesalers across the country and its year end was 30 September 20X1. The final audit is nearly complete and it is proposed that the financial statements and audit report will be signed on 13 December. Revenue for the year is $78 million and profit before taxation is $7·5 million. The following events have occurred subsequent to the year end.

Receivable

A customer of Humphries Co has been experiencing cash flow problems and its year-end balance is $0·3 million. The company has just become aware that its customer is experiencing significant going concern difficulties. Humphries believe that as the company has been trading for many years, they will receive some, if not full, payment from the customer; hence they have not adjusted the receivable balance.

Lawsuit

A key supplier of Humphries Co is suing them for breach of contract. The lawsuit was filed prior to the year end, and the sum claimed by them is $1 million. This has been disclosed as a contingent liability in the notes to the financial statements; however correspondence has just arrived from the supplier indicating that they are willing to settle the case for a payment by Humphries Co of $0·6 million. It is likely that the company will agree to this.

Warehouse

Humphries Co has three warehouses; following extensive rain on 20 November significant rain and river water flooded the warehouse located in Bass. All of the inventory was damaged and has been disposed of. The insurance company has already been contacted. No amendments or disclosures have been made in the financial statements.

---

131 **Which of the following best describes the definition of an adjusting event?**

A   An event which provides evidence of a condition arising after the year end which if material must be recognised in the financial statements

B   An event which provides evidence of a condition in existence at the year-end which if material must be recognised in the financial statements

C   An event which provides evidence of a condition arising after the year end which if material must be disclosed in the notes to the financial statements

D   An event which provides evidence of a condition in existence at the year-end which if material must be disclosed in the notes to the financial statements   **(2 marks)**

132 **Calculate the materiality level of the receivable and settlement figure for the lawsuit by reference to profit before tax and state whether they are material.**

	Calculation	Material	
		Yes	No
Receivable			
Lawsuit			

(2 marks)

133 State whether the above events are adjusting or non-adjusting.

	Adjusting	Non-adjusting
Receivable		
Lawsuit		
Warehouse		

(2 marks)

134 State whether each of the following procedures is appropriate or not in order to reach a conclusion on the issue concerning receivables?

Procedure	Appropriate	
	Yes	No
Contact the customer directly and enquire when they are likely to pay the outstanding balance		
Review correspondence between the customer and Humphries to assess whether there is any likelihood of payment		
Review the post year-end period to see if any payments have been received from the customer		
Inspect the original invoice and goods despatch note to confirm the customer received the goods and therefore owes the money		

(2 marks)

135 Assuming that the receivable and warehouse issued are resolved but the lawsuit issue remains unresolved, which FOUR of the following section titles must be included in the audit report?

Section Titles	Include in audit report
Auditor Responsibilities for the Audit of the Financial Statements	
Basis for opinion	
Basis for qualified opinion	
Key Audit Matters	
Opinion	
Qualified opinion	
Responsibilities of Management and Those Charged With Governance	

(2 marks)

The following scenario relates to questions 136 – 140

This objective test case question contains question types which will only appear in a computer-based exam, but this question provides valuable practice for all students whichever version of the exam they are taking

Greenfields Co specialises in manufacturing equipment which can help to reduce toxic emissions in the production of chemicals. The company has grown rapidly over the past eight years and this is due partly to the warranties that the company gives to its customers. It guarantees its products for five years and if problems arise in this period it undertakes to fix them, or provide a replacement product. You are the manager responsible for the audit of Greenfields and you are performing the final review stage of the audit and have come across the following two issues.

Receivable balance owing from Yellowmix Co

Greenfields has a material receivable balance owing from its customer, Yellowmix Co. During the year-end audit, your team reviewed the ageing of this balance and found that no payments had been received from Yellowmix for over six months, and Greenfields would not allow this balance to be circularised. Instead management has assured your team that they will provide a written representation confirming that the balance is recoverable.

Warranty provision

The warranty provision included within the statement of financial position is material. The audit team has performed testing over the calculations and assumptions which are consistent with prior years. The team has requested a written representation from management confirming the basis and amount of the provision are reasonable. Management has yet to confirm acceptance of this representation.

136 **Choose the appropriate words/phrases from the selection to complete the sentences below. Options may be selected more than once.**

A written representation _____ in respect of the receivable balance. This is because_____.

A written representation _____ in respect of the warranty provision. This is because_____.

A   Is appropriate

B   Is not appropriate

C   The matter is not material

D   The matter involves management judgement

E   Other procedures can be performed which provide more reliable evidence

F   An ISA specifically requires a written representation to be obtained for the item

(2 marks)

137 **Written representations are required by other international auditing standards (ISAs) in respect of particular areas of the audit. Which of the following areas of the audit require written representation to be obtained?**

Area of the audit	Required by an ISA	
	Yes	No
Fraud and error (ISA 240)		
Laws and regulations (ISA 250)		
Analytical procedures (ISA 520)		
Subsequent events (ISA 560)		

(2 marks)

138 **Assuming that the directors of Greenfields Co refuse to provide a written representation to the auditor, which of the following statements is correct?**

A The refusal to provide a written representation will only be a matter of concern if it relates to a material area of the financial statements

B The refusal to provide a written representation may cast doubt over management integrity and as such the reliability of other evidence provided by the client may be called into question

C The refusal to provide a written representation will result in the need for the auditor to resign from the engagement once the audit report has been issued

D The auditor will need to notify the shareholders of the issue in person **(2 marks)**

139 **Which TWO of the following audit reporting implications could result if Greenfields refuse to provide a written representation letter?**

A Unmodified opinion and report

B Unmodified opinion with emphasis of matter paragraph

C Qualified opinion due to material misstatement

D Qualified opinion due to an inability to obtain sufficient appropriate evidence

E Adverse opinion as the financial statements do not show a true and fair view

F Disclaimer of opinion as the auditor does not have sufficient appropriate evidence to be able to express an audit opinion **(2 marks)**

140 **Which THREE of the following MUST be included in every written representation according to ISA 580?**

Plans or intentions of management that affect carrying values of assets	
Confirmation from management that they have provided the auditor with all information and access to records during the audit	
Confirmation from management that the financial statements are accurate and there are no material misstatements	
Confirmation from management that all transactions have been reflected in the financial statements	
Confirmation from management that they have prepared the financial statements in accordance with the applicable financial reporting framework	

(2 marks)

Section 2

PRACTICE QUESTIONS

PLANNING AND RISK ASSESSMENT

141 VENUS *Walk in the footsteps of a top tutor*

ISA 210 *Agreeing the Terms of Audit Engagements* requires auditors to agree the terms of an engagement with those charged with governance and formalise these in an engagement letter.

Required:

(a) **Identify and explain TWO factors which would indicate that an engagement letter for an existing audit client should be revised.**   **(2 marks)**

(b) **List SIX matters which should be included within an audit engagement letter.**
                                                                                  (3 marks)

You have been asked by the audit engagement partner to gain an understanding about the new client as part of the planning process.

Required:

(c) **Identify FIVE sources of information relevant to gaining an understanding and describe how this information will be used by the auditor.**   **(5 marks)**

You are an audit supervisor of Pluto & Co and are currently planning the audit of your client, Venus Magnets Co (Venus) which manufactures decorative magnets. Its year end is 31 December 2015 and the forecast profit before tax is $9.6 million.

During the year, the directors reviewed the useful lives and depreciation rates of all classes of plant and machinery. This resulted in an overall increase in the asset lives and a reduction in the depreciation charge for the year.

Inventory is held in five warehouses and on 28 and 29 December a full inventory count will be held with adjustments for movements to the year end. This is due to a lack of available staff on 31 December. In October, there was a fire in one of the warehouses; inventory of $0.9 million was damaged and this has been written down to its scrap value of $0.2 million. An insurance claim has been submitted for the difference of $0.7 million. Venus is still waiting to hear from the insurance company with regards to this claim, but has included the insurance proceeds within the statement of profit or loss and the statement of financial position.

The finance director has informed the audit manager that the October and November bank reconciliations each contained unreconciled differences; however, he considers the overall differences involved to be immaterial.

A directors' bonus scheme was introduced during the year which is based on achieving a target profit before tax. In order to finalise the bonus figures, the finance director of Venus would like the audit to commence earlier so that the final results are available earlier this year.

Required:

(d)   Describe FIVE audit risks, and explain the auditor's response to each risk, in planning the audit of Venus Magnets Co.   **(10 marks)**

(Total: 20 marks)

142   SYCAMORE *Walk in the footsteps of a top tutor*

You are the audit supervisor of Maple & Co and are currently planning the audit of an existing client, Sycamore Science Co (Sycamore), whose year end was 30 April 2015. Sycamore is a pharmaceutical company, which manufactures and supplies a wide range of medical supplies. The draft financial statements show revenue of $35.6 million and profit before tax of $5.9 million.

Sycamore's previous finance director left the company in December 2014 after it was discovered that he had been claiming fraudulent expenses from the company for a significant period of time. A new finance director was appointed in January 2015 who was previously a financial controller of a bank, and she has expressed surprise that Maple & Co had not uncovered the fraud during last year's audit.

During the year Sycamore has spent $1.8 million on developing several new products. These projects are at different stages of development and the draft financial statements show the full amount of $1.8 million within intangible assets. In order to fund this development, $2.0 million was borrowed from the bank and is due for repayment over a ten-year period. The bank has attached minimum profit targets as part of the loan covenants.

The new finance director has informed the audit partner that since the year end there has been an increased number of sales returns and that in the month of May over $0.5 million of goods sold in April were returned.

Maple & Co attended the year-end inventory count at Sycamore's warehouse. The auditor present raised concerns that during the count there were movements of goods in and out the warehouse and this process did not seem well controlled.

During the year, a review of plant and equipment in the factory was undertaken and surplus plant was sold, resulting in a profit on disposal of $210,000.

Required:

(a)   State Maples & Co's responsibilities in relation to the prevention and detection of fraud and error.   **(5 marks)**

(b)   Describe EIGHT audit risks, and explain the auditor's response to each risk, in planning the audit of Sycamore Science Co.   **(16 marks)**

(c)   Explain the quality control procedures that Maple & Co should have in place during the engagement performance.   **(5 marks)**

(d) Sycamore's new finance director has read about review engagements and is interested in the possibility of Maple & Co undertaking these in the future. However, she is unsure how these engagements differ from an external audit and how much assurance would be gained from this type of engagement.

Required:

(i) **Explain the purpose of review engagements and how these differ from external audits; and** **(2 marks)**

(ii) **Describe the level of assurance provided by external audits and review engagements.** **(2 marks)**

(Total: 30 marks)

143 RECORDER COMMUNICATIONS *Walk in the footsteps of a top tutor*

(a) ISA 300 *Planning an Audit of Financial Statements* provides guidance to auditors. Planning an audit involves establishing the overall audit strategy for the engagement and developing an audit plan. Adequate planning benefits the audit of financial statements in several ways.

Required:

Explain the importance of audit planning. **(5 marks)**

Recorder Communications Co (Recorder) is a large mobile phone company which operates a network of stores in countries across Europe. The company's year end is 30 June. You are the audit senior of Piano & Co. Recorder is a new client and you are currently planning the audit with the audit manager. You have been provided with the following planning notes from the audit partner following his meeting with the finance director.

Recorder purchases goods from a supplier in South Asia and these goods are shipped to the company's central warehouse. The goods are usually in transit for two weeks and the company correctly records the goods when received. Recorder does not undertake a year-end inventory count, but carries out monthly continuous (perpetual) inventory counts and any errors identified are adjusted in the inventory system for that month. Manufacturers regularly bring out new models of mobile phones. When this happens, the old models have to be sold at a significant discount as customers usually want the latest model. Recorder has a number of older models in inventory.

During the year the company introduced a bonus based on sales for its sales persons. The bonus target was based on increasing the number of customers signing up for 24-month phone line contracts. This has been successful and revenue has increased by 15%, especially in the last few months of the year. The level of receivables is considerably higher than last year and there are concerns about the creditworthiness of some customers.

Recorder has a policy of revaluing its land and buildings and this year has updated the valuations of all land and buildings.

During the year the directors have each been paid a significant bonus, and they have included this within wages and salaries. Separate disclosure of the bonus is required by local legislation.

Required:

(b) Describe SEVEN audit risks, and explain the auditor's response to each risk, in planning the audit of Recorder Communications Co. **(14 marks)**

(c) Explain the audit procedures you should perform in order to place reliance on the continuous (perpetual) counts for year-end inventory. **(3 marks)**

(d) Describe substantive procedures you should perform to confirm the directors' bonus payments included in the financial statements. **(4 marks)**

The audit of Recorder is nearly complete and the audit report is due to be signed next week. The directors are refusing to adjust the valuation of inventory to the lower of cost and net realisable value. The difference is considered to have a material effect on the financial statements.

(e) Describe the impact on the audit report if the issue remains unresolved. **(4 marks)**

(Total: 30 marks)

144 KANGAROO CONSTRUCTION *Walk in the footsteps of a top tutor*

(a) Explain the concepts of materiality and performance materiality in accordance with ISA 320 *Materiality in Planning and Performing an Audit*. **(5 marks)**

(b) You are the audit senior of Rhino & Co and you are planning the audit of Kangaroo Construction Co (Kangaroo) for the year ended 31 March 2013. Kangaroo specialises in building houses and provides a five-year building warranty to its customers. Your audit manager has held a planning meeting with the finance director. He has provided you with the following notes of his meeting and financial statement extracts:

Kangaroo has had a difficult year; house prices have fallen and, as a result, revenue has dropped. In order to address this, management has offered significantly extended credit terms to their customers. However, demand has fallen such that there are still some completed houses in inventory where the selling price may be below cost. Cash flow issues have been alleviated partly due to the requirement for customers to pay a deposit of $5,000 to secure the house they wish to buy. The deposit is refundable until the house is 75% complete. At this stage the house is deemed to be built to the customer's specification and the deposit becomes non-refundable.

During the year, whilst calculating depreciation, the directors extended the useful lives of plant and machinery from three years to five years. This reduced the annual depreciation charge.

The directors need to meet a target profit before interest and taxation of $0.5 million in order to be paid their annual bonus. In addition, to try and improve profits, Kangaroo changed their main material supplier to a cheaper alternative. This has resulted in some customers claiming on their building warranties for extensive repairs. To help with operating cash flow, the directors borrowed $1 million from the bank during the year. This is due for repayment at the end of 2013.

Financial statement extracts for year ended 31 March

	DRAFT 2013 $m	ACTUAL 2012 $m
Revenue	12.5	15.0
Cost of sales	(7.0)	(8.0)
Gross profit	5.5	7.0
Operating expenses	(5.0)	(5.1)
Profit before interest and taxation	0.5	1.9
Inventory	1.9	1.4
Receivables	3.1	2.0
Cash	0.8	1.9
Trade payables	1.6	1.2
Loan	1.0	–

Required:

Using the information above:

(i)   Calculate SIX ratios, for BOTH years, which would assist the audit senior in planning the audit; and   **(6 marks)**

(ii)   Using the information provided and the ratios calculated, identify and describe SEVEN audit risks and explain the auditor's response to each risk in planning the audit of Kangaroo Construction Co.   **(14 marks)**

The audit of Kangaroo Construction is nearly complete and the audit report is due to be signed next week. Your audit work discovered that the warranty provision of $0.6m should be increased to $0.9m as a result of the increase in claims. The directors are refusing to make this adjustment.

(e)   Discuss the issue and describe the impact on the audit report if the issue remains unresolved.   **(5 marks)**

(Total: 30 marks)

145 SUNFLOWER STORES *Walk in the footsteps of a top tutor*

Sunflower Stores Co (Sunflower) operates 25 food supermarkets. The company's year end is 31 December 2012. The audit manager and partner recently attended a planning meeting with the finance director and have provided you with the planning notes below.

You are the audit senior, and this is your first year on this audit. In order to familiarise yourself with Sunflower, the audit manager has asked you to undertake some research in order to gain an understanding of Sunflower, so that you are able to assist in the planning process. He has then asked that you identify relevant audit risks from the notes below and also consider how the team should respond to these risks.

Sunflower has spent $1.6 million in refurbishing all of its supermarkets; as part of this refurbishment programme their central warehouse has been extended and a smaller warehouse, which was only occasionally used, has been disposed of at a profit. In order to finance this refurbishment, a sum of $1.5 million was borrowed from the bank. This is due to be repaid over five years.

The company will be performing a year-end inventory count at the central warehouse as well as at all 25 supermarkets on 31 December. Inventory is valued at selling price less an average profit margin as the finance director believes that this is a close approximation to cost.

Prior to 2012, each of the supermarkets maintained their own financial records and submitted returns monthly to head office. During 2012 all accounting records have been centralised within head office. Therefore at the beginning of the year, each supermarket's opening balances were transferred into head office's accounting records. The increased workload at head office has led to some changes in the finance department and in November 2012 the financial controller left. His replacement will start in late December.

Required:

(a) **List FIVE sources of information that would be of use in gaining an understanding of Sunflower Stores Co, and for each source describe what you would expect to obtain.** **(5 marks)**

(b) **Using the information provided, describe FIVE audit risks and explain the auditor's response to each risk in planning the audit of Sunflower Stores Co.** **(10 marks)**

(c) **The finance director of Sunflower Stores Co is considering establishing an internal audit department.**

Required:

Describe the factors the finance director should consider before establishing an internal audit department. **(5 marks)**

(Total: 20 marks)

146 ABRAHAMS *Walk in the footsteps of a top tutor*

(a) **Explain the components of audit risk and, for each component, state an example of a factor which can result in increased audit risk.** **(6 marks)**

Abrahams Co develops, manufactures and sells a range of pharmaceuticals and has a wide customer base across Europe and Asia. You are the audit manager of Nate & Co and you are planning the audit of Abrahams Co whose financial year end is 31 January. You attended a planning meeting with the finance director and engagement partner and are now reviewing the meeting notes in order to produce the audit strategy and plan. Revenue for the year is forecast at $25 million.

During the year the company has spent $2.2 million on developing several new products. Some of these are in the early stages of development whilst others are nearing completion. The finance director has confirmed that all projects are likely to be successful and so he is intending to capitalise the full $2.2 million.

Once products have completed the development stage, Abrahams begins manufacturing them. At the year end it is anticipated that there will be significant levels of work in progress. In addition the company uses a standard costing method to value inventory; the standard costs are set when a product is first manufactured and are not usually updated. In order to fulfil customer orders promptly, Abrahams Co has warehouses for finished goods located across Europe and Asia; approximately one third of these are third party warehouses where Abrahams just rents space.

In September a new accounting package was introduced. This is a bespoke system developed by the information technology (IT) manager. The old and new packages were not run in parallel as it was felt that this would be too onerous for the accounting team. Two months after the system changeover the IT manager left the company; a new manager has been recruited but is not due to start work until January.

In order to fund the development of new products, Abrahams has restructured its finance and raised $1 million through issuing shares at a premium and $2.5 million through a long-term loan. There are bank covenants attached to the loan, the main one relating to a minimum level of total assets. If these covenants are breached then the loan becomes immediately repayable. The company has a policy of revaluing land and buildings, and the finance director has announced that all land and buildings will be revalued as at the year end.

The reporting timetable for audit completion of Abrahams Co is quite short, and the finance director would like to report results even earlier this year.

Required:

(b)   **Using the information provided, identify and describe FIVE audit risks and explain the auditor's response to each risk in planning the audit of Abrahams Co.**

(10 marks)

(c)   **Describe substantive procedures you should perform to obtain sufficient appropriate evidence in relation to:**

(i)   **Inventory held at the third party warehouses; and**

(ii)   **Use of standard costs for inventory valuation.**

(4 marks)

(Total: 20 marks)

147   REDSMITH *Walk in the footsteps of a top tutor*

(a)   In agreeing the terms of an audit engagement, the auditor is required to agree the basis on which the audit is to be carried out. This involves establishing whether the preconditions for an audit are present and confirming that there is a common understanding between the auditor and management of the terms of the engagement.

Required:

Describe the process the auditor should undertake to assess whether the PRECONDITIONS for an audit are present.   (3 marks)

(b)   **List FOUR examples of matters the auditor may consider when obtaining an understanding of the entity.**   (2 marks)

(c)   You are the audit senior of White & Co and are planning the audit of Redsmith Co for the year ended 30 September 2010. The company produces printers and has been a client of your firm for two years; your audit manager has already had a planning meeting with the finance director. He has provided you with the following notes of his meeting and financial statement extracts.

Redsmith's management were disappointed with the 2009 results and so in 2010 undertook a number of strategies to improve the trading results. This included the introduction of a generous sales-related bonus scheme for their salesmen and a high profile advertising campaign. In addition, as market conditions are difficult for their customers, they have extended the credit period given to them.

The finance director of Redsmith has reviewed the inventory valuation policy and has included additional overheads incurred this year as he considers them to be production related. He is happy with the 2010 results and feels that they are a good reflection of the improved trading levels.

Financial statement extracts for year ended 30 September

	DRAFT 2010 $m	ACTUAL 2009 $m
Revenue	23.0	18.0
Cost of Sales	(11.0)	(10.0)
Gross profit	12.0	8.0
Operating expenses	(7.5)	(4.0)
Profit before interest and taxation	4.5	4.0
Inventory	2.1	1.6
Receivables	4.5	3.0
Cash	–	2.3
Trade payables	1.6	1.2
Overdraft	0.9	–

Required:

Using the information above:

(i)   **Calculate FIVE ratios, for BOTH years, which would assist the audit senior in planning the audit; and** **(5 marks)**

(ii) **From a review of the above information and the ratios calculated, explain FIVE audit risks and explain the auditor's response to each risk.**

(10 marks)

(Total: 20 marks)

148   SPECS4YOU *Walk in the footsteps of a top tutor*

ISA 230 *Audit Documentation* establishes standards and provides guidance regarding documentation in the context of the audit of financial statements.

Required:

(a)   List the purposes of audit working papers. **(3 marks)**

(b)   You have recently been promoted to audit manager in the audit firm of Trums & Co. As part of your new responsibilities, you have been placed in charge of the audit of Specs4You Co, a long established audit client of Trums & Co. Specs4You Co sells spectacles; the company owns 42 stores where customers can have their eyes tested and choose from a range of frames.

Required:

List the documentation that should be of assistance to you in familiarising yourself with Specs4You Co. Describe the information you should expect to obtain from each document. **(8 marks)**

(c)   The time is now towards the end of the audit, and you are reviewing working papers produced by the audit team. An example of a working paper you have just reviewed is shown below.

Client Name **Specs4You Co**   Year **end 30 April**   Page **xxxxxxx**
Working paper **Payables transaction testing**

Prepared by	Date
Reviewed by **CW**	Date **12 June 2007**

Audit assertion: To make sure that the purchases day book is correct.

Method: Select a sample of 15 purchase orders recorded in the purchase order system. Trace details to the goods received note (GRN), purchase invoice (PI) and the purchase day book (PDB) ensuring that the quantities and prices recorded on the purchase order match those on the GRN, PI and PDB.

Test details: In accordance with audit risk, a sample of purchase orders were selected from a numerically sequenced purchase order system and details traced as stated in the method. Details of items tested can be found on another working paper.

Results: Details of purchase orders were normally correctly recorded through the system. Five purchase orders did not have any associated GRN, PI and were not recorded in the PDB. Further investigation showed that these orders had been cancelled due to a change in spectacle specification. However, this does not appear to be a system deficiency as the internal controls do not allow for changes in specification.

Conclusion: Purchase orders are completely recorded in the purchase day book.

Required:

Explain why the working paper shown above does not meet the standards normally expected of a working paper. *Note:* **You are not required to reproduce the working paper.** **(9 marks)**

(Total: 20 marks)

INTERNAL CONTROLS AND AUDIT EVIDENCE

149 BRONZE   *Walk in the footsteps of a top tutor*

You are an audit senior of Scarlet & Co and are in the process of reviewing the systems testing completed on the payroll cycle of Bronze Industries Co (Bronze), as well as preparing the audit programmes for the final audit.

Bronze operate several chemical processing factories across the country, it manufactures 24 hours a day, seven days a week and employees work a standard shift of eight hours and are paid for hours worked at an hourly rate. Factory employees are paid weekly, with approximately 80% being paid by bank transfer and 20% in cash; the different payment methods are due to employee preferences and Bronze has no plans to change these methods. The administration and sales teams are paid monthly by bank transfer.

Factory staff are each issued a sequentially numbered clock card which details their employee number and name. Employees swipe their cards at the beginning and end of the eight-hour shift and this process is not supervised. During the shift employees are entitled to a 30-minute paid break and employees do not need to clock out to access the dining area. Clock card data links into the payroll system, which automatically calculates gross and net pay along with any statutory deductions. The payroll supervisor for each payment run checks on a sample basis some of these calculations to ensure the system is operating effectively.

Bronze has a human resources department which is responsible for setting up new permanent employees and leavers. Appointments of temporary staff are made by factory production supervisors. Occasionally overtime is required of factory staff, usually to fill gaps caused by staff holidays. Overtime reports which detail the amount of overtime worked are sent out quarterly by the payroll department to production supervisors for their review.

To encourage staff to attend work on time for all shifts Bronze pays a discretionary bonus every six months to factory staff; the production supervisors determine the amounts to be paid. This is communicated in writing by the production supervisors to the payroll department and the bonus is input by a clerk into the system.

For employees paid by bank transfer, the payroll manager reviews the list of the payments and agrees to the payroll records prior to authorising the bank payment. If any changes are required, the payroll manager amends the records. For employees paid in cash, the pay packets are prepared in the payroll department and a clerk distributes them to employees; as she knows most of these individuals she does not require proof of identity.

Required:

(a) Identify and explain FIVE internal control STRENGTHS in Bronze Industries Co's payroll system. **(5 marks)**

(b) In respect of the payroll system:

(i) Identify and explain SIX internal control deficiencies;

(ii) Recommend a control to address each of these deficiencies; and

(iii) Describe a test of control Scarlet & Co should perform to assess if each of these controls is operating effectively.

Note: The total marks will be split equally between each part. **(18 marks)** (c)　Describe substantive ANALYTICAL PROCEDURES you should perform to confirm Bronze Industries Co's payroll expense. **(3 marks)**

(d)　Explain the factors to be considered in determining the suitability of using analytical procedures as a substantive procedure. **(4 marks)**

(Total: 30 marks)

150　HUMMINGBIRD *Walk in the footsteps of a top tutor*

Hummingbird Scents Co (Hummingbird) manufactures and sells luxury toiletries; they have been trading for over 20 years and the company's year end is 30 September 2014. Hummingbird sells products to trade customers via its own website; this represents 60% of revenue. Remaining revenue is generated by contracts to supply toiletries to hotels. Below is a description of the sales system.

Hotel revenue

The hotel revenue is made up of four key customers. Hummingbird has one sales clerk, Brenda, who maintains all aspects of this revenue stream; Brenda receives customer orders, raises sales invoices and processes payments. In raising invoices, the sales system automatically inserts the online trade customer prices for products. However, each hotel customer has contracted prices which are lower than the online prices and hence Brenda manually edits the invoices prior to despatch.

Online revenue

New trade customers are set up in the sales ledger master file upon passing suitable credit checks, and a credit limit is set at this stage by the finance director. Customers place online orders up to their pre-set credit limit; they receive an email confirmation and the sales order interfaces into the despatch system. The order number is linked to the customer account number. Goods are despatched daily with a goods despatched note which is referenced to the sales order number but are not sequentially numbered. Hummingbird used to despatch goods via a reliable national courier company. However, to reduce costs they have changed to a cheaper local courier and some orders have been delivered to customers late.

Trade customers' sales invoices are automatically generated by the system on the day the online order is placed. The prices are inserted in accordance with the website rates. Occasionally Hummingbird makes special offers or discounts sales; when this occurs the master file data has to be amended to ensure that the correct prices are used on invoices. This task is usually performed by a senior sales ledger clerk.

Revenue and receivables records

On a monthly basis statements are sent to the hotel customers; a number of trade customers have been requesting monthly statements and Hummingbird is considering this request. The company only reconciles the sales ledger control account at the end of September in order to verify the year-end balance.

Required:

(a) As the external auditor of Hummingbird Co, write a report to management in respect of the sales system described above which:

    (i)   Identifies and explains SEVEN deficiencies in the sales system; and

    (ii)   Provides a recommendation to address each of these deficiencies.

    A covering letter IS required.

    Note: Up to two marks will be awarded within this requirement for presentation and the remaining marks will be split equally between each part.   **(16 marks)**

(b) Describe substantive procedures the auditor should perform to confirm Hummingbird Co's revenue.   **(4 marks)**

                                              (Total: 20 marks)

151 TROMBONE *Walk in the footsteps of a top tutor*

(a) ISA 315 Identifying and Assessing the Risks of Material Misstatement through Understanding the Entity and Its Environment describes the five components of an entity's internal control.

Required:

Identify and briefly explain the FIVE components of an entity's internal control.

                                                     (5 marks)

Trombone Co (Trombone) operates a chain of hotels across the country. Trombone employs in excess of 250 permanent employees and its year end is 31 August. You are the audit supervisor of Viola & Co and are currently reviewing the documentation of Trombone's payroll system, detailed below, in preparation for the interim audit.

Trombone's payroll system

Permanent employees work a standard number of hours per week as specified in their employment contract. However, when the hotels are busy, staff can be requested by management to work additional shifts as overtime. This can either be paid on a monthly basis or taken as days off.

Employees record any overtime worked and days taken off on weekly overtime sheets which are sent to the payroll department. The standard hours per employee are automatically set up in the system and the overtime sheets are entered by clerks into the payroll package, which automatically calculates the gross and net pay along with relevant deductions. These calculations are not checked at all. Wages are increased by the rate of inflation each year and the clerks are responsible for updating the standing data in the payroll system.

Employees are paid on a monthly basis by bank transfer for their contracted weekly hours and for any overtime worked in the previous month. If employees choose to be paid for overtime, authorisation is required by department heads of any overtime in excess of 30% of standard hours. If employees choose instead to take days off, the payroll clerks should check back to the 'overtime worked' report; however, this report is not always checked.

The 'overtime worked' report, which details any overtime recorded by employees, is run by the payroll department weekly and emailed to department heads for authorisation. The payroll department asks department heads to only report if there are any errors recorded. Department heads are required to arrange for overtime sheets to be authorised by an alternative responsible official if they are away on annual leave; however, there are instances where this arrangement has not occurred.

The payroll package produces a list of payments per employee; this links into the bank system to produce a list of automatic payments. The finance director reviews the total list of bank transfers and compares this to the total amount to be paid per the payroll records; if any issues arise then the automatic bank transfer can be manually changed by the finance director.

Required:

(b)   In respect of the payroll system of Trombone Co:

(i)   Identify and explain FIVE deficiencies;

(ii)   Recommend a control to address each of these deficiencies; and

(iii)   Describe a test of control Viola & Co should perform to assess if each of these controls is operating effectively.

Note: The total marks will be split equally between each part.   (15 marks)

(c)   Describe substantive procedures you should perform at the final audit to confirm the completeness and accuracy of Trombone Co's payroll expense.   (6 marks)

Trombone deducts employment taxes from its employees' wages on a monthly basis and pays these to the local taxation authorities in the following month. At the year end the financial statements will contain an accrual for income tax payable on employment income. You will be in charge of auditing this accrual.

Required:

(d)   Describe the audit procedures required in respect of the year end accrual for tax payable on employment income.   (4 marks)

(Total: 30 marks)

152   OREGANO *Walk in the footsteps of a top tutor*

You are a member of the recently formed internal audit department of Oregano Co (Oregano). The company manufactures tinned fruit and vegetables which are supplied to large and small food retailers. Management and those charged with governance of Oregano have concerns about the effectiveness of their sales and despatch system and have asked internal audit to document and review the system.

Sales and despatch system

Sales orders are mainly placed through Oregano's website but some are made via telephone. Online orders are automatically checked against inventory records for availability; telephone orders, however, are checked manually by order clerks after the call. A follow-up call is usually made to customers if there is insufficient inventory. When taking telephone orders, clerks note down the details on plain paper and afterwards they complete a three part pre-printed order form. These order forms are not sequentially numbered and are sent manually to both despatch and the accounts department.

As the company is expanding, customers are able to place online orders which will exceed their agreed credit limit by 10%. Online orders are automatically forwarded to the despatch and accounts department.

A daily pick list is printed by the despatch department and this is used by the warehouse team to despatch goods. The goods are accompanied by a despatch note and all customers are required to sign a copy of this. On return, the signed despatch notes are given to the warehouse team to file.

The sales quantities are entered from the despatch notes and the authorised sales prices are generated by the invoicing system. If a discount has been given, this has to be manually entered by the sales clerk onto the invoice. Due to the expansion of the company, and as there is a large number of sale invoices, extra accounts staff have been asked to help out temporarily with producing the sales invoices. Normally it is only two sales clerks who produce the sales invoices.

Required:

(a) Describe TWO methods for documenting the sales and despatch system; and for each explain an advantage and a disadvantage of using this method. **(6 marks)**

(b) List TWO control objectives of Oregano Co's sales and despatch system. **(2 marks)**

(c) Identify and explain SIX deficiencies in Oregano Co's sales and despatch system and provide a recommendation to address each of these deficiencies. **(12 marks)**

(Total: 20 marks)

153 FOX INDUSTRIES *Walk in the footsteps of a top tutor*

(a) ISA 260 *Communication with Those Charged with Governance* provides guidance to auditors in relation to communicating with those charged with governance on matters arising from the audit of an entity's financial statements.

Required:

(i) Explain why it is important that auditors communicate throughout the audit with those charged with governance; and **(2 marks)**

(ii) Describe THREE examples of matters that the auditors may communicate to those charged with governance. **(3 marks)**

Introduction

Fox Industries Co (Fox) manufactures engineering parts. It has one operating site and a customer base spread across Europe. The company's year end was 30 April 2013. Below is a description of the purchasing and payments system.

Purchasing system

Whenever production materials are required, the relevant department sends a requisition form to the ordering department. An order clerk raises a purchase order and contacts a number of suppliers to see which can despatch the goods first. This supplier is then chosen. The order clerk sends out the purchase order. This is not sequentially numbered and only orders above $5,000 require authorisation.

Purchase invoices are input daily by the purchase ledger clerk, who has been in the role for many years and, as an experienced team member, he does not apply any application controls over the input process. Every week the purchase day book automatically updates the purchase ledger, the purchase ledger is then posted manually to the general ledger by the purchase ledger clerk.

Payments system

Fox maintains a current account and a number of saving (deposit) accounts. The current account is reconciled weekly but the saving (deposit) accounts are only reconciled every two months.

In order to maximise their cash and bank balance, Fox has a policy of delaying payments to all suppliers for as long as possible. Suppliers are paid by a bank transfer. The finance director is given the total amount of the payments list, which he authorises and then processes the bank payments.

Required:

(b)   As the external auditors of Fox Industries Co, write a report to management in respect of the purchasing and payments system described above which:

(i)   Identifies and explains FOUR deficiencies in the system; and

(ii)   Explains the possible implication of each deficiency; and

(iii)   Provides a recommendation to address each deficiency.

A covering letter IS required.

Note: Up to two marks will be awarded within this requirement for presentation and the remaining marks will be split equally between each part.   (14 marks)

(c)   Identify and explain FOUR application controls that should be adopted by Fox Industries Co to ensure the completeness and accuracy of the input of purchase invoices.   (4 marks)

(d)   Describe substantive procedures the auditor should perform to confirm the bank and cash balance of Fox Industries Co at the year end.   (7 marks)

(Total: 30 marks)

154   LILY WINDOW GLASS   *Walk in the footsteps of a top tutor*

Lily Window Glass Co (Lily) is a glass manufacturer, which operates from a large production facility, where it undertakes continuous production 24 hours a day, seven days a week. Also on this site are two warehouses, where the company's raw materials and finished goods are stored. Lily's year end is 31 December.

Lily is finalising the arrangements for the year-end inventory count, which is to be undertaken on 31 December 2012. The finished windows are stored within 20 aisles of the first warehouse. The second warehouse is for large piles of raw materials, such as sand, used in the manufacture of glass. The following arrangements have been made for the inventory count:

The warehouse manager will supervise the count as he is most familiar with the inventory. There will be ten teams of counters and each team will contain two members of staff, one from the finance and one from the manufacturing department. None of the warehouse staff, other than the manager, will be involved in the count.

Each team will count an aisle of finished goods by counting up and then down each aisle. As this process is systematic, it is not felt that the team will need to flag areas once counted. Once the team has finished counting an aisle, they will hand in their sheets and be given a set for another aisle of the warehouse. In addition to the above, to assist with the inventory counting, there will be two teams of counters from the internal audit department and they will perform inventory counts.

The count sheets are sequentially numbered, and the product codes and descriptions are printed on them but no quantities. If the counters identify any inventory which is not on their sheets, then they are to enter the item on a separate sheet, which is not numbered. Once all counting is complete, the sequence of the sheets is checked and any additional sheets are also handed in at this stage. All sheets are completed in ink.

Any damaged goods identified by the counters will be too heavy to move to a central location, hence they are to be left where they are but the counter is to make a note on the inventory sheets detailing the level of damage.

As Lily undertakes continuous production, there will continue to be movements of raw materials and finished goods in and out of the warehouse during the count. These will be kept to a minimum where possible.

The level of work-in-progress in the manufacturing plant is to be assessed by the warehouse manager. It is likely that this will be an immaterial balance. In addition, the raw materials quantities are to be approximated by measuring the height and width of the raw material piles. In the past this task has been undertaken by a specialist; however, the warehouse manager feels confident that he can perform this task.

Required:

(a)   For the inventory count arrangements of Lily Window Glass Co:

   (i)   Identify and explain SIX deficiencies; and

   (ii)   Provide a recommendation to address each deficiency.

The total marks will be split equally between each part   **(12 marks)**

You are the audit senior of Daffodil & Co and are responsible for the audit of inventory for Lily. You will be attending the year-end inventory count on 31 December 2012.

In addition, your manager wishes to utilise computer-assisted audit techniques for the first time for controls and substantive testing in auditing Lily Window Glass Co's inventory.

Required:

(b)   Describe the procedures to be undertaken by the auditor DURING the inventory count of Lily Window Glass Co in order to gain sufficient appropriate audit evidence.   **(6 marks)**

(c)   For the audit of the inventory cycle and year-end inventory balance of Lily Window Glass Co:

(i)   Describe FOUR audit procedures that could be carried out using computer-assisted audit techniques (CAATS);

(ii)   Explain the potential advantages of using CAATs; and

(iii)   Explain the potential disadvantages of using CAATs.

The total marks will be split equally between each part   (12 marks)

(Total: 30 marks)

155   PEAR INTERNATIONAL   *Walk in the footsteps of a top tutor*

(a)   Auditors are required to document their understanding of the client's internal controls. There are various options available for recording the internal control system. Two of these options are narrative notes and internal control questionnaires.

Required:

Describe the advantages and disadvantages to the auditor of narrative notes and internal control questionnaires as methods for documenting a system.   **(5 marks)**

Pear International Co (Pear) is a manufacturer of electrical equipment. It has factories across the country and its customer base includes retailers as well as individuals, to whom direct sales are made through their website. The company's year end is 30 September 2012. You are an audit supervisor of Apple & Co and are currently reviewing documentation of Pear's internal control in preparation for the interim audit.

Pear's website allows individuals to order goods directly, and full payment is taken in advance. Currently the website is not integrated into the inventory system and inventory levels are not checked at the time when orders are placed.

Goods are despatched via local couriers; however, they do not always record customer signatures as proof that the customer has received the goods. Over the past 12 months there have been customer complaints about the delay between sales orders and receipt of goods. Pear has investigated these and found that, in each case, the sales order had been entered into the sales system correctly but was not forwarded to the despatch department for fulfilling.

Pear's retail customers undergo credit checks prior to being accepted and credit limits are set accordingly by sales ledger clerks. These customers place their orders through one of the sales team, who decides on sales discount levels.

Raw materials used in the manufacturing process are purchased from a wide range of suppliers. As a result of staff changes in the purchase ledger department, supplier statement reconciliations are no longer performed. Additionally, changes to supplier details in the purchase ledger master file can be undertaken by purchase ledger clerks as well as supervisors.

In the past six months Pear has changed part of its manufacturing process and as a result some new equipment has been purchased, however, there are considerable levels of plant and equipment which are now surplus to requirement. Purchase requisitions for all new equipment have been authorised by production supervisors and little has been done to reduce the surplus of old equipment.

Required:

(b)   In respect of the internal control of Pear International Co:

    (i)   Identify and explain FIVE deficiencies

    (ii)   Recommend a control to address each of these deficiencies; and

    (iii)   Describe a test of control Apple & Co would perform to assess if each of these controls is operating effectively.   **(15 marks)**

(c)   Describe substantive procedures you should perform at the year end to confirm each of the following for plant and equipment:

    (i)   Additions; and

    (ii)   Disposals.   **(6 marks)**

Pear's directors are considering establishing an internal audit department next year, and the finance director has asked what impact, if any, establishing an internal audit department would have on future external audits performed by Apple & Co.

Required:

(d)   Explain the potential impact on the work performed by Apple & Co during the interim and final audits, if Pear International Co was to establish an internal audit department.   **(4 marks)**

(Total: 30 marks)

156   GREYSTONE   **WALK IN THE FOOTSTEPS OF A TOP TUTOR**

(a)   Auditors have a responsibility under ISA 265 *Communicating Deficiencies in Internal Control to those Charged with Governance and Management,* to communicate deficiencies in internal controls. In particular SIGNIFICANT deficiencies in internal controls must be communicated in writing to those charged with governance.

Required:

Explain examples of matters the auditor should consider in determining whether a deficiency in internal controls is significant.   **(3 marks)**

Greystone Co is a retailer of ladies clothing and accessories. It operates in many countries around the world and has expanded steadily from its base in Europe. Its main market is aimed at 15 to 35 year olds and its prices are mid to low range. The company's year end was 30 September 2010.

In the past the company has bulk ordered its clothing and accessories twice a year. However, if their goods failed to meet the key fashion trends then this resulted in significant inventory write downs. As a result of this the company has recently introduced a just in time ordering system. The fashion buyers make an assessment nine months in advance as to what the key trends are likely to be, these goods are sourced from their suppliers but only limited numbers are initially ordered.

Ordering process

Each country has a purchasing manager who decides on the initial inventory levels for each store, this is not done in conjunction with store or sales managers. These quantities are communicated to the central buying department at the head office in Europe. An ordering clerk amalgamates all country orders by specified regions of countries, such as Central Europe and North America, and passes them to the purchasing director to review and authorise.

As the goods are sold, it is the store manager's responsibility to re-order the goods through the purchasing manager; they are prompted weekly to review inventory levels as although the goods are just in time, it can still take up to four weeks for goods to be received in store.

It is not possible to order goods from other branches of stores as all ordering must be undertaken through the purchasing manager. If a customer requests an item of clothing, which is unavailable in a particular store, then the customer is provided with other branch telephone numbers or recommended to try the company website.

Goods received and invoicing

To speed up the ordering to receipt of goods cycle, the goods are delivered directly from the suppliers to the individual stores. On receipt of goods the quantities received are checked by a sales assistant against the supplier's delivery note, and then the assistant produces a goods received note (GRN). This is done at quiet times of the day so as to maximise sales. The checked GRNs are sent to head office for matching with purchase invoices.

As purchase invoices are received they are manually matched to GRNs from the stores, this can be a very time consuming process as some suppliers may have delivered to over 500 stores. Once the invoice has been agreed then it is sent to the purchasing director for authorisation. It is at this stage that the invoice is entered onto the purchase ledger.

Required:

(b)   List THREE control objectives of Greystone's purchasing system.   **(3 marks)**

(c)   In respect of the purchasing system above:

    (i)   Identify and explain SIX deficiencies in that system

    (ii)   Provide a recommendation to address each deficiency

    (iii) Describe a test of control the auditor would perform to assess if each of these controls is operating effectively.   **(18 marks)**

(d)   Describe substantive procedures the auditor should perform on the year-end trade payables of Greystone Co.   **(6 marks)**

(Total: 30 marks)

157 SHINY HAPPY WINDOWS *Walk in the footsteps of a top tutor*

(a) Explain the terms 'control objectives' and 'control procedures' and explain the relationship between them. **(3 marks)**

(b) Shiny Happy Windows Co (SHW) is a window cleaning company. Customers' windows are cleaned monthly, the window cleaner then posts a stamped addressed envelope for payment through the customer's front door.

SHW has a large number of receivable balances and these customers pay by cheque or cash, which is received in the stamped addressed envelopes in the post. The following procedures are applied to the cash received cycle:

(1) A junior clerk from the accounts department opens the post and if any cheques or cash have been sent, she records the receipts in the cash received log and then places all the monies into the locked small cash box.

(2) The contents of the cash box are counted each day and every few days these sums are banked by which ever member of the finance team is available.

(3) The cashier records the details of the cash received log into the cash receipts day book and also updates the sales ledger.

(4) Usually on a monthly basis the cashier performs a bank reconciliation, which he then files, if he misses a month then he catches this up in the following month's reconciliation.

Required:

For the cash cycle of SHW:

(i) Identify and explain FOUR deficiencies in the system **(4 marks)**

(ii) Suggest controls to address each of these deficiencies; and **(4 marks)**

(iii) List tests of controls the auditor of SHW would perform to assess if the controls are operating effectively. **(4 marks)**

(c) Describe substantive procedures an auditor would perform in verifying a company's bank balance. **(5 marks)**

(Total: 20 marks)

158 MATALAS *Walk in the footsteps of a top tutor*

Matalas Co sells cars, car parts and petrol from 25 different locations in one country. Each branch has up to 20 staff working there, although most of the accounting systems are designed and implemented from the company's head office. All accounting systems, apart from petty cash, are computerised, with the internal audit department frequently advising and implementing controls within those systems.

Matalas has an internal audit department of six staff, all of whom have been employed at Matalas for a minimum of five years and some for as long as 15 years. In the past, the chief internal auditor appoints staff within the internal audit department, although the chief executive officer (CEO) is responsible for appointing the chief internal auditor. The chief internal auditor reports directly to the finance director. The finance director also assists the chief internal auditor in deciding on the scope of work of the internal audit department.

You are an audit manager in the internal audit department of Matalas. You are currently auditing the petty cash systems at the different branches. Your initial systems notes on petty cash contain the following information:

(1)   The average petty cash balance at each branch is $5,000.

(2)   Average monthly expenditure is $1,538, with amounts ranging from $1 to $500.

(3)   Petty cash is kept in a lockable box on a bookcase in the accounts office.

(4)   Vouchers for expenditure are signed by the person incurring that expenditure to confirm they have received re-imbursement from petty cash.

(5)   Vouchers are recorded in the petty cash book by the accounts clerk; each voucher records the date, reason for the expenditure, amount of expenditure and person incurring that expenditure.

(6)   Petty cash is counted every month by the accounts clerk, who is in charge of the cash. The petty cash balance is then reimbursed using the 'imprest' system and the journal entry produced to record expenditure in the general ledger.

(7)   The cheque to reimburse petty cash is signed by the accountant at the branch at the same time as the journal entry to the general ledger is reviewed.

Required:

(a)   **Explain the issues which limit the independence of the internal audit department in Matalas Co. Recommend a way of overcoming each issue.** **(8 marks)**

(b)   **Explain the internal control deficiencies in the petty cash system at Matalas Co. For each deficiency, recommend a control to overcome that deficiency.** **(12 marks)**

(Total: 20 marks)

159   ANDROMEDA *Walk in the footsteps of a top tutor*

(a)   **Explain FOUR factors which influence the reliability of audit evidence.** **(4 marks)**

Andromeda Industries Co (Andromeda) develops and manufactures a wide range of fast moving consumer goods. The company's year end is 31 December 2015 and the forecast profit before tax is $8.3 million. You are the audit manager of Neptune & Co and the year-end audit is due to commence in January. The following information has been gathered during the planning process:

Inventory count

Andromeda's raw materials and finished goods inventory are stored in 12 warehouses across the country. Each of these warehouses is expected to contain material levels of inventory at the year end. It is expected that there will be no significant work in progress held at any of the sites. Each count will be supervised by a member of Andromeda's internal audit department and the counts will all take place on 31 December, when all movements of goods in and out of the warehouses will cease.

Research and development

Andromeda spends over $2 million annually on developing new product lines. This year it incurred expenditure on five projects, all of which are at different stages of development. Once they meet the recognition criteria under IAS 38 Intangible Assets for development expenditure, Andromeda includes the costs incurred within intangible assets. Once production commences, the intangible assets are amortised on a straight line basis over five years.

Required:

(b) Describe audit procedures you would perform during the audit of Andromeda Industries Co:

    (i) BEFORE and DURING the inventory counts; and   (8 marks)

    (ii) In relation to research and development expenditure.   (4 marks)

(c) During the audit, the team discovers that one of the five development projects, valued at $980,000 and included within intangible assets, does not meet the criteria for capitalisation. The finance director does not intend to change the accounting treatment adopted as she considers this an immaterial amount.

Required:

Discuss the issue and describe the impact on the audit report, if any, if the issue remains unresolved.   (4 marks)

        (Total: 20 marks)

160 HAWTHORN *Walk in the footsteps of a top tutor*

(a) (i) Identify and explain FOUR financial statement assertions relevant to classes of transactions and events for the year under audit; and

    (ii) For each identified assertion, describe a substantive procedure relevant to the audit of REVENUE.   (8 marks)

(b) Hawthorn Enterprises Co (Hawthorn) manufactures and distributes fashion clothing to retail stores. Its year end was 31 March 2015. You are the audit manager and the year-end audit is due to commence shortly. The following three matters have been brought to your attention.

(i) **Supplier statement reconciliations**

Hawthorn receives monthly statements from its main suppliers and although these have been retained, none have been reconciled to the payables ledger as at 31 March 2015. The engagement partner has asked the audit senior to recommend the procedures to be performed on supplier statements.

        (3 marks)

(ii)   Bank reconciliation

During last year's audit of Hawthorn's bank and cash, significant cut off errors were discovered with a number of post year-end cheques being processed prior to the year end to reduce payables. The finance director has assured the audit engagement partner that this error has not occurred again this year and that the bank reconciliation has been carefully prepared. The audit engagement partner has asked that the bank reconciliation is comprehensively audited.

(4 marks)

(iii)   Receivables

Hawthorn's receivables ledger has increased considerably during the year, and the year-end balance is $2.3 million compared to $1.4 million last year. The finance director of Hawthorn has requested that a receivables circularisation is not carried out as a number of their customers complained last year about the inconvenience involved in responding. The engagement partner has agreed to this request, and tasked you with identifying alternative procedures to confirm the existence and valuation of receivables.

(5 marks)

Required:

Describe substantive procedures you would perform to obtain sufficient and appropriate audit evidence in relation to the above three matters.

Note: The mark allocation is shown against each of the three matters above.

(Total: 20 marks)

161   ROSE LEISURE CLUB   *Walk in the footsteps of a top tutor*

(a)   **Identify and explain each of the FIVE fundamental principles contained within ACCA's Code** *of Ethics and Conduct.*   **(5 marks)**

(b)   Rose Leisure Club Co (Rose) operates a chain of health and fitness clubs. Its year end was 31 October 2012. You are the audit manager and the year-end audit is due to commence shortly. The following three matters have been brought to your attention.

(i)   Trade payables and accruals

Rose's finance director has notified you that an error occurred in the closing of the purchase ledger at the year end. Rather than it closing on 1 November, it accidentally closed one week earlier on 25 October. All purchase invoices received between 25 October and the year end have been posted to the 2013 year-end purchase ledger.   **(6 marks)**

(ii)   Receivables

Rose's trade receivables have historically been low as most members pay monthly in advance. However, during the year a number of companies have taken up group memberships at Rose and hence the receivables balance is now material. The audit senior has undertaken a receivables circularisation for the balances at the year end; however, there are a number who have not responded and a number of responses with differences.   **(5 marks)**

(iii) Reorganisation

The company recently announced its plans to reorganise its health and fitness clubs. This will involve closing some clubs for refurbishment, retraining some existing staff and disposing of some surplus assets. These plans were agreed at a board meeting in October and announced to their shareholders on 29 October. Rose is proposing to make a reorganisation provision in the financial statements. **(4 marks)**

Required:

Describe substantive procedures you would perform to obtain sufficient and appropriate audit evidence in relation to the above three matters.

Note: The mark allocation is shown against each of the three matters above.

(Total: 20 marks)

162 PINEAPPLE BEACH HOTEL *Walk in the footsteps of a top tutor*

(a) (i) **Identify and explain FOUR financial statement assertions relevant to account balances at the year end; and**

(ii) **For each identified assertion, describe a substantive procedure relevant to the audit of year-end inventory.** **(8 marks)**

Pineapple Beach Hotel Co (Pineapple) operates a hotel providing accommodation, leisure facilities and restaurants. Its year end was 30 April 2012. You are the audit senior of Berry & Co and are currently preparing the audit programmes for the year end audit of Pineapple. You are reviewing the notes of last week's meeting between the audit manager and finance director where two material issues were discussed.

Depreciation

Pineapple incurred significant capital expenditure during the year on updating the leisure facilities for the hotel. The finance director has proposed that the new leisure equipment should be depreciated over 10 years using the straight-line method.

Food poisoning

Pineapple's directors received correspondence in March from a group of customers who attended a wedding at the hotel. They have alleged that they suffered severe food poisoning from food eaten at the hotel and are claiming substantial damages. Pineapple's lawyers have received the claim and believe that the lawsuit against the company is unlikely to be successful.

Required:

Describe substantive procedures to obtain sufficient and appropriate audit evidence in relation to the above two issues.

Note: The total marks will be split equally between each issue.

(8 marks)

(c) **List and explain the purpose of FOUR items that should be included on every working paper prepared by the audit team.** **(4 marks)**

(Total: 20 marks)

163 TIRROL **WALK IN THE FOOTSTEPS OF A TOP TUTOR**

Following a competitive tender, your audit firm Cal & Co has just gained a new audit client Tirrol Co. You are the manager in charge of planning the audit work. Tirrol Co's year end is 30 June 2009 with a scheduled date to complete the audit of 15 August 2009. The date now is 3 June 2009.

Tirrol Co provides repair services to motor vehicles from 25 different locations. All inventory, sales and purchasing systems are computerised, with each location maintaining its own computer system. The software in each location is the same because the programs were written specifically for Tirrol Co by a reputable software house. Data from each location is amalgamated on a monthly basis at Tirrol Co's head office to produce management and financial accounts.

You are currently planning your audit approach for Tirrol Co. One option being considered is to re-write Cal & Co's audit software to interrogate the computerised inventory systems in each location of Tirrol Co (except for head office) as part of inventory valuation testing. However, you have also been informed that any computer testing will have to be on a live basis and you are aware that July is a major holiday period for your audit firm.

Required:

(a) (i)   Explain the benefits of using audit software in the audit of Tirrol Co.
                                                                      (4 marks)

      (ii)   Explain the problems that may be encountered in the audit of Tirrol Co and
             for each problem, explain how that problem could be overcome.   **(10 marks)**

(b) Following a discussion with the management at Tirrol Co you now understand that the internal audit department are prepared to assist with the statutory audit. Specifically, the chief internal auditor is prepared to provide you with documentation on the computerised inventory systems at Tirrol Co. The documentation provides details of the software and shows diagrammatically how transactions are processed through the inventory system. This documentation can be used to significantly decrease the time needed to understand the computer systems and enable audit software to be written for this year's audit.

Required:

Explain how you will evaluate the computer systems documentation produced by the internal audit department in order to place reliance on it during your audit.

                                                                      (6 marks)

                                                               (Total: 20 marks)

THE FOLLOWING QUESTIONS ARE EXAM STANDARD BUT DO NOT REFLECT THE CURRENT EXAM FORMAT. THESE QUESTIONS PROVIDE VALUABLE PRACTICE FOR STUDENTS NEVERTHELESS.

AUDIT FRAMEWORK

164 CINNAMON *Walk in the footsteps of a top tutor*

Salt & Pepper & Co (Salt & Pepper) is which has seen its revenue decline steadily over the past few years.

Salt & Pepper, a firm of Chartered Certified Accountants, has recently been approached by a prospective new audit client, Cinnamon Brothers Co (Cinnamon), whose year end is 31 December. Cinnamon requires their audit to be completed by the end of February; however, this is a very busy time for Salt & Pepper and so it is intended to use more junior staff as they are available. Additionally, in order to save time and cost, Salt & Pepper have not contacted Cinnamon's previous auditors.

The firm is seeking to reduce audit costs and has therefore decided not to update the engagement letters of existing clients, on the basis that these letters do not tend to change much on a yearly basis. One of Salt & Pepper's existing clients has proposed that this year's audit fee should be based on a percentage of their final pre-tax profit. The partners are excited about this option as they believe it will increase the overall audit fee.

Required:

(a) Describe the steps that Salt & Pepper should take in relation to Cinnamon:

   (i) Prior to accepting the audit; and   (5 marks)

   (ii) To confirm whether the preconditions for the audit are in place. (3 marks)

(b) State FOUR matters that should be included within an audit engagement letter.

                                                                        (2 marks)

(c) Explain the quality control procedures Salt & Pepper should implement to ensure the audit is performed efficiently and effectively given the time pressure for completion and the use of junior staff.   (4 marks)

(d) (i) Identify and explain THREE ethical risks which arise from the above actions of Salt & Pepper & Co; and

   (ii) For each ethical risk explain the steps which Salt & Pepper & Co should adopt to reduce the risks arising.

   Note: The total marks will be split equally between each part.   (6 marks)

                                                                 (Total: 20 marks)

165 ORANGE FINANCIALS *Walk in the footsteps of a top tutor*

(a)   Explain the external auditors' responsibilities in relation to the prevention and detection of fraud and error.   **(4 marks)**

You are the audit manager of Currant & Co and you are planning the audit of Orange Financials Co (Orange), who specialise in the provision of loans and financial advice to individuals and companies. Currant & Co has audited Orange for many years.

The directors are planning to list Orange on a stock exchange within the next few months and have asked if the engagement partner can attend the meetings with potential investors. In addition, as the finance director of Orange is likely to be quite busy with the listing, he has asked if Currant & Co can produce the financial statements for the current year.

During the year, the assistant finance director of Orange left and joined Currant & Co as a partner. It has been suggested that due to his familiarity with Orange, he should be appointed to provide an independent partner review for the audit.

Once Orange obtains its stock exchange listing it will require several assignments to be undertaken, for example, obtaining advice about corporate governance best practice. Currant & Co is very keen to be appointed to these engagements, however, Orange has implied that in order to gain this work Currant & Co needs to complete the external audit quickly and with minimal questions/issues.

The finance director has informed you that once the stock exchange listing has been completed, he would like the engagement team to attend a weekend away at a luxury hotel with his team, as a thank you for all their hard work. In addition, he has offered a senior member of the engagement team a short-term loan at a significantly reduced interest rate.

Required:

(b)   (i)   Explain SIX ethical threats which may affect the independence of Currant & Co's audit of Orange Financials Co; and

   (ii)   For each threat explain how it might be reduced to an acceptable level.

                                                           (12 marks)

(c)   Orange is aware that subsequent to the stock exchange listing it will need to establish an audit committee and has asked for some advice in relation to this.

   Required:

   Explain the benefits to Orange of establishing an audit committee.   **(4 marks)**

                                                           (Total: 20 marks)

166 LV FONES *Walk in the footsteps of a top tutor*

(a) State the FIVE threats contained within ACCA's Code of Ethics and Conduct and for each threat list ONE example of a circumstance that may create the threat.

(5 marks)

You are the audit manager of Jones & Co and you are planning the audit of LV Fones Co, which has been an audit client for four years and specialises in manufacturing luxury mobile phones.

During the planning stage of the audit you have obtained the following information. The employees of LV Fones Co are entitled to purchase mobile phones at a discount of 10%. The audit team has in previous years been offered the same level of staff discount.

During the year the financial controller of LV Fones was ill and hence unable to work. The company had no spare staff able to fulfil the role and hence a qualified audit senior of Jones & Co was seconded to the client for three months. The audit partner has recommended that the audit senior work on the audit as he has good knowledge of the client. The fee income derived from LV Fones was boosted by this engagement and along with the audit and tax fee, now accounts for 16% of the firm's total fees.

From a review of the correspondence files you note that the partner and the finance director have known each other socially for many years and in fact went on holiday together last summer with their families. As a result of this friendship the partner has not yet spoken to the client about the fee for last year's audit, 20% of which is still outstanding.

Required:

(b) (i) Explain the ethical threats which may affect the independence of Jones & Co's audit of LV Fones Co. (5 marks)

(ii) For each threat explain how it might be avoided. (5 marks)

(c) Describe the steps an audit firm should perform prior to accepting a new audit engagement. (5 marks)

(Total: 20 marks)

167 SAXOPHONE ENTERPRISES *Walk in the footsteps of a top tutor*

Saxophone Enterprises Co (Saxophone) has been trading for 15 years selling insurance and has recently become a listed company. In accordance with corporate governance principles Saxophone maintains a small internal audit department. The directors feel that the team needs to increase in size and specialist skills are required, but they are unsure whether to recruit more internal auditors, or to outsource the whole function to their external auditors, Cello & Co.

Saxophone is required to comply with corporate governance principles in order to maintain its listed status; hence the finance director has undertaken a review of whether or not the company complies.

Bill Bassoon is the chairman of Saxophone, until last year he was the chief executive. Bill is unsure if Saxophone needs more non-executive directors as there are currently three non-executive directors out of the eight board members. He is considering appointing one of his close friends, who is a retired chief executive of a manufacturing company, as a non-executive director.

The finance director, Jessie Oboe, decides on the amount of remuneration each director is paid. Currently all remuneration is in the form of an annual bonus based on profits. Jessie is considering setting up an audit committee, but has not undertaken this task yet as she is very busy. A new sales director was appointed nine months ago. He has yet to undertake his board training as this is normally provided by the chief executive and this role is currently vacant.

There are a large number of shareholders and therefore the directors believe that it is impractical and too costly to hold an annual general meeting of shareholders. Instead, the board has suggested sending out the financial statements and any voting resolutions by email; shareholders can then vote on the resolutions via email.

Required:

(a) **Explain the advantages and disadvantages for each of Saxophone Enterprises Co AND Cello & Co of outsourcing the internal audit department.**

   Note: The total marks will be split as follows:

   Saxophone Enterprises Co (8 marks)

   Cello & Co (2 marks)   (10 marks)

(b) **In respect of the corporate governance of Saxophone Enterprises Co:**

   (i) **Identify and explain FIVE corporate governance weaknesses; and**

   (ii) **Provide a recommendation to address each weakness.**

   Note: The total marks will be split equally between each part.   (10 marks)

                                                                          (Total: 20 marks)

168   GOOFY   *Walk in the footsteps of a top tutor*

You are an audit manager in NAB & Co, a large audit firm which specialises in the audit of retailers. The firm currently audits Goofy Co, a food retailer, but Goofy Co's main competitor, Mickey Co, has approached the audit firm to act as auditors. Both companies are highly competitive and Goofy Co is concerned that if NAB & Co audits both companies then confidential information could pass across to Mickey Co.

Required:

(a) **Explain the safeguards that your firm should implement to ensure that this conflict of interest is properly managed.**   (4 marks)

Goofy Co's year end is 31 December, which is traditionally a busy time for NAB & Co. Goofy Co currently has an internal audit department of five employees but they have struggled to undertake the variety and extent of work required by the company, hence Goofy Co is considering whether to recruit to expand the department or to outsource the internal audit department. If outsourced, Goofy Co would require a team to undertake monthly visits to test controls at the various shops across the country, and to perform ad hoc operational reviews at shops and head office.

Goofy Co is considering using NAB & Co to provide the internal audit services as well as remain as external auditors.

Required:

(b) Discuss the advantages and disadvantages to both Goofy Co and NAB & Co of outsourcing their internal audit department. **(10 marks)**

(c) The audit engagement partner for Goofy Co has been in place for approximately six years and her son has just accepted a job offer from Goofy Co as a sales manager; this role would entitle him to shares in Goofy Co as part of his remuneration package. If NAB & Co is appointed as internal as well as external auditors, then Goofy Co has suggested that the external audit fee should be renegotiated with at least 20% of the fee being based on the profit after tax of the company as they feel that this will align the interests of NAB & Co and Goofy Co.

Required:

From the information in (c) explain the ethical threats which may affect the independence of NAB & Co in respect of the audit of Goofy Co, and for each threat explain how it may be reduced. **(6 marks)**

(Total: 20 marks)

169 MONTEHODGE *Walk in the footsteps of a top tutor*

(a) Discuss the advantages and disadvantages of outsourcing an internal audit department. **(8 marks)**

(b) MonteHodge Co has a sales income of $253 million and employs 1,200 people in 15 different locations. MonteHodge Co provides various financial services from pension and investment advice to individuals, to maintaining cash books and cash forecasting in small to medium-sized companies. The company is owned by six shareholders, who belong to the same family; it is not listed on any stock-exchange and the shareholders have no intention of applying for a listing. However, an annual audit is required by statute and additional regulation of the financial services sector is expected in the near future.

Most employees are provided with on-line, real-time computer systems, which present financial and stock market information to enable the employees to provide up-to-date advice to their clients. Accounting systems record income, which is based on fees generated from investment advice. Expenditure is mainly fixed, being salaries, office rent, lighting and heating, etc. Internal control systems are limited; the directors tending to trust staff and being more concerned with making profits than implementing detailed controls.

Four of the shareholders are board members, with one member being the chairman and chief executive officer. The financial accountant is not qualified, although has many years experience in preparing financial statements.

Required:

Discuss the reasons for and against having an internal audit department in MonteHodge Co. **(12 marks)**

(Total: 20 marks)

REVIEW AND REPORTING

170 CHESTNUT & CO *Walk in the footsteps of a top tutor*

(a) ISA 700 *Forming an Opinion and Reporting on Financial Statements* requires auditors to produce an audit report. This report should contain a number of consistent elements so that users are able to understand what the audit report means.

Required:

Describe FIVE elements of an unmodified auditor's report and for each explain why they are included.   **(5 marks)**

You are the audit manager of Chestnut & Co and are reviewing the key issues identified in the files of three audit clients.

Palm Industries Co (Palm)

Palm's year end was 31 March 2015 and the draft financial statements show revenue of $28.2 million, receivables of $5.6 million and profit before tax of $4.8 million. The fieldwork stage for this audit has been completed.

A customer of Palm owed an amount of $350,000 at the year end. Testing of receivables in April highlighted that no amounts had been paid to Palm from this customer as they were disputing the quality of certain goods received from Palm. The finance director is confident the issue will be resolved and no allowance for receivables was made with regards to this balance.

Ash Trading Co (Ash)

Ash is a new client of Chestnut & Co, its year end was 31 January 2015 and the firm was only appointed auditors in February 2015, as the previous auditors were suddenly unable to undertake the audit. The fieldwork stage for this audit is currently ongoing.

The inventory count at Ash's warehouse was undertaken on 31 January 2015 and was overseen by the company's internal audit department. Neither Chestnut & Co nor the previous auditors attended the count. Detailed inventory records were maintained but it was not possible to undertake another full inventory count subsequent to the year end.

The draft financial statements show a profit before tax of $2.4 million, revenue of $10.1 million and inventory of $510,000.

Bullfinch.com (Bullfinch)

Bullfinch.com is a website design company whose year end was 31 October 2015. The audit is almost complete and the financial statements are due to be signed shortly. Revenue for the year is $11.2 million and profit before tax is $3.8 million. A key customer, with a receivables balance at the year end of $283,000, has just notified Bullfinch.com that they are experiencing cash flow difficulties and so are unable to make any payments for the foreseeable future. The finance director has notified the auditor that he will write this balance off as an irrecoverable debt in the 2016 financial statements.

Required:

(b)   For each of the issues:

(i)   Discuss the issue, including an assessment of whether it is material;

(ii)   Recommend ONE procedure the audit team should undertake to try to resolve the issue; and

(iii)   Describe the impact on the audit report if the issue remains UNRESOLVED.

Notes:

1   Marks will be split equally between each issue.

2   Audit report extracts are NOT required.   **(15 marks)**

(Total: 20 marks)

171   CLARINET *Walk in the footsteps of a top tutor*

Clarinet Co (Clarinet) is a computer hardware specialist and has been trading for over five years. The company is funded partly through overdrafts and loans and also by several large shareholders; the year end is 30 April 2014.

Clarinet has experienced significant growth in previous years; however, in the current year a new competitor, Drums Design Co (Drums), has entered the market and through competitive pricing has gained considerable market share from Clarinet. One of Clarinet's larger customers has stopped trading with them and has moved its business to Drums. In addition, a number of Clarinet's specialist developers have left the company and joined Drums. Clarinet has found it difficult to replace these employees due to the level of their skills and knowledge. Clarinet has just received notification that its main supplier who provides the company with specialist electrical equipment has ceased to trade.

Clarinet is looking to develop new products to differentiate itself from the rest of its competitors. It has approached its shareholders to finance this development; however, they declined to invest further in Clarinet. Clarinet's loan is long term and it has met all repayments on time. The overdraft has increased significantly over the year and the directors have informed you that the overdraft facility is due for renewal next month, and they are confident it will be renewed.

The directors have produced a cash flow forecast which shows a significantly worsening position over the coming 12 months. They are confident with the new products being developed, and in light of their trading history of significant growth, believe it is unnecessary to make any disclosures in the financial statements regarding going concern.

At the year end, Clarinet received notification from one of its customers that the hardware installed by Clarinet for the customers' online ordering system has not been operating correctly. As a result, the customer has lost significant revenue and has informed Clarinet that they intend to take legal action against them for loss of earnings. Clarinet has investigated the problem post year end and discovered that other work-in-progress is similarly affected and inventory should be written down. The finance director believes that as this misstatement was identified after the year end, it can be amended in the 2015 financial statements.

Required:

(a) Describe the procedures the auditors of Clarinet Co should undertake in relation to the uncorrected inventory misstatement identified above. **(4 marks)**

(b) Explain SIX potential indicators that Clarinet Co is not a going concern. **(6 marks)**

(c) Describe the audit procedures which you should perform in assessing whether or not Clarinet Co is a going concern. **(6 marks)**

(d) The auditors have been informed that Clarinet's bankers will not make a decision on the overdraft facility until after the audit report is completed. The directors have now agreed to include some going concern disclosures.

Required:

Describe the impact on the audit report of Clarinet Co if the auditor believes the company is a going concern but that this is subject to a material uncertainty.

(4 marks)

(Total: 20 marks)

172   PAPRIKA *Walk in the footsteps of a top tutor*

(a) (i) Explain the meaning of the term 'pervasive' in the context of the audit report. **(2 marks)**

(ii) Explain the two types of modified opinions when there is an issue which is considered material and pervasive. **(2 marks)**

You are an audit manager in Brown & Co and you are nearing completion of the audit of Paprika & Co (Paprika). The audit senior has produced extracts below from the draft audit report for Paprika.

Auditor's responsibility

(1) Our responsibility is to express an opinion on all pages of the financial statements based on our audit.

(2) We conducted our audit in accordance with most of the International Standards on Auditing.

(3) Those standards require that we comply with ethical requirements and plan and perform the audit to obtain maximum assurance as to whether the financial statements are free from all misstatements whether caused by fraud or error.

(4) We have a responsibility to prevent and detect fraud and error and to prepare the financial statements in accordance with International Financial Reporting Standards.

(5) An audit involves performing procedures to obtain evidence about the amounts and disclosures in the financial statements. The procedures selected depend on the availability and experience of audit team members.

(6) We considered internal controls relevant to the entity; and express an opinion on the effectiveness of these internal controls.

(7) We did not evaluate the overall presentation of the financial statements, as this is management's responsibility.

(8) We considered the reasonableness of any new accounting estimates made by management. We did not review the appropriateness of accounting policies as these are the same as last year.

(9) In order to confirm raw material inventory quantities, we relied on the work undertaken by an independent expert.

Required:

(b) **Describe the factors to consider and steps Brown & Co should take, prior to placing reliance on the work of the independent expert, in order to confirm raw material quantities.** **(4 marks)**

(c) **For the above audit report extracts, identify and explain SIX elements of this report which require amendment.**

Note: Redrafted audit report extracts are not required. **(12 marks)**

(Total: 20 marks)

173 PANDA *Walk in the footsteps of a top tutor*

(a) **Explain the five elements of an assurance engagement.** **(5 marks)**

(b) Panda Co manufactures chemicals and has a factory and four offsite storage locations for finished goods. Panda Co's year end was 30 April 2013. The final audit is almost complete and the financial statements and audit report are due to be signed next week. Revenue for the year is $55 million and profit before taxation is $5.6 million.

The following two events have occurred subsequent to the year end. No amendments or disclosures have been made in the financial statements.

Event 1 – Defective chemicals

Panda Co undertakes extensive quality control checks prior to despatch of any chemicals. Testing on 3 May 2013 found that a batch of chemicals produced in April was defective. The cost of this batch was $0.85 million. In its current condition it can be sold at a scrap value of $0.1 million. The costs of correcting the defect are too significant for Panda Co's management to consider this an alternative option.

Event 2 – Explosion

An explosion occurred at the smallest of the four offsite storage locations on 20 May 2013. This resulted in some damage to inventory and property, plant and equipment. Panda Co's management have investigated the cause of the explosion and believe that they are unlikely to be able to claim on their insurance. Management of Panda Co has estimated that the value of damaged inventory and property, plant and equipment was $0.9 million and it now has no scrap value.

Required:

For each of the two events above:

(i) **Explain whether the financial statements require amendment; and**

(ii) **Describe audit procedures that should be performed in order to form a conclusion on any required amendment.**

Note: The total marks will be split equally between each event. **(12 marks)**

(c) The directors do not wish to make any amendments or disclosures to the financial statements for the explosion (event 2).

Required:

Explain the impact on the audit report should this issue remain unresolved.

(3 marks)

(Total: 20 marks)

174   VIOLET & CO   *Walk in the footsteps of a top tutor*

(a) **Explain the purpose of, and procedures for, obtaining written representations.**

(5 marks)

(b) The directors of a company have provided the external audit firm with an oral representation confirming that the bank overdraft balances included within current liabilities are complete.

Required:

Describe the relevance and reliability of this oral representation as a source of evidence to confirm the completeness of the bank overdraft balances.   (3 marks)

(c) You are the audit manager of Violet & Co and you are currently reviewing the audit files for several of your clients for which the audit fieldwork is complete. The audit seniors have raised the following issues:

Daisy Designs Co (Daisy)

Daisy's year end is 30 September, however, subsequent to the year end the company's sales ledger has been corrupted by a computer virus. Daisy's finance director was able to produce the financial statements prior to this occurring; however, the audit team has been unable to access the sales ledger to undertake detailed testing of revenue or year-end receivables. All other accounting records are unaffected and there are no backups available for the sales ledger. Daisy's revenue is $15.6m, its receivables are $3.4m and profit before tax is $2m.

Fuchsia Enterprises Co (Fuchsia)

Fuchsia has experienced difficult trading conditions and as a result it has lost significant market share. The cash flow forecast has been reviewed during the audit fieldwork and it shows a significant net cash outflow. Management are confident that further funding can be obtained and so have prepared the financial statements on a going concern basis with no additional disclosures; the audit senior is highly sceptical about this. The prior year financial statements showed a profit before tax of $1.2m; however, the current year loss before tax is $4.4m and the forecast net cash outflow for the next 12 months is $3.2m.

Required:

For each of the two issues:

(i)   Discuss the issue, including an assessment of whether it is material;

(ii)   Recommend procedures the audit team should undertake at the completion stage to try to resolve the issue; and

(iii)   Describe the impact on the audit report if the issue remains unresolved.

Notes: 1   The total marks will be split equally between each issue.

             2   Audit report extracts are NOT required.   **(12 marks)**

                                                                          (Total: 20 marks)

175   MINNIE   *Walk in the footsteps of a top tutor*

You are the audit manager of Daffy & Co and you are briefing your team on the approach to adopt in undertaking the review and finalisation stage of the audit. In particular, your audit senior is unsure about the steps to take in relation to uncorrected misstatements.

During the audit of Minnie Co the following uncorrected misstatement has been noted.

The property balance was revalued during the year by an independent expert valuer and an error was made in relation to the assumptions provided to the valuer.

Required:

(a)   Explain the term 'misstatement' and describe the auditor's responsibility in relation to misstatements.   **(4 marks)**

(b)   Describe the factors Daffy & Co should consider when placing reliance on the work of the independent valuer.   **(4 marks)**

(c)   The following additional issues have arisen during the course of the audit of Minnie Co. Profit before tax is $10m.

       (i)   Depreciation has been calculated on the total of land and buildings. In previous years it has only been charged on buildings. Total depreciation is $2.5m and the element charged to land only is $0.7m.   **(4 marks)**

       (ii)   Minnie Co's computerised wages program is backed up daily, however for a period of two months the wages records and the back-ups have been corrupted, and therefore cannot be accessed. Wages and salaries for these two months are $1.1m.   **(4 marks)**

       (iii) Minnie Co's main competitor has filed a lawsuit for $5m against them alleging a breach of copyright; this case is ongoing and will not be resolved prior to the audit report being signed. The matter is correctly disclosed as a contingent liability.   **(4 marks)**

Required:

Discuss each of these issues and describe the impact on the audit report if the above issues remain unresolved.

Note: Audit report extracts are NOT required.   **(Total: 20 marks)**

Section 3

ANSWERS TO OBJECTIVE TEST CASE QUESTIONS

AUDIT FRAMEWORK

1   A

This is a well-known definition that has been derived from the guidance in the UK Corporate Governance Code.

2   D

Audit, remuneration and nomination committees are fundamental corporate governance best practice. The risk committee is generally a voluntary committee. In the absence of a risk committee, controls would be addressed by the audit committee.

3   C

NEDs should not be paid a bonus and therefore the acceptance of the fixed fee is an advantage. Also NEDs should seek re-election by shareholders at regular intervals and therefore long term fixed contracts are not practical. Independence is a great advantage for NEDs to be able to represent shareholders within the boardroom. A lack of relevant retail experience is the only real disadvantage in the list.

4   B

The lack of independence due to the relationship with the CEO along with the request for a fixed seven year contract when NEDs should seek regular re-election from shareholders are both disadvantages to him taking a NED position.

5   D

An audit committee will not **implement** controls themselves neither have they responsibility for preparing the financial statements. The audit committee focus on financial reporting integrity and as part of this will monitor and review internal audit effectiveness.

6   B

Statement 1 is not correct as internal audit (IA) should not report to the finance director as this would impact on their independence. Some of the internal controls and functions IA review are the responsibility of the finance director and they may not act on any recommendations which appear to criticise their department. Statement 2 is correct as companies are not required to implement and maintain an IA function. Corporate governance principles recommend that listed companies maintain an IA function. If an IA function is not in place the company should assess the need for one on an annual basis.

7   A

Internal audit should not implement their own recommendations. This could create a self-review threat.

8   C

An outsourced firm is likely to be more independent as they are not employees of the company. The outsourced firm is responsible for staffing and bears the risk of staffing issues such as staff turnover. An outsourced firm is likely to have less awareness of the client's risks. Flexibility is reduced as the internal auditor is not an employee and cannot be controlled in the same way.

9   B

It will generally be the role of the HR and/or operational departments to instigate disciplinary proceedings against employees.

10   D

All are legitimate limitations of an internal audit function.

11   D

The conceptual framework provides guidelines with the objective that the auditor chooses the most appropriate course of action in the circumstances. This allows flexibility to deal with all possible situations. The guidelines followed are professional guidance but are not legal requirements.

12   A

Professional scepticism refers to the state of mind the auditor should maintain whilst performing the audit. With regards to independence there is an overriding requirement to be independent rather than it being a specific principle.

13   C

As Foliage is a listed company, Jane Leaf should not serve as the independent review partner for a period of two years.

14   B

Bark & Co should assess whether audit and non-audit fees would represent more than 15% of gross practice income for two consecutive years. If the recurring fees are likely to exceed 15% of annual practice income this year, additional consideration should be given as to whether the taxation and non-audit assignments should be undertaken by the firm. In addition, if the fees do exceed 15% then this should be disclosed to those charged with governance at Foliage. It is highly unlikely Bark will need to resign as auditors.

15   A

There will be a familiarity between the audit manager in their new capacity at Bark and the audit team. The audit team may be too trusting of their previous colleague. A self-review threat would be created if an employee of the client joined the audit firm and was assigned to the audit of their previous employer. A self-interest threat would have arisen during the recruitment process as the judgement of the audit manager may have been affected by the desire to be appointed financial controller. As the audit manager has been recruited this threat is no longer present.

16   A

The audit team may be too trusting of or too sympathetic to the financial controller because of their previous relationship with him (familiarity threat). A self-review threat would apply if the financial controller was now employed as an auditor and assigned to the audit of the previous employer.

17   A

A self-interest threat would be created as the audit team may not wish to upset the client in any way for fear of losing the discount.

18   B

A discount of 40% is highly unlikely to be a modest sum and therefore the most appropriate option is to reject the discount. Approval would be sought from the audit partner not the audit manager. The ACCA Code of Ethics allows acceptance of goods and hospitality that are considered trivial or modest.

19   C

The social relationship gives rise to a familiarity threat and the outstanding fees give rise to self-interest and intimidation threats.

20   D

Discussion and a repayment plan is the best option to both keep the audit client and also ensure that all outstanding fees are repaid.

21 A

Confidential information is any information which is not publicly available. Auditors are privileged to have access to this information through their right to have access to all books and records, information and explanations of a client. The primary reason for maintaining confidentiality is to maintain the trust of a client and maintain the reputation of the firm and the profession. The threat of being sued should not be the primary reason.

22 B

The audit teams of each client would sign a confidentiality agreement but it would not be necessary to have all employees of the firm sign confidentiality agreements.

23 TRUE, FALSE, FALSE

Long association creates a familiarity threat. Contingent fees are specifically prohibited by the ACCA Code of Ethics for audit and assurance work. Self-review is the core threat created with internal auditors and external auditors being from the same firm although it could also create self-interest and intimidation threats if fee levels from the one client become excessive.

24 B and F

A is incorrect as internal auditors are not required to be members of any professional body. C is incorrect as external auditors report to shareholders rather than those charged with governance. D is incorrect as internal auditors can be independent of the company, for example, if the internal audit function has been outsourced. E is incorrect as they should not implement their own recommendations otherwise it may create a self-review threat when they come to appraise the new controls at a later date.

25 B and C

In the case of situations A and D, the auditor has an obligation to disclose details of their clients' affairs to third parties.

26 B, D

Shareholders appoint the directors. The board sets the strategy for the company.

27 B, C, D and E

The finance director lacks independence therefore their presence will not increase the independent effectiveness of the audit committee. Whilst an audit committee can assist effective risk management it will not directly impact the external risks faced by the business.

28   DEFICIENCY, STRENGTH, DEFICIENCY, DEFICIENCY

	Strength	Deficiency
Mr Osbourne is the chairman and chief executive of Cameron		✓
All of the current NEDs are independent	✓	
The finance director will head the newly formed audit committee		✓
The remuneration of each director is decided by Mr Osbourne		✓

29   1D, 2C

To balance the board of directors, two more non-executive directors need to be appointed. It is unlikely that a company would reduce the number of directors to achieve a balance. Directors, both executive and non-executive, should be appointed based on experience and ability to do the job.

30   C and D

A risk committee is not mandatory and if one does not exist then the audit committee will ensure risk management responsibilities are fulfilled. A remuneration committee of independent NEDs should decide on executive director remuneration.

31

	True	False
An audit must be performed in accordance with International Standards on Auditing	✓	
International Standards on Auditing are legal requirements		✓
Where there is a difference between the requirements of an ISA and local law, local law should be followed	✓	
Before an ISA is issued an Exposure Draft must first have been published	✓	

ISAs are professional guidance but are not legal requirements.

32

	Benefit	Limitation
An audit may highlight deficiencies in internal controls which will be communicated to management	✓	
An audit provides management with assurance that they have prepared their financial statements in accordance with the appropriate financial reporting framework	✓	
Sampling will be used		✓
Evidence is persuasive rather than conclusive		✓

33

	Right	Duty	Neither
Attend board meetings of the company			✓
Access to all books and records of the company	✓		
Provide an opinion on the financial statements		✓	
Receive notice of general meetings of the company	✓		

The auditor has a right to receive notice of, attend and be heard at the general meetings of the company. The auditor has no right to attend board meetings of the company.

34   C

ISAs are issued to provide guidance to auditors. By following ISAs, audits will be consistently performed. Whilst this should reduce the risk of issuing an incorrect opinion, it does not guarantee all opinions will be correct.

35   C

There is no minimum post qualification experience requirement to be allowed to sign off an audit report. An auditor must be a member of a recognised supervisory body and must have an audit practising certificate to be allowed to sign off an audit report.

PLANNING AND RISK ASSESSMENT

36   B

Obtaining an understanding of the entity is performed at the planning stage which usually takes place before the year end. Therefore subsequent events cannot be considered at this point in time.

37   B

Detection risk is greater due to the lack of knowledge of the client. In order to address this, the auditor must spend time obtaining that knowledge.

38   A

A is only 1.3% of profit and less than 0.1% of revenue and therefore too low a level based on the standard benchmark calculations. The others all lie within the benchmarks of materiality for profit and revenue.

39   D

Results of previous audits and the need to maintain professional scepticism should be included in an audit strategy not the audit engagement letter.

40   A

Professional scepticism does not require the auditor to assume the financial statements are materially misstated but does require them to be alert to the possibility of misstatement.

41   A

Statement 1 is incorrect as ISAs are issued by the International Auditing and Assurance Standards Board rather than the IASB who issue accounting standards. Statement 2 is incorrect as ISAs do not override local legislation.

42   B

The risk of revenue cut off errors increases with employees aiming to maximise their current year bonus. The increased risk of a reduction in profits as a result of irrecoverable debts is a business risk. Revenue is more likely to be overstated in order to achieve a higher bonus. The bonus would have no impact on the customer response level to direct confirmation requests.

43   C

Statement 1 refers to the use of analytical procedures at the final review or completion stage of the audit. Statement 2 refers to the use of analytical procedures to obtain substantive evidence during the fieldwork stage of the audit.

44   A

Cut-off testing would not provide relevant evidence to the potential valuation issue caused by the increased risk of irrecoverable debts.

45

Receivables days	34.9 days	(121/1267) × 365
Payables days	31.5 days	(87.5/1013) × 365
Inventory days	21.6 days	(60/1013) × 365
Quick ratio	2.8	(121 + 123)/87.5

46   C

Quality control standards are developed to help reduce the risk of issuing an inappropriate opinion which will maintain confidence in the profession and protect the firm's reputation.

47   D

Audit work must be reviewed by someone more senior than the person who performed the work.

48   A

By not testing the sample sizes documented in the audit plan the audit plan has not been followed. Sample sizes will have been chosen based on the judgement of the auditor responsible for planning taking into consideration the requirement to obtain sufficient appropriate evidence. It is not acceptable to defer conclusions to the audit manager. If the sample sizes are considered acceptable at the lower quantities, the audit plan should be updated to reflect this. However, sample sizes should not be reduced simply to save time. If sufficient appropriate evidence is not obtained, material misstatements may go undetected and an inappropriate audit opinion could be issued.

49   B

Up to the date of the audit report the auditor must perform procedures to identify subsequent events and ensure they have been appropriately reflected in the financial statements. It is only after the audit report has been signed that they only need to take action if they become aware of any subsequent events. Enquiry alone is not sufficient. Choosing to rely only on enquiry of management demonstrates a lack of professional scepticism.

50   C

The firm would not report their staff to the ACCA. The matter will be dealt with internally through communication and training. Disciplinary measures may be taken by the firm if they consider it necessary to do so.

51

	20X3	**20X2**
Gross margin	44.0% (5.5/12.5 × 100)	46.7% (7/15 × 100)
Operating margin	4.0% (0.5/12.5 × 100)	12.7% (1.9/15 × 100)

Formulae:

Gross margin = gross profit/revenue × 100

Operating margin = operating profit (PBIT)/revenue × 100

52

	20X3	**20X2**
Receivables days	91 (3.1/12.5 × 365)	49 (2/15 × 365)
Payables days	83 (1.6/7 × 365)	55 (1.2/8 × 365)

Formulae:

Receivables days = receivables/revenue × 365

Payables days = payables/cost of sales × 365

53   A, B and F

A, B and F are audit risks as they clearly describe how the financial statements may be materially misstated. C, D and E are business risks as they describe issues the directors would be concerned about but which would not necessarily result in the financial statements being materially misstated.

54   B and C

Statements B and C will allow the auditor to make an assessment of the appropriateness of the change. Statement A explains the audit risk rather than providing a response. Statement D is of no audit value as it is known the policy has changed in the year.

55   TRUE, TRUE

	True	False
Risk of material misstatement The risk that the financial statements are materially misstated prior to audit. This consists of two components – Inherent risk and Control risk	✓	
Performance materiality The amount set by the auditor at less than materiality for the financial statements as a whole to reduce to an appropriately low level the probability that the aggregate of uncorrected and undetected misstatements exceeds materiality for the financial statements as a whole	✓	

INTERNAL CONTROLS

56   C

Risk assessment refers to the company's own processes for determining the business risks to be managed.

57   B

Narrative notes can be lengthy for large complex systems which limits their usefulness.

58   A

Controls can be overstated by the simple ticking of a box and hence the auditor will perform a walk through test to confirm the accuracy of the system documentation.

59   A

The goods received should be agreed to the purchase order before signing the delivery note to ensure that Coastal Co does not accept goods not required. The supplier's delivery note will record what has been sent which may not be the same as the purchase order.

60   D

Pre-printed payroll sheets ensure that only genuine employees are paid. Quarterly reviews of standing data ensure that unauthorised amendments are identified and resolved.

61   TRUE, TRUE, TRUE, FALSE

Narrative notes	True	False
Simple to record	✓	
Facilitates understanding by junior team members	✓	
Can be cumbersome	✓	
Usually very easy to identify missing controls		✓

62   TRUE, FALSE, FALSE, TRUE

Internal control questionnaires	True	False
A timely method of systems documentation	✓	
Does not consider all likely controls in a system		✓
Overstatement of controls present unlikely to occur		✓
Unusual controls may be missed	✓	

63   1C, 2A, 3D, 4B

Deficiency		Explanation	
1	Availability of inventory is not checked at the time of ordering	C	Risk of orders not being fulfilled on a timely basis
2	Telephone orders are not recorded immediately	A	Risk of incorrect orders being despatched
3	Order forms are not sequentially numbered	D	Orders may go missing leading to unfulfilled orders
4	The online ordering system allows customers to go over their credit limit	B	Risk of irrecoverable debts

64   A and D

The system should not allow credit limits to be exceeded by any amount. Changes to credit limits should only be performed by a responsible senior official.

65   D and E

Requisitions and discounts received are elements of a purchases system. A control objective should also refer to the risk the control is designed to mitigate, rather than the control itself.

66

	General	Application
Daily back up of the system	✓	
Authorisation of purchase orders		✓
Minimum order quantities		✓
Automatic updating of inventory once goods are sold		✓

67 C

The purpose of test data is to test the computerised controls within the system. When using test data, the external auditor is in effect auditing 'through the computer'.

68 A

CAATs are usually expensive to set up but become more cost effective over time.

69 B

Tracing a transaction through the system to ensure it is recorded in the sales day book is a substantive procedure testing the assertion of completeness.

70 C

A, B and D are true. C is false as the auditor must always evaluate the work before relying on it to ensure it is relevant and reliable for external audit purposes. The presence of an audit committee does not guarantee this.

AUDIT EVIDENCE

71 C

Occurrence is an assertion relevant to transactions and events. Inventory is an account balance.

72 B

Reviewing the inventory count instructions and then observing that the instructions are followed during the count are both tests of control and will provide the auditor with evidence the controls over inventory are operating effectively. The other two tests are substantive in nature providing evidence towards the valuation and cut-off assertions.

73 C

C is a substantive procedure regarding inventory valuation. Statement A provides evidence of completeness. Statement B provides evidence of cut-off. Statement D provides evidence of completeness and existence.

74   C

Statements 2 and 3 provide evidence for existence. Statement 1 relates to completeness and statement 4 relates to valuation.

75   D

A direct confirmation will confirm the amount outstanding but not the intention of the customer to pay this amount. Reviewing post year-end receipts will confirm actual recoverability of the outstanding balance.

76   A

Analytical procedures must be used at the planning stage but are not mandatory as a substantive procedure. Statement 2 is correct as the auditor will assess risk using a variety of techniques at the planning stage.

77   D

All are valid analytical procedures with a proof in total calculation being an example of a substantive analytical procedure.

78   A

Not all suppliers issue supplier statements. Lack of supplier reconciliations can mean misstatements within payables and accruals go undetected. Supplier statements are third party evidence making them more reliable than client generated evidence.

79   C

There is no suggestion of any issue that would cause the auditor to consider resigning. The audit team should be fully briefed and advised to be vigilant. The FD should also be advised that their assistance is likely to be requested by the audit team in the absence of an FC.

80   B

1, 2 and 3 are all valid sources of evidence. It would not be appropriate or professional for the auditor to arrange a telephone conversation with the financial controller, especially when legal proceedings are ongoing.

81   C

A, B and D are purposes of planning an audit.

82   A

The audit strategy is derived at the planning stage of the audit. Results of substantive analytical audit procedures would only be known after the work has been performed.

83   B

Recalculating the size of the fraud would not assist in the detection of further frauds. Reporting the matter to the police would be a management function and therefore not an audit procedure to detect further frauds. A discussion with management would be useful to identify any other suspected frauds. Searching for duplicate bank account numbers would identify possible other frauds that are occurring.

84   D

Fraud is an intentional act and therefore usually concealed by the perpetrator which makes it more difficult to identify than errors – whether they are simple mistakes or errors of judgment.

85   A

3 and 4 are tests of control not substantive procedures.

86   A

Statement 1 is correct. Cut-off testing must be performed and inventory must be counted at least once per year. Surprise counts are not a standard external audit test.

87   B

Items not present on the sheets but in the warehouse being recorded on count sheets is a strength. Process 1 is a deficiency as counters may just agree with the quantity on the sheet and not actually count the goods. Process 3 will lead to understatement of inventory. Old or damaged items should be included until they are sold or scrapped. Process 4 could result in errors as the finance department may not fully understand the adjustments to be made. Process 5 could result in cut-off errors as it will be difficult to identify goods already counted or not counted if movements are happening during the counting process.

88   C

If the timetable is not monitored then some areas could be missed and all inventory not counted at least once a year.

89   A

This test primarily confirms existence.

90   D

Post year-end sales invoices will give the most reliable evidence of net realisable value. A selling price list may not reflect the actual price charged, for example, if discounts are regularly given to customers. Payments to suppliers will verify the cost of the inventory. Written representation from management from management does not provide the most reliable source of evidence in this case.

91   B

Whilst other procedures may be necessary the appropriate first response is to send a follow up request.

92   D

At this stage of the audit there is no need to consider a modified report especially as many differences will be reconciled. Written representations are not appropriate in this matter where sufficient appropriate evidence is obtainable.

93   A

B verifies existence and classification; C verifies rights and obligations; D verifies valuation.

94   C

The independent 3rd party report is most reliable with the work performed by the audit junior next. The audit junior is using information provided by the client and therefore less reliable than the independent report. Documentary evidence is more reliable than verbal confirmations.

95   1C, 2A, 3D, 4B

Casting the non-current asset register means to recalculate. Physical verification of assets is inspection. Checking the reconciliation of the asset register to the nominal ledge would require the auditor to re-perform the reconciliation. Discussion with management regarding the basis for depreciation would involve enquiry of why they have chosen the rates they are using.

96   A

Monetary unit sampling involves testing every $nth starting at a random point.

97   C

Systematic sampling is where a sample is chosen with a constant interval. The starting point is chosen randomly.

98   D

There is not enough information in the scenario to conclude whether Statement A is correct. Often, testing high value items enables the auditor to test a high proportion of the balance by testing fewer items, increasing the efficiency of the test. Sampling requires every item in the population to have a chance of selection. By only testing balances over a certain amount, the balances below the threshold do not have a chance of selection. Stratified sampling involves breaking down the population into sub-populations such as the balances above and below a certain amount. However, stratified sampling would require items within each sub-population to be tested. As the balances below the threshold are not being tested this does not meet the criteria for stratified sampling. Therefore, this is a means of selecting items to test but does not represent sampling.

99   B

The sample should be extended before any further action is taken. The matter may need to be discussed with the audit senior or manager and the client but further evidence should be obtained first. The audit opinion will only be modified if the errors are material and if they are not corrected by the client. This is the final action to be taken rather than the initial course of action.

100   A

The time the auditor has available should not influence their audit procedures. In order to sample from a population, the population must be complete, accurate and appropriate for the purpose of the test. If the size of the population is small, sampling may not provide the most efficient method of obtaining evidence. Therefore the size of the population would need to be considered.

101   C

Inspection of credit check reports is a test of control, not a substantive procedure.

102   A

Greater volumes can be tested using CAATs. Statement B is a description of test data not audit software. CAATs are usually expensive to set up. The need for specialist expertise is seen as a disadvantage.

103   D

All are procedures that could be performed using audit software.

104   C

The fact that there are 600 customers at Delphic makes the use of audit software much more beneficial to an auditor

105   B

As the system within the computer is not audited the audit trail can be difficult to follow and direct evidence cannot be obtained.

106   D

NFPs are likely to have a finance person in charge of the finances. Some NFPs are required by law to have an audit such as government bodies. Charities are required to be audited if they are of a certain size. Although ISAs are written for audits of companies, they should still be followed in an audit of an NFP. Additional standards specific to the audit of certain types of NFP may be applicable.

107   C

All risks given are relevant to NFP organisations.

108   D

The intended user of an audit report for a company is usually the shareholders. A not-for-profit organisation does not have shareholders. The responsible party for both a company and a NFP will be the directors. Auditors will be the practitioner and all audits require sufficient appropriate evidence on which to base the audit opinion.

109   B

The financial statements may still be manipulated to show a break even position or to meet a specific target or objective imposed on the organisation. Audit reports are publicly available as taxpayers have a right to see the financial statements and associated audit report. The time required for the audit will depend on many factors such as complexity of the organisation and its transactions, the volume of transactions, etc, as is the case with company audits.

110   C

A local government department needs to ensure it has enough income to pay its expenses. A cut in funding from central government means the organisation must either find income from other sources or must cut its costs, or a combination of both. An audit report for a government department may need to refer to going concern uncertainties in the same way as for a company.

REVIEW AND REPORTING

111   B

The Chairman's statement forms part of the other information published with the financial statements. Other information may be financial or non-financial. The auditor must read this information to ensure it is consistent with the financial statements and their knowledge of the entity obtained during the audit. There is no requirement to provide an opinion on the Chairman's statement.

112   D

The audit report should include a section headed 'Other Information' which describes the auditor's responsibilities in respect of the other information, such as the Chairman's statement. The inconsistency between the Chairman's statement and the financial statements should be described in this section.

113   C

Inconsistencies between the other information and the financial statements may undermine the credibility of the audit report as it may be perceived that the auditor has not identified the inconsistencies and therefore the audit was not performed properly. If the inconsistencies are not brought to the attention of the user they may be misled by the incorrect or inconsistent information.

114 C

Notes to the financial statements form part of the financial statements and are subject to audit.

115 B

The auditor must read the other information to ensure it is consistent with the financial statements and their knowledge of the entity obtained during the audit. They do not audit the other information. As assurance conclusion is not expressed on the other information.

116 A

An emphasis of matter paragraph, if included, would modify the audit report.

117 B

Statements 1 and 2 do not affect the audit opinion as they do not affect the true and fair view of the financial statements.

118 D

Although only a benchmark, a matter is material if it is in excess of ½ – 1% of revenue. The receivable is 2.5% of revenue and therefore likely to be considered material on this basis.

119 C

From the scenario the customer has agreed the balance is outstanding but is struggling to make any payments. Confirming an already confirmed balance will not provide evidence over the level of adjustment required.

120 A

If the matter were deemed material the financial statements would be materially misstated. A qualified opinion would be required. As the matter is only 2.5% of revenue it is not pervasive.

121 A

Calculation of key ratios may identify indicators of going concern issues which need to be investigated further through audit procedures. However, the ratios do not provide evidence that the company is or is not a going concern. Ratios are calculated using historical information and the client may have already taken action to improve their financial position since that information was created.

122 B

Whilst customer service levels may deteriorate due to fewer staff, the going concern issue is more linked to the expertise of the staff. Without the specialist knowledge of overseas locations, MMT is unlikely to be able to differentiate its services from its competitors. This will have a greater detrimental effect on the survival of the company.

123 C

The opinion will not be modified if the disclosures are adequate. The report will need to include a section referring to the Material Uncertainty Related to Going Concern.

124 D

If the basis of preparation is wrong the financial statements will be materially misstated to such an extent they do not give a true and fair view. This is material and pervasive which would require an adverse opinion.

125 D

A Basis for opinion section is included in all audit reports. This section explains that the auditor has conducted the audit in accordance with ISAs.

126 A and D

A and D describe matters that are material and pervasive. A represents 86% of PBT therefore is deemed pervasive. B represents 3.4% of PBT therefore is not material. C represents 41% of PBT therefore is material but not pervasive. D affects the basis of preparation of the financial statements therefore is deemed pervasive.

127 1D, 2B, 3A, 4E, 5C

Element	Purpose
1 Title	Clearly identifies the report as an Independent Auditor's Report (D)
2 Addressee	Identifies the intended user of the report (B)
3 Basis for opinion	Provides a description of the professional standards applied during the audit to provide confidence to users that the report can be relied upon (A)
4 Key audit matters	Draws attention to any other significant matters of which the users should be aware (E)
5 Name of engagement partner	To identify the person responsible for the audit opinion in case of any queries (C)

128 B

As the claim is only possible to succeed a contingent liability disclosure is required. A provision would only be required if the claim was probable to succeed. At 10.3% of PBT, the claim is material, being greater than 5% of PBT.

129 1E

The matter is correctly treated in the financial statements therefore the opinion should be unmodified. As Paddington has sufficient cash to make the settlement there is no uncertainty facing the company.

130 1B, 2C, 3D, 4A

131   B

An adjusting event is one which provides evidence of a condition in existence at the year end and therefore requires adjustment. Adjustment means the financial statements should recognise the corresponding debit and credit to adjust the figures presented in the financial statements.

132

	Calculation	Material	
		Yes	No
Receivable	4% PBT (0.3/7.5 × 100)		✓
Lawsuit	8% PBT (0.6/7.5 × 100)	✓	

133

	Adjusting	Non-adjusting
Receivable	✓	
Lawsuit	✓	
Warehouse		✓

The receivable and lawsuit are both issues that were in existence at the year end. The warehouse was damaged in November, almost two months after the year end therefore the condition was not in existence at the year end.

134

Procedure	Appropriate	
	Yes	No
Contact the customer directly and enquire when they are likely to pay the outstanding balance		✓
Review correspondence between the customer and Humphries to assess whether there is any likelihood of payment	✓	
Review the post year-end period to see if any payments have been received from the customer	✓	
Inspect the original invoice and goods despatch note to confirm the customer received the goods and therefore owes the money		✓

It would not be appropriate to contact the customer directly to enquire about payment of the outstanding balance. The auditor would have already inspected the original invoice and goods despatch note when the audit fieldwork was taking place. At the completion stage, the auditor would perform follow up procedures focusing on subsequent events such as whether payment had been received since the last time after date payments were checked and reviewing any correspondence that had been received since the last time a review of correspondence had taken place.

135

Section Titles	Include in audit report
Auditor Responsibilities for the Audit of the Financial Statements	✓
Basis for opinion	
Basis for qualified opinion	✓
Key Audit Matters	
Opinion	
Qualified opinion	✓
Responsibilities of Management and Those Charged With Governance	✓

As the adjustment is material, the opinion will need to be modified. The issue is material but not pervasive therefore a qualified opinion will be required. The section will be titled 'Qualified Opinion' and will be followed by a 'Basis for Qualified Opinion' section. Responsibilities of both management and auditors are included in every audit report. Key audit matters are only compulsory for listed companies. As the scenario does not specify that Humphries is a listed client, it cannot be assumed that a Key Audit Matters section must be included in the audit report.

136 B, E, A, D

A written is not appropriate in respect of the receivable balance. This is because other procedures can be performed which provide more reliable evidence.

A written representation is appropriate in respect of the warranty provision. This is because the matter involves management judgement.

The client cannot confirm with confidence that the customer will pay their outstanding balance. Therefore a written representation is not appropriate. Other procedures provide more reliable evidence such as after date cash testing. The warranty provision is decided by management based on their experience and judgement. As a result there are limited other procedures that can be performed that would provide sufficient appropriate evidence. Therefore a written representation is appropriate.

137

Area of the audit	Required by an ISA	
	Yes	No
Fraud and error (ISA 240)	✓	
Laws and regulations (ISA 250)	✓	
Analytical procedures (ISA 520)		✓
Subsequent events (ISA 560)	✓	

138 B

The refusal to provide a written representation may cast doubt over the reliability of any other evidence provided by the client which means it will have a material effect. The auditor will only need to consider resignation from the engagement if the auditor believes the client lacks integrity and believes the same issues could arise in future audits that would make the auditor-client relationship untenable. The shareholders will be made aware of the issue if the audit report is modified as the auditor will need to provide an explanation of why the audit report is being modified. The auditor will not need to specifically notify the shareholders of the issue in person.

139 D and F

Written representations are required by ISA 580. Therefore without a written representation the auditor does not have sufficient appropriate evidence. If the auditor considers this to be material but not pervasive a qualified opinion will be issued. If it is deemed pervasive a disclaimer of opinion will be issued.

140

Plans or intentions of management that affect carrying values of assets	
Confirmation from management that they have provided the auditor with all information and access to records during the audit	✓
Confirmation from management that the financial statements are accurate and there are no material misstatements	
Confirmation from management that all transactions have been reflected in the financial statements	✓
Confirmation from management that they have prepared the financial statements in accordance with the applicable financial reporting framework	✓

Section 4

ANSWERS TO PRACTICE QUESTIONS

PLANNING AND RISK ASSESSMENT

141 VENUS   *Walk in the footsteps of a top tutor*

Key answer tips

Requirements (a) and (b) cover knowledge of engagement letters. For part (a) think of sensible reasons why a contract with a client may need to be amended. Part (b) has been examined many times before and students should be able to score reasonably well on this.

In part (c) you are asked for sources of information, i.e. where can an auditor obtain information to help plan the audit. Make sure you include an explanation of how the information will be used to score the full mark.

Part (d) asks for audit risks which are examined at every sitting. Audit risks need to relate to either a risk of material misstatement or a detection risk. For risk of material misstatement, identify a balance in the scenario that is at risk of misstatement and explain why you believe it could be misstated. This is usually because the client has failed to apply the relevant IFRS correctly. The IFRSs examinable for ACCA paper F3 are examinable for paper F8. Detection risks are the risks the auditor does not detect material misstatements in the financial statements e.g. when it is a new audit client or if there is a tight reporting deadline.

For the response, make sure it relates to the risk, not the balance in general. Try and be as specific as possible, simply saying more testing is required will not be sufficient. State the nature of the tests that should be performed.

A 2 column table should be used to keep the risks in line with the responses and to make sure you address both parts of the requirement.

(a)   Engagement letters

Engagement letters for recurring/existing clients should be revised if any of the following factors are present:

- Any indication that the entity misunderstands the objective and scope of the audit, as this misunderstanding would need to be clarified.

- Any revised or special terms of the audit engagement, as these would require inclusion in the engagement letter.

- A recent change of senior management or significant change in ownership. The letter is signed by a director on behalf of those charged with governance; if there have been significant changes in management they need to be made aware of what the audit engagement letter includes.

- A significant change in nature or size of the entity's business. The approach taken by the auditor may need to change to reflect the change in the entity and this should be clarified in the engagement letter.

- A change in legal or regulatory requirements. The engagement letter is a contract; hence if legal or regulatory changes occur, then the contract could be out of date.

- A change in the financial reporting framework adopted in the preparation of the financial statements. The engagement letter clarifies the role of auditors and those charged with governance, it identifies the reporting framework of the financial statements and if this changes, then the letter requires updating.

- A change in other reporting requirements. Other reporting requirements may be stipulated in the engagement letter; hence if these change, the letter should be updated.

(b)   Matters to be included in an audit engagement letter

- The objective and scope of the audit

- The responsibilities of the auditor

- The responsibilities of management

- Identification of the financial reporting framework for the preparation of the financial statements

- Expected form and content of any reports to be issued

- Elaboration of the scope of the audit with reference to legislation

- The form of any other communication of results of the audit engagement

- The fact that some material misstatements may not be detected

- Arrangements regarding the planning and performance of the audit, including the composition of the audit team

- The expectation that management will provide written representations

- The basis on which fees are computed and any billing arrangements

- A request for management to acknowledge receipt of the audit engagement letter and to agree to the terms of the engagement

- Arrangements concerning the involvement of internal auditors and other staff of the entity

- Any obligations to provide audit working papers to other parties

- Any restriction on the auditor's liability

- Arrangements to make available draft financial statements and any other information

- Arrangements to inform the auditor of facts which might affect the financial statements, of which management may become aware during the period from the date of the auditor's report to the date the financial statements are issued.

(c)   **Understanding an entity**

Prior year financial statements

Provides information in relation to the size of a company as well as the key accounting policies, disclosure notes and whether the audit opinion was modified or not.

Discussions with the previous auditors/access to their files

Provides information on key issues identified during the prior year audit as well as the audit approach adopted.

Prior year report to management

If this can be obtained from the previous auditors or from management, it can provide information on the internal control deficiencies noted last year. If these have not been rectified by management, then they could arise in the current year audit as well and may impact the audit approach.

Accounting systems notes/procedural manuals

Provides information on how each of the key accounting systems operates and this will be used to identify areas of potential control risk and help determine the audit approach.

Discussions with management

Provides information in relation to the business, any important issues which have arisen or changes to accounting policies from the prior year.

Review of board minutes

Provides an overview of key issues which have arisen during the year and how those charged with governance have addressed them.

Current year budgets and management accounts

Provides relevant financial information for the year to date. It will help the auditor during the planning stage for preliminary analytical review and risk identification.

Company website

Recent press releases from the company may provide background on the business during the year as this will help in identifying the key audit risks.

Financial statements of competitors

This will provide information about the company's competitors, in relation to their financial results and their accounting policies. This will be important in assessing the performance in the year and also when undertaking the going concern review.

(d)   Audit risk and auditor's responses

Audit risk	Auditor's response
The directors have reviewed the asset lives and depreciation rates of plant and machinery, resulting in the depreciation charge reducing. Under IAS 16 *Property, Plant and Equipment*, asset lives should be reviewed annually, and if the asset lives have increased as a result of this review such that the depreciation decreases, then this change may be reasonable.	Discuss with the directors the rationale for any extensions of asset lives and reduction of depreciation rates. The revised useful life of a sample of assets should be compared to how often these assets are replaced, as this provides evidence of the useful life of assets.
However, there is a risk that this reduction has occurred in order to achieve profit targets, due to the introduction of the bonus system. If this is the case, then plant and machinery is overvalued and profit overstated.	
Due to staff availability, the company is planning to undertake a full year-end inventory count days before the year end and then adjust for movements to the year end.	During the final audit the year-end inventory adjustments schedule should be reviewed in detail and supporting documentation obtained for all adjusting items.
If the adjustments are not completed accurately, then the year-end inventory could be under or overstated.	The audit team should increase the extent of inventory cut-off testing at the year end.
In October, a fire damaged inventory such that it has been written down from $0.9m to $0.2m which is its scrap value. This write down should have been charged to profit or loss.	Discuss with management the basis of the $0.2m scrap value attributed.
If the goods remain unsold after the year end, there is the risk that the scrap value is overstated and inventory overvalued.	Review whether any of the goods were sold pre or post year end and at what value; this should assess whether the attributed scrap value is reasonable. If none have been sold, discuss with management the possibility of further write downs.
An insurance claim for $0.7m has been submitted and the proceeds included within profit or loss.	Discuss with management whether any response has been received from the insurance company and review the related correspondence. If virtually certain, the treatment adopted is correct.
However, the company has not received a reply from the insurance company and this would therefore represent a possible contingent asset. To comply with IAS 37 *Provisions, Contingent Liabilities and Contingent Assets*, this should not be recognised until the receipt is virtually certain. With no response to date, the inclusion of this sum overstates profit and receivables.	If not, management should be requested to remove it from profit and receivables. If the receipt is probable, the auditor should request management include a contingent asset disclosure note.

Audit risk	Auditor's response
The bank reconciliations for October and November both contain unreconciled amounts, and the finance director believes the overall differences to be immaterial.	Discuss this issue with the finance director and request that the December reconciliation is fully reconciled. The reconciling items should be tested in detail and agreed to supporting documentation.
Errors in bank reconciliations could actually represent large errors which net off to a small amount. If the differences are not fully reconciled, it could result in bank balances being under or overstated.	
In addition, unreconciled amounts in the bank could have arisen due to fraud.	Throughout the audit, the team should be alert to the risk of fraud and maintain professional scepticism.
A directors' bonus scheme was introduced which is based on achieving a target profit before tax. There is a risk the directors might feel under pressure to manipulate the results through the judgements taken or through the use of provisions.	Throughout the audit, the team will need to be alert to this risk and maintain professional scepticism.
	Detailed review and testing on judgemental decisions, including treatment of provisions, and compare treatment against prior years. Any journal adjustments affecting profit should be tested in detail.
	In addition, a written representation should be obtained from management confirming the basis of any significant judgements.
The finance director has requested that the audit commence earlier than normal as he wishes to report results earlier. A reduction in the audit timetable will increase detection risk and place additional pressure on the team in obtaining sufficient and appropriate evidence.	The timetable should be confirmed with the finance director. If it is to be reduced, then consideration should be given to performing an interim audit in late December or early January; this would then reduce the pressure on the final audit.
The finance director has requested that the audit commence earlier than normal as he wishes to report results earlier. The finance team will have less time to prepare the financial information leading to an increased risk of errors arising in the financial statements.	The team needs to maintain professional scepticism and be alert to the increased risk of errors occurring.

ACCA marking scheme

			Marks
(a)	1 mark for each factor identified and adequately explained.		
	• Entity misunderstands the objective and scope of the audit		
	• Revised or special terms of the audit		
	• Recent change of senior management/change in ownership		
	• Change in nature or size of the entity's business		
	• Change in legal or regulatory requirements		
	• Change in the financial reporting framework		
	• Change in other reporting requirements		
		Maximum	**2**
(b)	½ mark per valid point.		
	• Objective/scope		
	• Responsibilities of auditor		
	• Responsibilities of management		
	• Identification of framework for financial statements		
	• Form/content reports		
	• Elaboration of scope		
	• Form of communications		
	• Some misstatements may be missed		
	• Arrangement for audit		
	• Written representations required		
	• Basis of fees/billing		
	• Management acknowledge letter		
	• Internal auditor arrangements		
	• Obligations to provide working papers to others		
	• Restriction on auditor's liability		
	• Arrangements to make draft financial statements available		
	• Arrangements to inform auditors of subsequent events		
		Max	**3**
(c)	½ mark for source of documentation and ½ mark for describing relevance of info, maximum of 2½ marks for sources and 2½ marks for relevance.		
	• Prior year financial statements		
	• Previous auditor/access to their files		
	• Prior year report to management		
	• Accounting systems notes		
	• Discussions with management		
	• Review of board minutes		
	• Current year budgets and management accounts		
	• Company website		
	• Financial statements of competitors		
		Max	**5**
(d)	Up to 1 mark per well described risk and up to 1 mark for each well explained response.		
	• Depreciation rates and asset lives		
	• Adjustments for movements in inventory to the year-end date		
	• Write down of inventory		
	• Contingent asset		
	• Unreconciled differences on bank reconciliations		
	• Manipulation of profit due to directors' bonus		
	• Reporting timetable shortened		
		Max	**10**
Total			**20**

Examiner's comments

Candidates were presented with a question at this sitting based on a manufacturing company and asked to assess audit risk and responses. As noted in previous Examiner's reports; a fundamental factor in planning and assessing the risks of an audit of an entity is an assessment of audit risk, and this remains a highly examinable area. Audit risk questions typically require a number of audit risks to be identified (½ marks each), explained (½ marks each) and an auditor's response to each risk (1 mark each). Performance was mixed. It was encouraging that candidates generally identified the issues correctly from the scenario. However, candidates sometimes did not explain how each issue could impact on the audit risk and therefore were not awarded the full mark. To explain the audit risk candidates need to state for each issue if this could result in a balance being over stated, under stated, misstated, misclassified, a going concern problem or refer to a relevant assertion. In addition, many candidates misunderstood the implication of the inventory being counted before the year-end and thought the problem was the lack of staff for the count as opposed to the roll forward adjustments which would be necessary.

The provision of relevant auditor's responses continues to be a poorly attempted area and candidates are once again reminded to ensure that this area of the syllabus is adequately studied and practised. While an auditor's response does not have to be a detailed audit procedure, rather it should set out an approach the audit team will take to address the identified risk, the responses given were sometimes either too weak (e.g. in response to the directors' bonus being based on profits a weak response was to 'audit the profit or loss account') or, did not address the issue (e.g. in response to the un-reconciled differences on the bank reconciliation, a weak response was to 'obtain a bank confirmation') It was pleasing to note that few candidates discussed business risks. A minority of candidates however did propose, in relation to the director's bonus being based on profits, the inappropriate response that the auditor should inform management not to base bonuses on profit levels in the future.

It was also pleasing to note that many candidates presented their answers well using a two-column approach with audit risk in one column and the related response in the other column.

142 SYCAMORE *Walk in the footsteps of a top tutor*

Key answer tips

Requirements (a) (c) and (d) require repetition of information from the text book – responsibilities of the auditor in respect of fraud and error, quality control procedures and the difference between an audit and a review engagement. Quality control is new to the syllabus. Any students resitting this paper should make sure they have familiarised themselves with this new syllabus area.

In part (b) audit risks need to relate to either a risk of material misstatement or a detection risk. For risk of material misstatement, identify a balance in the scenario that is at risk of misstatement and explain why you believe it could be misstated. This is usually because the client has failed to apply the relevant IFRS correctly. The IFRSs examinable for ACCA paper F3 are examinable for paper F8. Detection risks are the risks the auditor does not detect material misstatements in the financial statements e.g. when it is a new audit client or if there is a tight reporting deadline.

For the response, make sure it relates to the risk, not the balance in general. Try and be as specific as possible, simply saying more testing is required will not be sufficient. State the nature of the tests that should be performed.

A 2 column table should be used to keep the risks in line with the responses and to make sure you address both parts of the requirement.

(a) **Fraud responsibility**

Maple & Co must conduct an audit in accordance with ISA 240 *The Auditor's Responsibilities Relating to Fraud in an Audit of Financial Statements* and are responsible for obtaining reasonable assurance that the financial statements taken as a whole are free from material misstatement, whether caused by fraud or error.

In order to fulfil this responsibility, Maple & Co is required to identify and assess the risks of material misstatement of the financial statements due to fraud.

They need to obtain sufficient appropriate audit evidence regarding the assessed risks of material misstatement due to fraud, through designing and implementing appropriate responses. In addition, Maple & Co must respond appropriately to fraud or suspected fraud identified during the audit.

When obtaining reasonable assurance, Maple & Co is responsible for maintaining professional scepticism throughout the audit, considering the potential for management override of controls and recognising the fact that audit procedures which are effective in detecting error may not be effective in detecting fraud.

To ensure that the whole engagement team is aware of the risks and responsibilities for fraud and error, ISAs require that a discussion is held within the team. For members not present at the meeting, Sycamore's audit engagement partner should determine which matters are to be communicated to them.

If fraud is detected, the auditor must report this to management and those charged with governance.

(b) **Audit risks and auditors' responses**

Audit risks	Auditor's responses
Sycamore's previous finance director left in December after it was discovered that he had been committing fraud with regards to expenses claimed.	Discuss with the new finance director what procedures they have adopted to identify any further frauds by the previous finance director.
There is a risk that he may have undertaken other fraudulent transactions; these would need to be written off in the statement of profit or loss. If these have not been uncovered, the financial statements could include errors.	In addition, the team should maintain their professional scepticism and be alert to the risk of further fraud and errors.

Audit risks	Auditor's responses
The new finance director was appointed in January 2015 and was previously a financial controller of a bank.	During the audit, careful attention should be applied to any changes in accounting policies and in particular any key judgemental decisions made by the finance director.
Sycamore is a pharmaceutical company which is very different to a bank; there is a risk that the new finance director is not sufficiently competent to prepare the financial statements, leading to errors.	
During the year, Sycamore has spent $1.8 million on developing new products; these are at different stages and the total amount has been capitalised as an intangible asset.	A breakdown of the development expenditure should be reviewed and tested in detail to ensure that only projects which meet the capitalisation criteria are included as an intangible asset, with the balance being expensed.
However, in order to be capitalised it must meet all of the criteria under IAS 38 *Intangible Assets*. There is a risk that some projects may not reach final development stage and hence should be expensed rather than capitalised. Intangible assets and profit could be overstated.	
Sycamore has borrowed $2.0 million from the bank via a ten-year loan. This loan needs to be correctly split between current and non-current liabilities in order to ensure correct disclosure.	During the audit, the team would need to confirm that the $2.0 million loan finance was received. In addition, the split between current and non-current liabilities and the disclosures for this loan should be reviewed in detail to ensure compliance with relevant accounting standards.
Also as the level of debt has increased, there should be additional finance costs. There is a risk that this has been omitted from the statement of profit or loss, leading to understated finance costs and overstated profit.	The finance costs should be recalculated and any increase agreed to the loan documentation for confirmation of interest rates and cashbook and bank statements to confirm the amount was paid and is not therefore a year-end payable.
The loan has a minimum profit target covenant. If this is breached, the loan would be instantly repayable.	Review the covenant calculations prepared by Sycamore and identify whether any defaults have occurred; if so, determine the effect on the company.
There is a risk the liability is incorrectly allocated as a non-current liability rather than a current liability if the covenant is breached.	Review the disclosure of the loan as a current liability.

Audit risks	**Auditor's responses**
If the company does not have sufficient cash flow to meet this loan repayment, then there could be going concern implications.	Review cash flow forecasts and enquire of management how they will deal with any need to make the loan repayment.
There is a risk of inadequate disclosure of going concern issues.	
In addition, there is a risk of manipulation of profit to ensure that covenants are met.	The team should maintain their professional scepticism and be alert to the risk that profit has been overstated to ensure compliance with the covenant.
There have been a significant number of sales returns made subsequent to the year end. As these relate to pre year-end sales, they should be removed from revenue in the draft financial statements and the inventory reinstated.	Review a sample of the post year-end sales returns and confirm if they relate to pre year-end sales, that the revenue has been reversed and the inventory included in the year-end ledgers.
If the sales returns have not been correctly recorded, then revenue will be overstated and inventory understated.	In addition, the reason for the increased level of returns should be discussed with management. This will help to assess if there are underlying issues with the net realisable value of inventory.
During Sycamore's year-end inventory count there were movements of goods in and out. If these goods in transit were not carefully controlled, then goods could have been omitted or counted twice. This would result in inventory being under or overstated.	During the final audit, the goods received notes and goods despatched notes received during the inventory count should be reviewed and followed through into the inventory count records as correctly included or not.
Surplus plant and equipment was sold during the year, resulting in a profit on disposal of $210,000. As there is a minimum profit loan covenant, there is a risk that this profit on disposal may not have been correctly calculated, resulting in overstated profits.	Recalculate the profit and loss on disposal calculations and agree all items to supporting documentation.
Significant profits or losses on disposal are an indication that the depreciation policy of plant and equipment may not be appropriate. Depreciation may be overstated as a result.	Discuss the depreciation policy for plant and equipment with the finance director to assess its reasonableness.

(c)   **Quality control**

Briefing/direction of the team

The audit team should be informed of their responsibilities, the objectives of their work, the nature of the client's business and any other relevant information to enable them to perform their work efficiently and effectively. This will enable them to identify material misstatements and know which areas require greater attention.

Supervision – tracking the progress of the audit

The audit supervisor should keep track of the progress of the audit in order to ensure the work is being completed on time or whether action needs to be taken such as bringing in additional staff to help complete the work or whether to agree an extended deadline with the client.

Supervision – addressing significant matters

The audit supervisor will also ensure that significant matters are being dealt with promptly. If issues are resolved as soon as they are identified the audit is more likely to be completed within the agreed timeframe.

Supervision – considering competence of team

The audit supervisor will consider the competence of the audit team and will provide additional coaching if required. The supervisor should be available for the team members to refer to in case of any queries.

Consultation

Consultation will be required where the team does not have the necessary expertise. The audit supervisor should identify any areas where consultation with an expert is required and make arrangements for such consultation whether this is referring the matter to another person within the audit firm or using an external expert.

Review of work

Each team member's work should be reviewed by someone more senior. This is to ensure the work has been to the required standard. The reviewer may identify additional work that needs to be performed before a conclusion can be drawn reducing the risk that material misstatements go undetected.

EQCR

An engagement quality control review will be necessary for listed clients and other high risk clients, for example to provide an additional safeguard for clients where independence issues have been identified. The engagement quality control reviewer should be someone independent of the audit team who has no prior knowledge of the client and is able to assess the judgemental areas of the audit with an objective mind. The EQCR will review the proposed audit opinion and assess whether there is sufficient appropriate evidence to support that opinion before it is issued.

Documentation

Audit work must be documented to provide evidence that the work was performed in accordance with professional standards and provides a basis for the audit opinion issued. Documentation should enable an experienced auditor to understand the nature, timing and extent of the procedures performed, the results of those procedures and any significant judgements formed. If the audit report is called into question at a later date, the audit documentation should be able to prove that the auditor had performed the audit to the required level of quality. Documentation therefore provides protection in the event of a negligence claim.

(d) **(i)** **Review engagements**

Review engagements are often undertaken as an alternative to an audit, and involve a practitioner reviewing financial data, such as six-monthly figures. This would involve the practitioner undertaking procedures to state whether anything has come to their attention which causes the practitioner to believe that the financial data is not in accordance with the financial reporting framework.

A review engagement differs to an external audit in that the procedures undertaken are not nearly as comprehensive as those in an audit, with procedures such as analytical review and enquiry used extensively. In addition, the practitioner does not need to comply with ISAs as these only relate to external audits.

(ii) **Levels of assurance**

The level of assurance provided by audit and review engagements is as follows:

External audit

This provides comfort that the financial statements present fairly in all material respects (or are true and fair) and are free of material misstatements.

A high but not absolute level of assurance is provided. This is known as reasonable assurance.

Review engagements

The practitioner gathers sufficient evidence to be satisfied that the subject matter is plausible.

In this case negative assurance is given whereby the practitioner confirms that nothing has come to their attention which indicates that the subject matter contains material misstatements.

ACCA Marking scheme		
		Marks
(a)	Up to 1 mark per point.	
	— Per ISA 240 – obtain reasonable assurance that the financial statements are free from material misstatement, whether caused by fraud or error	
	— Identify and assess the risks of material misstatement due to fraud	
	— Obtain sufficient appropriate audit evidence	
	— Respond appropriately to fraud or suspected fraud identified during the audit	
	— Maintain professional scepticism throughout the audit	
	— Discussion within the engagement team	
	— Report fraud to management and those charged with governance	
	Max	**5**
(b)	Up to 1 mark per well described risk and up to 1 mark for each well explained response. Overall max of 8 marks for risks and 8 marks for responses.	
	— Fraud of previous finance director	
	— Competence of new finance director	
	— Treatment of capitalised development expenditure	
	— New loan finance – split between current and non-current	
	— Completeness of finance costs	
	— Loan covenants – risk of incorrect disclosure of loan as non-current liability if covenant is breached and loan is repayable	
	— Loan covenants – going concern risk if breached	

		– Loan covenants – risk of manipulation to show compliance			
		– Post year-end sales returns			
		– Goods in and out during the inventory count			
		– Profit on disposal – incorrect calculation			
		– Profit on disposal – inappropriate depreciation rate			
			Max	16	
(c)		Up to 1 mark per well explained valid point.			
		– Briefing/direction of the team			
		– Supervision – tracking the progress of the audit			
		– Supervision – addressing significant matters			
		– Supervision – considering competence of team			
		– Consultation			
		– Review of work			
		– EQCR			
		– Documentation			
			Max	5	
(d)	(i)	Up to 1 mark per well explained valid point.			
		– Description of review engagements			
		– Difference to external audit			
			Max	2	
	(ii)	Up to 1 mark per well described valid point.			
		– Level of assurance of external audit			
		– Level of assurance of review engagements			
			Max	2	
Total				30	

Examiner's comments

Part (a) required an explanation of auditor's responsibilities in relation to the prevention and detection of fraud and error. This question was answered unsatisfactorily and candidates need to be better prepared to tackle questions on core auditor responsibilities. The question required candidates to discuss the auditor's responsibilities in this area; it did not require an explanation of directors' responsibilities. Unfortunately many candidates wasted time providing this and there were no marks available for this. In addition some answers strayed into providing procedures for detecting fraud and error rather than just addressing responsibilities. Candidates are again reminded to read the question carefully and to ensure that they are answering the question that has been set. The majority of candidates were able to gain marks for reporting fraud to management or those charged with governance, for the auditors' general responsibility to detect material misstatements caused by fraud or error or that the auditors are not responsible for preventing fraud or error.

Part (b) required an identification and description of audit risks from the scenario and the relevant auditor's response for each. Performance on this question was mixed and performance in relation to this core area of the syllabus remains overall disappointing. Candidates who scored well in this question went on to describe how the point identified from the scenario was an audit risk by referring to the assertion and the account balance impacted. As in previous diets, a significant number of candidates tended to only identify facts from the scenario such as 'the previous finance director had been claiming fraudulent expenses from the company' but failed to describe how this results in an audit risk, thus limiting the marks that can be scored to ½ marks. To gain the full 1 mark candidates needed to refer to the risk of other fraudulent expenses being claimed resulting in an impact on profit, as the financial statement impact must be referred to. Only by connecting the fact from the scenario to the relevant assertion and area of the financial statements will the candidate have adequately explained the audit risk. Unfortunately many candidates yet again focused on business risks rather than audit risks, and explained the risk in terms of the impact on Sycamore rather than the financial statements risk and hence how it affects the auditor. As in previous sittings, many candidates performed poorly with regards to the auditor's responses. Many candidates gave business advice, such as undertaking quality control procedures over inventory to prevent the increased level of sales returns. In addition a significant proportion of candidates failed to appreciate that the inventory count had already occurred, hence auditor responses focused on procedures to adopt at the count were not relevant in the circumstances. Audit responses need to be practical and should relate to the approach (i.e. what testing) the auditor will adopt to assess whether the balance is materially misstated or not. Once again this was due to a failure to read the scenario carefully. Candidates should read the questions carefully and plan an appropriate response. Many candidates presented their answers well as they adopted a two column approach with audit risk in one column and the related response next to it. Future candidates must take note audit risk is and will continue to be an important element of the syllabus and must be understood, and they would benefit from practising audit risk questions.

Part (di) required an explanation of the purpose of review engagements and how they differed to an external audit and (dii) tested the levels of assurance for audits and review engagements. Overall this question was answered unsatisfactorily. Few candidates were able to explain the purpose of a review engagement and many candidates failed to score any marks for (di). Where the question was attempted many candidates repeated points that were then given in (dii). Candidates performed better in (dii) and many produced clear and concise answers which addressed the levels of assurance for each specified type of engagements. A minority of candidates however just referred to positive and negative assurance without linking them back to the two types of engagements.

143 RECORDER COMMUNICATIONS *Walk in the footsteps of a top tutor*

Key answer tips

Part (a) is a straightforward knowledge question. Notice that the question asks for the importance of planning. Answers which just state what activities are performed at the planning stage will not score marks. As planning is the most important stage of the process, students should be aware of the reasons why it is important to plan the audit.

Audit risks need to relate to either a risk of material misstatement or a detection risk. For risk of material misstatement, identify a balance in the scenario that is at risk of misstatement and explain why you believe it could be misstated. This is usually because the client has failed to apply the relevant IFRS correctly. The IFRSs examinable for ACCA paper F3 are examinable for paper F8. Detection risks are the risks the auditor does not detect material misstatements in the financial statements e.g. when it is a new audit client or if there is a tight reporting deadline. For the response, make sure it relates to the risk, not the balance in general. Try and be as specific as possible, simply saying more testing is required will not be sufficient. State the nature of the tests that should be performed.

A 2 column table should be used to keep the risks in line with the responses and to make sure you address both parts of the requirement.

Parts (c) and (d) require procedures over two very specific areas. Make sure you give specific answers that address the requirement.

Part (e) asks for audit reporting implications of an unresolved issue. To earn the marks you have to state your justification for the audit opinion you are suggesting. You should also consider any other modifications to the audit report that might be required such as a 'basis for' paragraph.

(a) Importance of audit planning

- It helps the auditor to devote appropriate attention to important areas of the audit.

- It helps the auditor to identify and resolve potential problems on a timely basis.

- It helps the auditor to properly organise and manage the audit engagement so that it is performed in an effective and efficient manner.

- It assists in the selection of engagement team members with appropriate levels of capabilities and competence to respond to anticipated risks and the proper assignment of work to them.

- It facilitates the direction and supervision of engagement team members and the review of their work.

- It assists, where applicable, in the coordination of work done by experts.

(b) Audit risks and responses

Audit risk	Auditor's response
Recorder Communications Co (Recorder) is a new client for Piano & Co. As the team is not so familiar with the accounting policies, transactions and balances of Recorder, there will be an increased detection risk on the audit.	Piano & Co should ensure they have a suitably experienced team. Also, adequate time should be allocated for team members to obtain an understanding of the company and the risks of material misstatement.
Recorder purchases their goods from South Asia and the goods are in transit for two weeks. At the year end there is a risk that the cut-off of inventory, purchases and payables may not be accurate. The company correctly accounts for goods when they receive them. Therefore at the year end only goods which have been received into the warehouse should be included in the inventory balance and a respective payables balance recognised.	The audit team should undertake detailed cut-off testing of goods in transit from the suppliers in South Asia to ensure that the cut-off is complete and accurate.

Audit risk	**Auditor's response**
The company undertakes continuous (perpetual) inventory counts at its central warehouse. Under such a system all inventory must be counted at least once a year with adjustments made to the inventory records.	The completeness of the continuous (perpetual) inventory counts should be reviewed. In addition, the level of adjustments made to inventory should be considered to assess whether reliance on the inventory records at the year end will be acceptable.
Inventory could be under or overstated if the continuous (perpetual) inventory counts are not complete and the inventory records accurately updated for adjustments.	
A sales-related bonus scheme has been introduced in the year; this may lead to sales cut-off errors with employees aiming to maximise their current year bonus.	Increased sales cut-off testing will be performed along with a review of any post year-end cancellations of contracts as they may indicate cut-off errors.
Receivables are considerably higher than the prior year and there are concerns about the creditworthiness of some customers.	Extended post year-end cash receipts testing and a review of the aged receivables ledger to be performed to assess valuation. Also consider the adequacy of any allowance for receivables.
There is a risk that some receivables may be overvalued as they are not recoverable.	
In addition, receivables could be overstated as a result of the bonus scheme; some of the customers signed up for contracts may not actually exist.	External confirmation of receivables to confirm that customers exist and represent valid amounts due.
Recorder has a policy of revaluing its land and buildings and these valuations have been updated during the year.	Discuss with management the process adopted for undertaking the valuation, including whether the whole class of assets was revalued and if the valuation was undertaken by an expert. This process should be reviewed for compliance with IAS 16.
Property, plant and equipment could be under or overvalued if the recent valuation has not been carried out in accordance with IAS 16 *Property, Plant and Equipment* and adequate disclosures may not have been made in the financial statements.	
	Review the disclosures of the revaluation in the financial statements for compliance with IAS 16.
The directors have each been paid a significant bonus and separate disclosure of this in the financial statements is required by local legislation.	Discuss this matter with management and review the disclosure in the financial statements to ensure compliance with local legislation.
The directors' remuneration disclosure will not be complete and accurate if the bonus paid is not disclosed in accordance with the relevant local legislation.	

(c)   Audit procedures for continuous (perpetual) inventory counts

- Attend at least one of the continuous (perpetual) inventory counts to review whether the controls over the inventory count are adequate.

- Confirm that all of the inventory lines have been counted or are due to be counted at least once a year by reviewing the schedules of counts undertaken/due to be undertaken.

- Review the adjustments made to the inventory records on a monthly basis to gain an understanding of the level of differences arising on a month by month basis.

- Discuss with management how they will ensure that year-end inventory will not be under or overstated. If significant differences consistently arise, this could indicate that the inventory records are not adequately maintained.

- Consider attending the inventory count at the year end to undertake test counts of inventory from records to floor and from floor to records in order to confirm the existence and completeness of inventory.

(d)   Substantive procedures for directors' bonus and remuneration

- Obtain a schedule of the directors' remuneration including the bonus paid and cast the addition of the schedule to confirm arithmetical accuracy.

- Agree the individual bonus payments to the payroll records.

- Inspect the cash book and bank statements to confirm the amount of each bonus paid.

- Review the board minutes to confirm whether any additional bonus payments relating to this year have been agreed.

- Obtain a written representation from management confirming the completeness of directors' remuneration including the bonus.

- Review any disclosures made of the bonus and assess whether these are in compliance with local legislation.

(e)   Audit report implications

- Failure to value inventory at the lower of cost and net realisable value will mean Recorder has not complied with the requirements of IAS 2 *Inventories*.

- The financial statements will be materially misstated due to overstatement of inventory, although the issue is unlikely to be pervasive.

- The audit opinion should be qualified with the 'except for' wording.

- A basis for qualified opinion will be required to explain the material misstatement to the users of the financial statements and quantify the financial effect of the misstatement on the financial statements.

- The basis for paragraph should be positioned below the opinion section within the audit report.

			Marks
(a)	Up to 1 mark per well explained point.		
	– Important areas of the audit		
	– Identify potential problems		
	– Effective and efficient audit		
	– Selection of engagement team members and assignment of work		
	– Direction, supervision and review		
	– Coordination of work	Max	5
(b)	Up to 1 mark per well described risk and up to 1 mark for each well explained response. Overall maximum of 7 marks for risks and 7 marks for responses.		
	– New client leading to increased detection risk		
	– Cut-off of goods in transit		
	– Continuous (perpetual) inventory counts		
	– Inventory valuation		
	– Sales cut-off		
	– Receivables – overvaluation		
	– Receivables – existence		
	– Valuation of land and buildings		
	– Directors' bonus remuneration	Max	14
(c)	Up to 1 mark per well explained procedure.		
	– Attend one of the continuous (perpetual) inventory counts to review whether the controls are adequate		
	– Review the schedule of counts to confirm completeness of all inventory lines		
	– Review the adjustments made to the inventory records to gain an understanding of the level of differences arising		
	– If significant differences, discuss with management how they will ensure that year-end inventory will not be under or overstated		
	– Attend the inventory count at the year end to undertake test counts to confirm the completeness and existence of inventory	Max	3
(d)	Up to 1 mark per well described procedure.		
	– Cast schedule of directors' remuneration including the bonus paid		
	– Agree the individual bonus payments to the payroll records		
	– Confirm the amount of each bonus paid by agreeing to the cash book and bank statements		
	– Review the board minutes to confirm whether any additional bonus payments relating to this year have been agreed		
	– Obtain written representation from management		
	– Review disclosures and assess whether these are in compliance with local legislation	Max	4
(e)	Up to 1 mark per well explained valid point		
	– Failure to comply with IAS 2 – inventory overstated		
	– Material misstatement – not pervasive		
	– Qualified opinion – except for		
	– Basis for qualified opinion	Max	4
Total			20

Examiner's comments

Part (a) required candidates to explain the importance of audit planning. Candidates' performance was satisfactory on this question. Many candidates were able to confidently identify that planning resulted in sufficient attention being devoted to important areas/audit risks, selection of an appropriate audit team, an efficient and effective audit and resolution of issues in a timely manner. Where candidates did not score enough marks to pass, this tended to be because they focused on the contents of an audit strategy and plan, which was not the specific focus of the question. Often candidates identified the procedures which would be considered prior to planning, such as confirming the independence of auditors or used to obtain an understanding of the entity resulting in some candidates focusing on what was done at the planning stage rather than explaining the importance of planning.

Part (b) required identification and description of audit risks from the scenario and the auditor's response for each. Performance on this question was mixed. The scenario contained significantly more than the number of risks required and so candidates were able to easily identify enough risks, and strong answers went on to describe how the point identified from the scenario was an audit risk by referring to the assertion and the account balance impacted. As in previous diets, some candidates tended to only identify facts from the scenario such as 'Recorder purchases goods from a supplier in South Asia and the goods are in transit for two weeks' but failed to describe how this could impact audit risk; this would only have scored ½ marks. To gain 1 mark the point needed to be developed to also explain that this could result in issues over the completeness of inventory. More so than in previous diets, candidates disappointingly provided business risks rather than audit risks with answers such as stock outs due to the two week transit period and possible damage to inventory during transit. As a result these candidates then provided responses related to how management should address these business risks rather than how the auditor should respond. This meant that out of a potential 2 marks per risk, candidates would only score ½ marks for the identification of the issue from the scenario. Some candidates also identified irrelevant risks such as Recorder undertaking continuous inventory counts. While an audit risk was present around inventory in relation to the effectiveness of the perpetual inventory system, very few candidates explained the risk in this manner instead focusing on the lack of a full year-end count. This demonstrated a lack of understanding of continuous inventory counts. Additionally, many candidates performed poorly with regards to the auditor's responses. Many candidates gave business advice, such as changing the salesmen's bonus structure or provided vague responses such as perform detailed substantive testing or maintain professional scepticism. Responses which start with 'ensure that......' are unlikely to score marks as they usually fail to explain exactly how the auditor will address the audit risk.

Audit responses need to be practical and should relate to the approach (i.e. what testing) the auditor will adopt to assess whether the balance is materially misstated or not. Most candidates presented their answers well, adopting a two column approach with audit risk in one column and the related response next to it. This helps candidates to ensure that for every risk identified there is a related response and candidates are encouraged to continue to use this approach where appropriate.

Part (c) required procedures the auditor should perform in order to place reliance on the continuous counts for inventory. Candidates' performance was disappointing. Many candidates provided lengthy answers on procedures to be carried out when attending a year-end inventory count or procedures to verify valuation or completeness/existence of inventory, suggesting that a significant proportion of candidates do not understand continuous inventory counts, the risks associated with this and therefore the areas the auditor needs to focus on. A small proportion of candidates correctly identified that it was important to confirm if all inventory items were counted at least once a year and also to assess the level of adjustments made during these counts. Inventory is a key element of the financial statements and candidates need to be able to provide relevant procedures for both full year-end counts as well as continuous counting.

Part (d) required substantive procedures for confirming the directors' bonus payment made during the year. Candidates' performance was disappointing. Unfortunately, many candidates focused on the authorisation of the bonus; this is not a substantive procedure and would not have scored any marks. A significant minority thought that the directors' bonus was based on sales which was not the case. The scenario stated that salesmen's bonuses were based on sales, hence candidates either confused these two items or failed to read the scenario properly. They then looked to recalculate the bonus based on sales levels which was not appropriate in the circumstances. A number of vague procedures were suggested such as obtaining written representations or reading board minutes without explaining what for. Analytical procedures were suggested; however they were unlikely to be valid procedures as bonuses by their nature tend to vary each year.

144 KANGAROO CONSTRUCTION *Walk in the footsteps of a top tutor*

Key answer tips

Audit risks need to relate to either a risk of material misstatement or a detection risk. For risk of material misstatement, identify a balance in the scenario that is at risk of misstatement and explain why you believe it could be misstated. Detection risks are the risks the auditor does not detect material misstatements in the financial statements e.g. when it is a new audit client or if there is a tight reporting deadline.

For the response, make sure it relates to the risk, not the balance in general. Try and be as specific as possible, simply saying more testing is required will not be sufficient. State the nature of the tests that should be performed.

A 2 column table should be used to keep the risks in line with the responses and to make sure you address both parts of the requirement.

(a) Materiality and performance materiality

Materiality and performance materiality are dealt with under ISA 320 *Materiality in Planning and Performing an Audit*. Auditors need to establish the materiality level for the financial statements as a whole, as well as assess performance materiality levels, which are lower than the overall materiality.

Materiality is defined in ISA 320 as follows:

'Misstatements, including omissions, are considered to be material if they, individually or in the aggregate, could reasonably be expected to influence the economic decisions of users taken on the basis of the financial statements.'

In assessing the level of materiality, there are a number of areas that should be considered. First the auditor must consider both the amount (quantity) and the nature (quality) of any misstatements, or a combination of both. The quantity of the misstatement refers to the relative size of it and the quality refers to an amount that might be low in value but due to its prominence could influence the user's decision, for example, directors' transactions.

Materiality is often calculated using benchmarks such as 5% of profit before tax or 1% of total revenue or total expenses. These values are useful as a starting point for assessing materiality.

The assessment of what is material is ultimately a matter of the auditor's professional judgement, and it is affected by the auditor's perception of the financial information needs of users of the financial statements and the perceived level of risk; the higher the risk, the lower the level of overall materiality.

In assessing materiality, the auditor must consider that a number of errors each with a low value may, when aggregated, amount to a material misstatement.

In calculating materiality, the auditor should also set the performance materiality level. Performance materiality is normally set at a level lower than overall materiality. It is used for testing individual transactions, account balances and disclosures. The aim of performance materiality is to reduce the risk that the total of errors in balances, transactions and disclosures does not in total exceed overall materiality.

Tutorial note

Award marks for ISA 320 definition of performance materiality below:

'Performance materiality means the amount or amounts set by the auditor at less than materiality for the financial statements as a whole to reduce to an appropriately low level the probability that the aggregate of uncorrected and undetected misstatements exceeds materiality for the financial statements as a whole. If applicable, performance materiality also refers to the amount or amounts set by the auditor at less than the materiality level or levels for particular classes of transactions, account balances or disclosures.'

(b) (i)   Ratios

Tutor's top tips

Ratios are relationships between different numbers in the financial statements. Percentage movements year to year are trends. The question asks for ratios therefore there will be no marks for calculating the percentage decrease in revenue/cost of sales.

Ratios to assist the audit supervisor in planning the audit:

	2013	2012
Gross margin	5.5/12.5 = 44%	7/15 = 46.7%
Operating margin	0.5/12.5 = 4%	1.9/15 = 12.7%
Inventory days	1.9/7 * 365 = 99 days	1.4/8 * 365 = 64 days
Inventory turnover	7/1.9 = 3.7	8/1.4 = 5.7
Receivable days	3.1/12.5 * 365 = 91 days	2.0/15 * 365 = 49 days
Payable days	1.6/7 * 365 = 83 days	1.2/8 * 365 = 55 days
Current ratio	5.8/2.6 = 2.2	5.3/1.2 = 4.4
Quick ratio	(5.8 – 1.9)/2.6 = 1.5	(5.3 – 1.4)/1.2 = 3.3

(ii) **Audit risks and responses**

Audit risk	**Audit response**
Receivable days have increased from 49 to 91 days and management has significantly extended the credit terms given to customers. This leads to an increased risk of recoverability of receivables as they may be overvalued.	Extended post year-end cash receipts testing and a review of the aged receivables ledger to be performed to assess valuation.
Due to the fall in demand for Kangaroo Construction Co's (Kangaroo) houses, there are some houses where the selling price may be below cost. IAS 2 *Inventories* requires that inventory should be stated at the lower of cost and NRV. In addition, inventory days have increased from 64 to 99 days and inventory turnover has fallen from 5.7 in 2012 to 3.7 in the current year. There is a risk that inventory is overvalued.	Detailed cost and net realisable value (NVR) testing to be performed and the aged inventory report to be reviewed to assess whether inventory requires writing down.
A deposit of $5,000 is paid by customers and is refundable until the house reaches 75% completion. There is a risk that the deposit is recognised as revenue when it is paid instead of when the revenue is earned. Revenue could be overstated as a result.	A schedule of houses which have been reserved but not completed should be obtained and the sales day book reviewed to ensure the $5,000 deposit has only been recognised for houses that have reached a 75% stage of completion.

Audit risk	Audit response
The directors have extended the useful lives of plant and machinery from three to five years, resulting in the depreciation charge reducing. Under IAS 16 *Property, Plant and Equipment*, useful lives are to be reviewed annually, and if asset lives have genuinely increased, then this change is reasonable.	Discuss with the directors the rationale for extending the useful lives. Also, the five year life should be compared to how often these assets are replaced, as this provides evidence of the useful life of assets.
However, there is a risk that this reduction has occurred in order to achieve profit targets. If this is the case, then plant and machinery is overvalued and profit overstated.	
The directors need to reach a profit level of $0.5 million in order to receive their annual bonus. There is a risk that they might feel under pressure to manipulate the results through the judgements taken or through the use of provisions.	Throughout the audit, the team will need to be alert to this risk and maintain professional scepticism. They will need to carefully review judgemental decisions and compare treatment against prior years. In addition, a written representation should be obtained from management confirming the basis of any significant judgements.
Due to a change in material supplier, the quality of products used has deteriorated and this has led to customers claiming on their five-year building warranty. If the overall number of people claiming on the warranty is likely to increase, then the warranty provision should possibly be higher. If the directors have not increased the level of the provision, then there is a risk the provision is understated.	Review the level of the warranty provision in light of the increased level of claims to confirm completeness of the provision.
Kangaroo has borrowed $1.0m from the bank via a short-term loan. This loan needs to be repaid in 2013 and so should be disclosed as a current liability.	During the audit, the team would need to check that the $1.0m loan finance was received. In addition, the disclosures for this loan should be reviewed in detail to ensure compliance with relevant accounting standards and legislation.

Audit risk	Audit response
In addition, Kangaroo may have given the bank a charge over its assets as security for the loan. There is a risk that the disclosure of any security given is not complete.	The loan correspondence should be reviewed to ascertain whether any security has been given, and this bank should be circularised as part of the bank confirmation process.
The current and quick ratios have decreased from 4.4 to 2.2 and 3.3 to 1.5 respectively. In addition, the cash balances have decreased over the year, there is a fall in demand and Kangaroo have taken out a short-term loan of $1 million, which needs to be repaid in 2013.	Detailed going concern testing to be performed during the audit and discussed with the directors to ensure that the going concern basis is reasonable.
Although all ratios are above the minimum levels, this is still a significant decrease and along with the fall in both operating and gross profit margins, as well as the significant increase in payable days could be evidence of going concern difficulties.	The team should discuss with the directors how the short-term loan of $1.0 million will be repaid later in 2013.

(c)   Audit reporting implications

- The increase in warranty provision required of $0.3m represents 60% of profit before tax (0.3/0.5 × 100) which is material to the financial statements.

- The financial statements are materially misstated due to understatement of the warranty provision. This may be considered material or material and pervasive.

- If considered material, the audit opinion should be qualified with the 'except for' wording.

- If deemed material and pervasive the audit opinion should be adverse with the wording stating that the financial statements do not show a true and fair view.

- A basis for qualified opinion or basis for adverse opinion would be required to explain the misstatement arising due to understatement of the warranty provision. The basis for paragraph would explain the financial effect of the issue on the financial statement.

- The basis for paragraph should be positioned below the opinion section within the audit report.

		ACCA marking scheme		
				Marks
(a)		Up to 1 mark per well explained point:		
		• Materiality for financial statements as a whole and also performance materiality levels		
		• Definition of materiality		
		• Amount or nature of misstatements, or both		
		• 5% profit before tax or 1% revenue or total expenses		
		• Judgement, needs of users and level of risk		
		• Small errors aggregated		
		• Performance materiality		
			Max	**5**
(b)	(i)	½ mark per ratio calculation per year.		
		• Gross margin		
		• Operating margin		
		• Inventory days		
		• Inventory turnover		
		• Receivable days		
		• Payable days		
		• Current ratio		
		• Quick ratio		
			Max	**6**
	(ii)	Up to 1 mark per well described audit risk and up to 1 mark per well explained audit response		
		• Receivables valuation		
		• Inventory valuation		
		• Revenue recognition - deposit		
		• Depreciation of plant and machinery		
		• Management manipulation of profit to reach bonus targets		
		• Completeness of warranty provision		
		• Disclosure of bank loan – split between current and non-current		
		• Disclosure of bank loan - security		
		• Going concern risk		
			Max	**14**
(c)		Up to 1 mark per well explained valid point		
		• Materiality calculation		
		• Misstatement may be material or material and pervasive		
		• If material – qualified 'except for'		
		• If pervasive – adverse 'FS do not show TFV'		
		• Basis for paragraph		
		• Position of Basis for paragraph		
				5
Total				**20**

Examiner's comments

Part (a) required an explanation of the concepts of materiality and performance materiality. Candidates' performed well on this question. The vast majority of candidates were able to score marks on the definition of materiality, provision of some benchmarks for the calculations and a reference to performance materiality being at a lower level. These points would have achieved a pass for this part of the question. An adequate level of detail was provided for this 'explain' requirement by the majority of candidates. Some candidates just gave a definition of materiality and nothing else; this would have gained a maximum of 1 mark.

Part (b) (i) required candidates to calculate ratios for 2012 and 2013 to assist in planning the audit. This question was answered very well by the vast majority of candidates with many scoring full marks. Some candidates attempted to calculate ratios despite there being inadequate data available, namely return on capital employed and gearing. Candidates need to think about the information provided in the scenario prior to calculating ratios. In order to gain the ½ mark available for each year a relevant ratio had to be calculated. Some candidates did not bring a calculator into the exam and hence were unable to calculate the final ratios; these candidates would not be able to score the available marks. Future candidates are reminded, once again, to bring a calculator into the F8 exam as they are often required.

Part (b) (ii) required a description of audit risks from the scenario and ratios calculated and the auditor's response for each. Performance on this question was once again unsatisfactory. The scenario contained more than the required number of risks and so candidates were able to easily identify enough risks. They then went on to describe how the point identified from the scenario or movement in a ratio was an audit risk by referring to the assertion and the account balances impacted. The improvement in this area noted in December 2012 has been reversed and the proportion of candidates who described the audit risk adequately has declined in this session. Some candidates tended to only identify facts from the scenario such as 'Kangaroo has completed houses in inventory where selling price may be below cost' but failed to explain how this could impact audit risk; this would only have scored ½ marks. To gain a full 1 mark they needed to refer to the risk of the inventory being overvalued. Where candidates did attempt to cover the assertion it was often vague; for example stating that 'inventory may be misstated', this is not sufficient to gain the ½ mark available. Additionally, many candidates used the ratios calculated in part (bi) and then gave a detailed analytical review of the ratio movements, commenting on ratio increases and decreases, but with no link at all to the audit risks. It was not uncommon to see very lengthy answers with no audit risks; this just puts the candidate under time pressure. Many candidates focused on business risks rather than audit risks and hence provided responses related to how management should address these business risks. For example, the scenario stated that 'Kangaroo had changed their main supplier to a cheaper alternative and as a result warranty claims had increased'. Some candidates answered 'this would lead to the company's reputation suffering as the quality of their buildings would decline'. The suggested auditor's response was 'to change back to a more expensive supplier'. Neither the risk nor the response has been related to the financial statements and hence would only gain a ½mark being the identification of the fact from the scenario.

Additionally, candidates performed inadequately with regards to the auditor's responses. As detailed above some candidates gave business advice, other responses focused more on repeating what the appropriate accounting treatment should be, therefore for the risk of inventory valuation due to number of houses where selling price was below cost, the response given was 'inventory should be valued at the lower of cost and NRV', this is not a valid audit response. Responses which start with 'ensure that......' are unlikely to score marks as they usually fail to explain exactly how the auditor will address the audit risk. Also some responses were weak such as 'discuss with the directors' without making it clear what would be discussed and how this would gather evidence. Audit responses need to be practical and should relate to the approach the auditor will adopt to assess whether the balance is materially misstated or not.

Most candidates presented their answers well as they adopted a two column approach with audit risk in one column and the related auditor's response next to it.

145 SUNFLOWER STORES *Walk in the footsteps of a top tutor*

(a)   Understanding an entity

Key answer tips

The question asks for sources of information and the information you would expect to obtain to gain an understanding of Sunflower Stores. Make sure you suggest information that would help you gain an understanding and not substantively test the financial statements. Think about what information you would require at the planning stage of the audit specifically. Suggesting information such as bank letters and receivables circularisations will not score marks as these are obtained at the substantive testing stage not the planning stage. The source is 'where' the information will come from.

Source of information	Information expect to obtain
Prior year audit file	Identification of issues that arose in the prior year audit and how these were resolved. Also whether any points brought forward were noted for consideration for this year's audit.
Prior year financial statements	Provides information in relation to the size of the entity as well as the key accounting policies and disclosure notes.
Accounting systems notes	Provides information on how each of the key accounting systems operates.
Discussions with management	Provides information in relation to any important issues which have arisen or changes to the company during the year.
Current year budgets and management accounts of Sunflower Stores Co (Sunflower)	Provides relevant financial information for the year to date. Will help the auditor to identify whether Sunflower has changed materially since last year. In addition, this will be useful for preliminary analytical review and risk identification.
Permanent audit file	Provides information in relation to matters of continuing importance for the company and the audit team, such as statutory books information or important agreements.
Sunflower's website	Recent press releases from the company may provide background on changes to the business during the year as this could lead to additional audit risks.

Source of information	Information expect to obtain
Prior year report to management	Provides information on the internal control deficiencies noted in the prior year; if these have not been rectified by management then they could arise in the current year audit as well.
Financial statements of competitors	This will provide information about Sunflower's competitors, in relation to their financial results and their accounting policies. This will be important in assessing Sunflower's performance in the year and also when undertaking the going concern review.

(b)   Audit risks and auditor responses

Tutor's top tips

Audit risks need to relate to either a risk of material misstatement or a detection risk. For risk of material misstatement, identify a balance in the scenario that is at risk of misstatement and explain why you believe it could be misstated. Detection risks are the risks the auditor does not detect material misstatements in the financial statements e.g. when it is a new audit client or if there is a tight reporting deadline.

For the response, make sure it relates to the risk, not the balance in general. Try and be as specific as possible, simply saying more testing is required will not be sufficient. State the nature of the tests that should be performed.

A 2 column table should be used to keep the risks in line with the responses and to make sure you address both parts of the requirement.

Audit risk	Auditor response
Sunflower has spent $1.6m on refurbishing its 25 food supermarkets. This expenditure needs to be reviewed to assess whether it is of a capital nature and should be included within non-current assets or expensed as repairs.	Review a breakdown of the costs and agree to invoices to assess the nature of the expenditure and, if capital, agree to inclusion within the asset register and, if repairs, agree to the statement of profit or loss.
During the year a small warehouse has been disposed of at a profit. The asset needs to have been correctly removed from property plant and equipment to ensure the non-current asset register is not overstated, and the profit on disposal should be included within the statement of profit or loss.	Review the non-current asset register to ensure that the asset has been removed. Also confirm the disposal proceeds as well as recalculating the profit on disposal. Consideration should be given as to whether the profit on disposal is significant enough to warrant separate disclosure within the statement of profit or loss.

Audit risk	*Auditor response*
Sunflower has borrowed $1.5m from the bank via a five year loan. This loan needs to be correctly split between current and non-current liabilities.	During the audit the team would need to confirm that the $1.5m loan finance was received. In addition, the split between current and non-current liabilities and the disclosures for this loan should be reviewed in detail to ensure compliance with relevant accounting standards.
In addition, Sunflower may have given the bank a charge over its assets as security for the loan. There is a risk that the disclosure of any security given is not complete.	The loan agreement should be reviewed to ascertain whether any security has been given, and this bank should be circularised as part of the bank confirmation process.
Sunflower will be undertaking a number of simultaneous inventory counts on 31 December including the warehouse and all 25 supermarkets. It is not practical for the auditor to attend all of these counts; hence it may not be possible to gain sufficient appropriate audit evidence over inventory counts.	The team should select a sample of sites to visit. It is likely that the warehouse contains most goods and therefore should be selected. In relation to the 25 supermarkets, the team should visit those with material inventory balances and/or those with a history of inventory count issues.
Sunflower's inventory valuation policy is selling price less average profit margin. Inventory should be valued at the lower of cost and net realisable value (NRV) and if this is not the case, then inventory could be under or overvalued.	Testing should be undertaken to confirm cost and NRV of inventory and that on a line-by-line basis the goods are valued correctly.
IAS 2 *Inventories* allows this as an inventory valuation method as long as it is a close approximation to cost. If this is not the case, then inventory could be under or overvalued.	In addition, valuation testing should focus on comparing the cost of inventory to the selling price less margin to confirm whether this method is actually a close approximation to cost.
The opening balances for each supermarket have been transferred into the head office's accounting records at the beginning of the year. There is a risk that if this transfer has not been performed completely and accurately, the opening balances may not be correct.	Discuss with management the process undertaken to transfer the data and the testing performed to confirm the transfer was complete and accurate. Computer-assisted audit techniques could be utilised by the team to sample test the transfer of data from each supermarket to head office to identify any errors.

Audit risk	*Auditor response*
There has been an increased workload for the finance department, the financial controller has left and his replacement will only start in late December.	The team should remain alert throughout the audit for additional errors within the finance department.
This increases the inherent risk within Sunflower as errors may have been made within the accounting records by the overworked finance team members. The new financial controller may not be sufficiently experienced to produce the financial statements and resolve any audit issues.	In addition, discuss with the finance director whether he will be able to provide the team with assistance for any audit issues the new financial controller is unable to resolve.

(c) **Internal audit department**

Prior to establishing an internal audit (IA) department, the finance director of Sunflower should consider the following:

(i)   The costs of establishing an IA department will be significant, therefore prior to committing to these costs and management time, a cost benefit analysis should be performed.

(ii) The size and complexity of Sunflower should be considered. The larger, more complex and diverse a company is, then the greater the need for an IA department. At Sunflower there are 25 supermarkets and a head office and therefore it would seem that the company is diverse enough to gain benefit from an IA department.

(iii) The role of any IA department should be considered. The finance director should consider what tasks he would envisage IA performing. He should consider whether he wishes them to undertake inventory counts at the stores, or whether he would want them to undertake such roles as internal controls reviews.

(iv) Having identified the role of any IA department, the finance director should consider whether there are existing managers or employees who could perform these tasks, therefore reducing the need to establish a separate IA department. This would however have implications on independence of the function.

(v)   The finance director should assess the current control environment and determine whether there are departments or stores with a history of control deficiencies. If this is the case, then it increases the need for an IA department.

(vi) If the possibility of fraud is high, then the greater the need for an IA department to act as both a deterrent and also to possibly undertake fraud investigations. As Sunflower operates 25 food supermarkets, it will have a significant risk of fraud of both inventory and cash.

(vii) The desire of senior management to have assurance and advice on risk and control.

(viii) The desire to be seen to be adopting best practice voluntarily to increase confidence of shareholders and other stakeholders.

	ACCA marking scheme	
		Marks
(a)	½ mark for source of documentation and ½ mark for information expect to obtain, max of 2½ marks for sources and 2½ marks for information expect	
	– Prior year audit file	
	– Prior year financial statements	
	– Accounting systems notes	
	– Discussions with management	
	– Permanent audit file	
	– Current year budgets and management accounts	
	– Sunflower's website	
	– Prior year report to management	
	– Financial statements of competitors	
	Max	**5**
(b)	Up to 1 mark per well described risk and up to 1 mark for each well explained response.	
	Treatment of $1.6m refurbishment expenditure	
	Disposal of warehouse	
	Bank loan of $1.5m	
	Attendance at year-end inventory counts	
	Inventory valuation	
	Transfer of opening balances from supermarkets to head office	
	Increased inherent risk of errors in finance department and new financial controller	
	Max	**10**
(c)	Up to 1 mark per well described point	
	Costs versus benefits of establishing an internal audit (IA) department	
	Size and complexity of Sunflower should be considered	
	The role of any IA department should be considered	
	Whether existing managers/employees can undertake the roles required	
	Whether the control environment has a history of control deficiencies	
	Whether the possibility of fraud is high	
	Management need for assurance on risk and controls	
	Increase confidence of shareholders and stakeholders	
	Max	**5**
Total		**20**

Examiner's comments

Part (a) required a list of five sources of information for gaining an understanding of Sunflower and what each source would be used for. Candidates' performance on this question was unsatisfactory. A significant proportion of candidates did not seem to understand what was required from them for this question. They did not seem to understand what a 'source of information' was and so failed to list where they would obtain information from such as prior year financial statements or last year's audit file. Some were able to explain what they would want to gain knowledge on e.g. audit risks or accounting policies but did not tie this into the source of information. In addition the question requirement related to gaining an understanding of Sunflower, this is part of the planning process, however a significant proportion of candidates gave sources of information relevant to carrying out the audit fieldwork, such as bank letters, written representations or receivables circularisation. Most candidates' confused requirements a and b and so gave sources of information relevant to auditing the risks from requirement b. These points were not relevant to gaining an understanding of Sunflower and hence scored no marks.

Part (b) required a description of audit risks from the scenario and the auditor's response for each. Performance on this question was mixed, although slightly better than when audit risk was last tested.

The scenario contained many more than the required number of risks and so many candidates were able to easily identify enough risks, they then went on to describe how the point identified from the scenario was an audit risk by referring to the assertion and the account balance impacted. There seemed to be a higher proportion of candidates this session who described the audit risk adequately. Some candidates tended to only identify facts from the scenario such as 'Sunflower has spent $1.6 million in refurbishing all of its supermarkets' but failed to explain how this could impact audit risk; this would only have scored ½ marks. To gain 1 mark they needed to refer to the risk of the expenditure not being correctly classified between capital and repairs resulting in misstated expenses or non-current assets. Additionally, candidates were able to identify the fact from the question but then focused on categorising this into an element of the audit risk model such as inherent or control risk. The problem with this approach is that just because they have stated an issue could increase control risk does not mean that they have described the audit risk and so this does not tend to score well.

The area where most candidates performed inadequately is with regards to the auditor's responses. Some candidates gave business advice such as, for the risk of the finance director (FD) leaving early, that 'the auditor should ask management to replace the FD quicker' this is not a valid audit response. Other responses focused more on repeating what the appropriate accounting treatment should be, therefore for the risk of inventory valuation due to the policy of valuing at selling price less margin, the response given was 'inventory should be valued at the lower of cost and NRV', again this is not a valid audit response. Responses which start with 'ensure that......' are unlikely to score marks as they usually fail to explain exactly how the auditor will address the audit risk. Also some responses were too vague such as 'increase substantive testing' without making it clear how, or in what area, this would be addressed. Audit responses need to be practical and should relate to the approach the auditor will adopt to assess whether the balance is materially misstated or not.

A significant minority of candidates misread the scenario and where it stated that it was the first year on this audit for the senior, candidates seemed to think that it was the first year for the firm as a whole and so identified an audit risk of Sunflower being a new client with higher detection risk. This scored no marks as it was not the first year of the audit, candidates must read the scenario more carefully.

Most candidates presented their answers well as they adopted a two column approach with audit risk in one column and the related response next to it.

Part (c) required candidates to describe factors the finance director should consider before establishing an internal audit (IA) department. Performance was unsatisfactory on this part of the question. Many candidates were able to gain a few marks with points on considering cost and benefits of the IA department and whether it should be outsourced or run in house. However, this seemed to be the limit of most candidates' knowledge in this area. Unfortunately many candidates strayed into the area of who IA should report to and the qualifications and independence of the department; these are factors to consider when running IA as opposed to whether or not to establish an IA department. Once again, candidates must answer the question set and not the one they wish had been asked.

146 ABRAHAMS *Walk in the footsteps of a top tutor*

Key answer tips

Part (a) is a purely knowledge based requirement covering the components of audit risk. Be careful not to mix up the definition of detection risk with the definition of audit risk.

Part (b) is a core topic in the F8 syllabus – audit risk and the auditor's response. The auditor's response should be directly linked to the audit risks explained and therefore a columnar approach is appropriate. This is a skills based question – the answers must relate to the issues presented in the scenario. Each sufficiently explained audit risk will be awarded 1 mark and each appropriate response a further mark. You therefore need to explain five audit risks for 10 marks. A 2 column table should be used to keep the risks in line with the responses and to make sure you address both parts of the requirement.

(a) Components of audit risk

Inherent risk

The susceptibility of an assertion about a class of transaction, account balance or disclosure to a misstatement that could be material, either individually or when aggregated with other misstatements, before consideration of any related controls.

Inherent risk is affected by the nature of an entity and factors which can result in an increase include:

- Changes in the industry it operates in.

- Operations that are subject to a high degree of regulation.

- Going concern and liquidity issues including loss of significant customers.

- Developing or offering new products or services, or moving into new lines of business. – Expanding into new locations.

- Application of new accounting standards.

- Accounting measurements that involve complex processes.

- Events or transactions that involve significant accounting estimates.

- Pending litigation and contingent liabilities.

Control risk

The risk that a misstatement that could occur in an assertion about a class of transaction, account balance or disclosure and that could be material, either individually or when aggregated with other misstatements, will not be prevented, or detected and corrected, on a timely basis by the entity's internal control.

The following factors can result in an increase in control risk:

- Lack of personnel with appropriate accounting and financial reporting skills.

- Changes in key personnel including departure of key management.

- Deficiencies in internal control, especially those not addressed by management.

- Changes in the information technology (IT) environment.

- Installation of significant new IT systems related to financial reporting.

Detection risk

The risk that the procedures performed by the auditor to reduce audit risk to an acceptably low level will not detect misstatement that exists and that could be material, either individually or when aggregated with other misstatements.

Detection risk is affected by sampling and non-sampling risk and factors which can result in an increase include:

- Inadequate planning.

- Inappropriate assignment of personnel to the engagement team.

- Failing to apply professional scepticism.

- Inadequate supervision and review of the audit work performed.

- Inappropriate sampling techniques performed.

- Inappropriate sample sizes.

(b) **Audit risks and responses**

Audit risk	Audit response
The finance director of Abrahams is planning to capitalise the full $2.2 million of development expenditure incurred. However in order to be capitalised it must meet all of the criteria under IAS 38 *Intangible Assets*.	A breakdown of the development expenditure should be reviewed and tested in detail to ensure that only projects which meet the capitalisation criteria are included as an intangible asset, with the balance being expensed.
There is a risk that some projects may not reach final development stage and hence should be expensed rather than capitalised. Intangible assets could be overstated and this risk is increased due to the loan covenant requirements to maintain a minimum level of assets.	
The inventory valuation method used by Abrahams is standard costing. This method is acceptable under IAS 2 *Inventories;* however, only if standard cost is a close approximation to actual cost.	The standard costs used for the inventory valuation should be tested in detail and compared to actual cost. If there are significant variations this should be discussed with management, to ensure that the valuation is appropriate.
Abrahams has not updated their standard costs from when the product was first developed and hence there is a risk that the standard costs could be out of date, resulting in over or undervalued inventory.	

Audit risk

The work in progress balance at the year end is likely to be material; however there is a risk that due to the nature of the production process the audit team may not be sufficiently qualified to assess the quantity and value of work in progress leading to misstated work in progress.

Over one-third of the warehouses of Abrahams belong to third parties. Sufficient and appropriate evidence will need to be obtained to confirm the quantities of inventory held in these locations in order to verify completeness and existence.

In September Abrahams Co introduced a new accounting system. This is a critical system for the accounts preparation and if there were any errors that occurred during the changeover process, these could impact on the final amounts in the trial balance.

The new accounting system is bespoke and the IT manager who developed it has left the company already and his replacement is not due to start until just before the year end. The accounting personnel who are using the system may have encountered problems and without the IT manager's support, errors could be occurring in the system due to a lack of knowledge and experience. This could result in significant errors arising in the financial statements.

Significant finance has been obtained in the year, $1 million of equity finance and $2.5 million of long-term loans. This finance needs to be accounted for correctly, with adequate disclosure made. The equity finance needs to be allocated correctly between share capital and share premium, and the loan should be presented as a non-current liability.

Audit response

Consideration should be given as to whether an independent expert is required to value the work in progress. If so this will need to be arranged with consent from management and in time for the year-end count.

Additional procedures will be required to ensure that inventory quantities have been confirmed for both third party and company owned locations.

The new system will need to be documented in full and testing should be performed over the transfer of data from the old to the new system.

This issue should be discussed with the finance director to understand how he is addressing this risk of misstatement. In addition, the team should remain alert throughout the audit for evidence of such errors.

Check that the split of the equity finance is correct and that total financing proceeds of $3.5 million were received. In addition, the disclosures for this finance should be reviewed in detail to ensure compliance with relevant accounting standards.

Audit risk	**Audit response**
The loan has a number of covenants attached to it. If these are breached then the loan would be instantly repayable and would be classified as a current liability. This could result in the company being in a net current liability position. If the company did not have sufficient cash flow to meet this loan repayment then there could be going concern implications.	Review the covenant calculations prepared by Abrahams Co and identify whether any defaults have occurred; if so then determine the effect on the company. The team should maintain their professional scepticism and be alert to the risk that assets have been overstated to ensure compliance with covenants.
The land and buildings are to be revalued at the year end, it is likely that the revaluation needs to be carried out and recorded in accordance with IAS 16 *Property, Plant and Equipment*; otherwise non-current assets may be incorrectly valued.	Review the reasonableness of the valuation and recalculate the revaluation surplus/deficit to ensure that land and buildings are correctly valued.
The reporting timetable for Abrahams Co is likely to be reduced. The previous timetable was already quite short and any further reductions will increase detection risk and place additional pressure on the team in obtaining sufficient and appropriate evidence.	The timetable should be confirmed with the financial director. If it is to be reduced then consideration should be given to performing an interim audit in late December or early January, this would then reduce the pressure on the final audit.

(c)   (i)   **Procedures to confirm inventory held at third party locations**

- Send a letter requesting direct confirmation of inventory balances held at year end from the third party warehouse providers used by Abrahams Co regarding quantities and condition.

- Attend the inventory count (if one is to be performed) at the third party warehouses to review the controls in operation to ensure the completeness and existence of inventory.

- Inspect any reports produced by the auditors of the warehouses in relation to the adequacy of controls over inventory.

- Inspect any documentation in respect of third party inventory.

(ii)   **Procedures to confirm use of standard costs for inventory valuation**

- Discuss with management of Abrahams Co the basis of the standard costs applied to the inventory valuation, and how often these are reviewed and updated.

- Review the level of variances between standard and actual costs and discuss with management how these are treated.

- Obtain a breakdown of the standard costs and agree a sample of these costs to actual invoices or wage records to assess their reasonableness.

	ACCA marking scheme	
		Marks
(a)	Up to 1 mark for each component of audit risk (if just a component is given without an explanation then just give 0.5) and up to 1 mark for each example of factor which increases risk.	
	Inherent risk	
	Control risk	
	Detection risk	
	Max	**6**
(b)	Up to 1 mark per well explained risk and up to 1 mark for each well explained response	
	Development expenditure treatment	
	Standard costing for valuation of inventory	
	Expert possibly required in verifying work in progress	
	Third party inventory locations	
	New accounting system introduced in the year	
	Lack of support by IT staff on new system may result in errors in accounting system	
	New finance obtained; loans and equity finance treatment	
	Loan covenants and risk of going concern problems	
	Revaluation of land and buildings	
	Reduced reporting timetable	
	Max	**10**
(c)	1 mark per well explained procedure, maximum of 2 marks for each of (i) and (ii)	
	(i) Third party locations	
	• Letter requesting direct confirmation	
	• Attend inventory count	
	• Review other auditor reports and documentation	
	Max	**2**
	(ii) Standard costing	
	• Discuss with management basis of standard costs	
	• Review variances	
	• Breakdown of standard costs and agree to actual costs	
	Max	**2**
Total		**20**

147 REDSMITH *Walk in the footsteps of a top tutor*

Key answer tips

Part (a) is a purely knowledge based requirement covering part of ISA 210 *Agreeing the Terms of Audit Engagements*. It is a difficult requirement – you either know the answer or you don't. A common sense approach will not help you here. If you don't have the knowledge, move on and try to compensate by scoring well on other requirements.

Part (b) is another purely knowledge based requirement, but a common sense approach will score well here. If you don't know the requirements of ISA 315 you can still score well by thinking generally about the areas/matters that of which the auditor should obtain an understanding.

Part (c) is a core topic in the F8 syllabus – audit risk and the auditor's response. The auditor's response should be directly linked to the audit risks explained and therefore a columnar approach is appropriate. This is a skills based question – the answers must relate to the issues presented in the scenario. Each sufficiently explained audit risk will be awarded 1 mark and each appropriate response a further mark.

(a)   Preconditions for an audit

ISA 210 *Agreeing the Terms of Audit Engagements* provides guidance to auditors on the steps they should take in accepting a new audit or continuing on an existing audit engagement. It sets out a number of processes that the auditor should perform including agreeing whether the preconditions are present, agreement of audit terms in an engagement letter, recurring audits and changes in engagement terms.

To assess whether the preconditions for an audit are present the auditor must determine whether the financial reporting framework to be applied in the preparation of the financial statements is acceptable. In considering this the auditor should assess the nature of the entity, the nature and purpose of the financial statements and whether law or regulations prescribes the applicable reporting framework.

In addition they must obtain the agreement of management that it acknowledges and understands its responsibility for the following:

- Preparation of the financial statements in accordance with the applicable financial reporting framework, including where relevant their fair presentation

- For such internal control as management determines is necessary to enable the preparation of financial statements that are free from material misstatement, whether due to fraud or error; and

- To provide the auditor with access to all relevant information for the preparation of the financial statements, any additional information that the auditor may request from management and unrestricted access to persons within the entity from whom the auditor determines it necessary to obtain audit evidence.

If the preconditions for an audit are not present, the auditor shall discuss the matter with management. Unless required by law or regulation to do so, the auditor shall not accept the proposed audit engagement:

- If the auditor has determined that the financial reporting framework to be applied in the preparation of the financial statements is unacceptable; or

- If management agreement of their responsibilities has not been obtained.

(b) **Matters to consider in obtaining an understanding of the entity:**

- The market and its competition
- Legislation and regulation
- Regulatory framework
- Ownership of the entity
- Nature of products/services and markets
- Location of production facilities and factories
- Key customers and suppliers
- Capital investment activities
- Accounting policies and industry specific guidance
- Financing structure
- Significant changes in the entity on prior years.

Tutor's top tips

Note the requirement asks for matters to consider in obtaining an understanding of the entity. Procedures that the auditor should perform or sources from which they would obtain this understanding will not score any marks. Also note the verb requirement 'list' and the number of marks available. With a 'list' requirement, each appropriate matter listed will be awarded ½ mark. The length of points provided in the model answer is appropriate for ½ mark.

(c) **(i)** **Ratios to assist the audit supervisor in planning the audit:**

	2010	2009
Gross margin	12/23 = 52.2%	8/18 = 44.4%
Operating margin	45/23 = 19.6%	4/18 = 22.2%
Inventory days	21/11 * 365 = 70 days	16/10 * 365 = 58 days
Receivable days	45/23 * 365 = 71 days	30/18 * 365 = 61 days
Payable days	16/11 * 365 = 53 days	12/10 * 365 = 44 days
Current ratio	66/25 = 2.6	69/12 = 5.8
Quick ratio	(66 – 21)/25 = 1.8	(69 – 16)/12 = 4.4

Tutor's top tips

Be sure to calculate ratios and not trends in order to score well in part (i). Simple % increases will not be awarded marks. The auditor will calculate ratios as part of the analytical review required at the planning stage. You should expect to be examined on the practical application of skills required during the audit process.

(ii)   Audit risks and responses

Audit risk	Response to risk
Management were disappointed with 2009 results and hence undertook strategies to improve the 2010 trading results. There is a risk that management might feel under pressure to manipulate the results through the judgements taken or through the use of provisions.	Throughout the audit the team will need to be alert to this risk. They will need to carefully review judgemental decisions and compare treatment against prior years.
A generous sales-related bonus scheme has been introduced in the year, this may lead to sales cut-off errors with employees aiming to maximise their current year bonus.	Increased sales cut-off testing will be performed along with a review of post year-end sales returns as they may indicate cut-off errors.
Revenue has grown by 28% in the year however, cost of sales has only increased by 10%. This increase in sales may be due to the bonus scheme and the advertising however, this does not explain the increase in gross margin. There is a risk that sales may be overstated.	During the audit a detailed breakdown of sales will be obtained, discussed with management and tested in order to understand the sales increase.
Gross margin has increased from 44.4% to 52.2%. Operating margin has decreased from 22.2% to 19.6%. This movement in gross margin is significant and there is a risk that costs may have been omitted or included in operating expenses rather than cost of sales. There has been a significant increase in operating expenses which may be due to the bonus and the advertising campaign but could be related to the misclassification of costs.	The classification of costs between cost of sales and operating expenses will be compared with the prior year to ensure consistency.

Audit risk	Response to risk
The finance director has made a change to the inventory valuation in the year with additional overheads being included. In addition inventory days have increased from 58 to 70 days. There is a risk that inventory is overvalued.	The change in the inventory policy will be discussed with management and a review of the additional overheads included performed to ensure that these are of a production nature. Detailed cost and net realisable value testing to be performed and the aged inventory report to be reviewed to assess whether inventory requires writing down.
Receivable days have increased from 61 to 71 days and management have extended the credit period given to customers. This leads to an increased risk of recoverability of receivables.	Extended post year-end cash receipts testing and a review of the aged receivables ledger to be performed to assess valuation.
The current and quick ratios have decreased from 5.8 to 2.6 and 4.4 to 1.8 respectively. In addition the cash balances have decreased significantly over the year. Although all ratios are above the minimum levels, this is still a significant decrease and along with the increase of sales could be evidence of overtrading which could result in going concern difficulties.	Detailed going concern testing to be performed during the audit and discussed with management to ensure that the going concern basis is reasonable.

Tutor's top tips

Take care to describe audit risks in part (c) and not business risks or interpretations of the ratios. Audit risk is the risk of giving an inappropriate opinion – you should describe the potential for misstatement in the financial statements or explain how detection risk is increased – be specific. Link the ratios you calculate in part (i) to the information given about the entity described when explaining the audit risk. The auditor's response must directly relate to the risk described – describe a procedure that would help the auditor detect any misstatement that may exist.

ACCA marking scheme

			Marks
(a)	Up to 1 mark per valid point		
	– ISA 210 provides guidance		
	– Determination of acceptable framework		
	– Agreement of management responsibilities		
	– Preparation of financial statements with applicable framework		
	– Internal controls		
	– Provide auditor with relevant information and access		
	– If preconditions are not present discuss with management		
	– Decline if framework unacceptable		
	– Decline if agreement of responsibilities not obtained		
		Max	**3**
(b)	½ mark per example of matter to consider in obtaining an understanding of the nature of an entity.		
		Max	**2**
(c) (i)	½ mark per ratio calculation per year.		
	– Gross margin		
	– Operating margin		
	– Inventory days		
	– Receivable days		
	– Payable days		
	– Current ratio		
	– Quick ratio		
		Max	**5**
(ii)	Up to 1 mark per well explained audit risk and up to 1 mark per audit response		
	– Management manipulation of results		
	– Sales cut-off		
	– Revenue growth		
	– Misclassification of costs between cost of sales and operating		
	– Inventory valuation		
	– Receivables valuation		
	– Going concern risk		
		Max	**10**
Total			**20**

148 SPECS4YOU *Walk in the footsteps of a top tutor*

Key answer tips

Parts (a) and (b) are book knowledge. Part (c) expects you to apply that knowledge to identify deficiencies in a working paper, illustrating that memorising without understanding is insufficient.

(a) The purposes of audit working papers include:

– To assist with the planning and performance of the audit.

– To assist in the supervision and review of audit work.

– To record the audit evidence resulting from the audit work performed to support the auditor's opinion.

(b) **Familiarisation**

Documentation	Information obtained
Memorandum and articles of association	Details of the objectives of Specs4You, its permitted capital structure and the internal constitution of the company.
Most recent published financial statements	Provide detail on the size of the company, profitability, etc. as well as any unusual factors such as loans due for repayment.
Most recent management accounts/budgets/cash flow information	Determine the current status of the company including ongoing profitability, ability to meet budget, etc. as well as identifying any potential going concern problems.
Organisation chart of Specs4You	To identify the key managers and employees in the company and other people to contact during the audit.
Industry data on spectacle sales	To find out how Specs4You is performing compared to the industry standards. This will help to highlight any areas of concern, for example higher than expected cost of sales, for investigation on the audit.
Financial statements of similar entities	To compare the accounting policies of Specs4You and obtain additional information on industry standards.
Prior year audit file	To establish what problems were encountered in last year's audit, how those problems were resolved and identify any areas of concern for this year's audit.
Search of Internet news sites	To find out whether the company has any significant news stories (good or bad) which may affect the audit approach.

(c) The audit working paper does not meet the standards normally expected in a working paper because:

- The page reference is unclear making it very difficult to either file the working paper in the audit file or locate the working paper should there be queries on it.

- It is not clear what the client year-end date is – the year is missing. The working paper could easily be filed in the wrong year's audit file.

- There is no signature of the person who prepared the working paper. This means it is unclear who to address queries to regarding the preparation or contents of the working paper.

- There is evidence of a reviewer's signature. However, given that the reviewer did not query the lack of preparer's signature or other omissions noted below, the effectiveness of the review must be put in question.

- The test 'objective' is vague – it is not clear what 'correct' means for example, it would be better to state the objective in terms of assertions such as completeness or accuracy.

- The test objective is also stated as an audit assertion. This is not the case as no audit assertions are actually listed here.

- It is not clear how the number for testing was determined. This means it will be very difficult to determine whether sufficient audit evidence was obtained for this test.

- Stating that details of testing can be found on another working paper is insufficient – time will be wasted finding the working paper, if it has, in fact, been included in the audit working paper file.

- Information on the results of the test is unclear – the working paper should clearly state the results of the test without bias. The preparer appears to have used personal judgement which is not appropriate as the opinion should be based on the facts available, not speculation.

- The conclusion provided does not appear to be consistent with the results of the test. Five errors were found therefore it is likely that there are some systems deficiencies.

	ACCA marking scheme		Marks
(a)	1 mark for each purpose		
	– Assist planning and performance of audit		
	– Assist supervision and review		
	– Support audit opinion		
		Max	**3**
(b)	½ per item of documentation and ½ for the information it provides		
	– Memorandum and articles of association		
	– Published FS		
	– Management accounts		
	– Budgets/forecasts		
	– Organisation chart		
	– Industry data		
	– Competitor FS		
	– Prior year audit file		
	– Internet/press articles		
		Max	**8**
(c)	Up to 1 mark per point		
	– Page reference		
	– Year end		
	– Name of preparer		
	– Objective/assertion		
	– Justification of sample size		
	– No reference of other working paper		
	– Results of the test unclear		
	– Conclusion inconsistent		
	– Results of the test unclear		
		Max	**9**
Total			**20**

INTERNAL CONTROLS AND AUDIT EVIDENCE

149   BRONZE   *Walk in the footsteps of a top tutor*

Key answer tips

This question covers both strengths and deficiencies of a payroll system. For the strengths, identify the controls that you can see in place. For the deficiencies identify the controls that are missing from the system.

In part (c) you are asked for analytical procedures to confirm payroll. An analytical procedure requires the auditor to form an expectation of the payroll figure to compare with the client's actual figure to assess whether it looks reasonable. Comparisons with prior year, comparison with budget and performing a proof in total would be typical analytical procedures for payroll.

(a)   Bronze Industries Co (Bronze) payroll system internal control strengths

Strengths in Bronze's payroll system are as follows:

- Factory staff are each issued a sequentially numbered clock card which details their employee number and name. This should ensure that employees are only paid for hours they have worked and that the payroll records record completely all employees, as any gaps in the sequence would be identified.

- The payroll system automatically calculates gross and net pay along with any statutory deductions. This should reduce the risk of employees' wages and statutory deductions being incorrect as there is a reduced risk of errors occurring.

- A sample of the calculations made by the automated system is checked by the payroll supervisor to ensure the system is operating effectively; this tests the automated controls within the system.

- Bronze has a human resources department which is responsible for setting up new permanent employees and leavers. Having a segregation of roles between human resources and payroll departments reduces the risk of fictitious employees being set up and also being paid.

- The discretionary bonus is communicated in writing to the payroll department. As this is in writing rather than verbal, this reduces the risk of the bonus being recorded at an incorrect amount in the payroll records.

- For employees paid by bank transfer, the list of the payments is reviewed in detail and agreed to the payroll records prior to authorising the bank payment. This reduces the risk of fraudulent payments being made through the creation of fictitious employees and other employees being omitted from the payment run.

(b) Bronze payroll system deficiencies and controls

Deficiencies	Controls	Test of control
Employees swipe their cards at the beginning and end of the eight-hour shift; this process is not supervised. This could result in a number of employees being swiped in as present when they are not. This will result in a substantially increased payroll cost for Bronze.	The clocking in and out process should be supervised by a responsible official to prevent one individual clocking in multiple employees. A supervisor should undertake a random check of employees by reviewing who has logged in with a swipe card and confirming visually that the employee is present.	Observe the clocking in and out process to ensure it is supervised by a responsible official. Enquire of the supervisor whether they perform a random check of employees.
Employees are entitled to a 30-minute paid break and do not need to clock out to access the dining area. Employees could be taking excessive breaks resulting in a decrease in productivity and increased payroll costs.	Employees should be allocated set break times and there should be a supervisor present to ensure that employees only take the breaks they are entitled to.	Review the rota for break-times to ensure break times are formally communicated to staff. Observe the dining area during break times to ensure a supervisor is present.
Although there is a human resources department, appointments of temporary staff are made by factory production supervisors. The supervisor could appoint unsuitable employees and may not carry out all the required procedures for new joiners. This could result in these temporary employees not receiving the correct pay and relevant statutory deductions.	All appointment of staff, whether temporary or permanent, should only be made by the human resources department.	Inspect the HR procedures manual to ensure that appointments of staff are the responsibility of the HR department. For a sample of employees employed by Bronze, inspect the employee's file to ensure the appropriate checks were carried out by the HR department prior to employment.

Deficiencies	Controls	Test of control
Overtime reports which detail the amount of overtime worked are sent out quarterly by the payroll department to production supervisors for review. These reports are reviewed after the payments have been made which could result in unauthorised overtime or amounts being paid incorrectly and Bronze's payroll cost increasing.	All overtime should be authorised by a responsible official prior to the payment being processed by the payroll department. This authorisation should be evidenced in writing.	Inspect the overtime reports for evidence of a responsible official's signature authorising the overtime prior to the payment being processed.
Production supervisors determine the amount of the discretionary bonus to be paid to employees. Production supervisors are not senior enough to determine this as they could pay extra bonuses to friends or family members.	The bonus should be determined by a more senior individual, such as the production director, and this should be communicated in writing to the payroll department.	Inspect the communication of bonuses to the payroll department and ensure it is sent by a senior official.
The bonus is input by a clerk into the payroll system. There is no indication that this input process is reviewed. This could result in input errors or the clerk could fraudulently change the amounts leading to incorrect bonus payments.	Once the clerk has input the bonus amounts, all entries should be double checked against the written confirmation from the production director by another member of the team to identify any amounts entered incorrectly.	Observe the payroll clerk inputting the bonus amounts and subsequent check against the written confirmation from the production director by a different member of the team.

Deficiencies	Controls	Test of control
The payroll manager reviews the bank transfer listing prior to authorising the payments and also amends the payroll records for any changes required. There is a lack of segregation of duties as it is the payroll team which processes the amounts and the payroll manager who authorises payments. The manager could fraudulently increase the amounts to be paid to certain employees, process this payment as well as amend the records.	The payroll manager should not be able to process changes to the payroll system as well as authorise payments. The authorisation of the bank transfer listing should be undertaken by an individual outside the payroll department, such as the finance director.	Inspect the payroll bank transfer listing for the authorisation signature. Ensure the signature is of a person outside of the payroll department and of suitable authority such as the finance director.
A payroll clerk distributes cash pay packets to employees without requesting proof of identity. Even if most employees are known to the clerk, there is a risk that without identity checks wages could be paid to incorrect employees.	The payroll clerks should be informed that all cash wages can only be paid upon sight of the employee's clock card and photographic identification as this confirms proof of identity.	Observe the process of wage collection to ensure that employees can only collect their wages on production of their clock card and photographic ID.

(c) **Substantive analytical procedures to confirm payroll expense**

- Compare the total payroll expense to the prior year and investigate any significant differences.

- Review monthly payroll charges, compare this to the prior year and budgets and discuss with management any significant variances.

- Compare overtime pay as a percentage of factory normal hours pay to investigate whether it is at a similar level to the prior year and within an acceptable range. Investigate any significant differences.

- Perform a proof in total of total wages and salaries, incorporating joiners and leavers and any pay increase. Compare this to the actual wages and salaries in the financial statements and investigate any significant differences.

(d)   Suitability of analytical procedures

- Nature of the balance or class of transactions. Analytical procedures are more suitable to large volume transactions that are predictable over time such as payroll, sales, and expenses.

- Reliability of the information being analysed. If the information being analysed is unreliable, the results of the analytical procedures will be unreliable. Reliability of the information will be affected by source, nature and effectiveness of internal controls.

- Relevance to the assertion being tested. Analytical procedures would usually not be used to test the existence assertion of a tangible asset such as inventory or property, plant and equipment as physical inspection of the asset would provide more reliable evidence.

- Precision of expectation. The auditor should consider whether a sufficiently precise expectation can be developed to be able to identify a material misstatement. If not, there is limited use in using analytical procedures.

- Amount of difference between expected amounts and recorded amounts that is acceptable. This will depend on the level of materiality and the desired level of assurance required by the auditor.

ACCA marking scheme		Marks
(a)	Up to 1 mark each per well explained strength. If not well explained, then just give ½ mark for each, overall maximum of 5 marks for 5 points • Sequentially numbered clock cards • Automatic calculations of gross, net pay and deductions • Sample of calculations double checked • Separate human resources and payroll department • Bonus communicated in writing to payroll • List of bank payments agreed in detail to payroll records **Max**	**5**
(b)	Up to 1 mark each per well explained deficiency, recommendation and test of control. If not well explained, then just give ½ mark for each. • Clock in/out process unsupervised • Employee breaks not monitored • Temporary staff are not appointed by human resources department • Overtime report reviewed after payment • Authorisation of discretionary bonus • No input checks over entry of bonus into payroll • Payroll manager reviews the bank transfer listing prior to payment and can change payroll records • No identity checks prior to cash wages pay out **Max**	**18**
(c)	Up to 1 mark per well described procedure, overall maximum of 3 marks. • Compare total payroll expense to the prior year and investigate any significant differences • Review monthly payroll charges, compare to the prior year, budgets, discuss with management • Compare overtime pay as a percentage of factory normal hours against prior year, investigate any significant differences • Perform a proof in total of total wages and salaries, compare to actual, and investigate any significant differences **Max**	**3**

(d)	Up to 1 mark per point		
	• Nature of the balance or class of transactions		
	• Reliability of the information being analysed		
	• Relevance to the assertion being tested		
	• Precision of expectation		
	• Amount of difference between expected amounts and recorded amounts that is acceptable	Max	4
Total			30

Examiner's comments

Internal control questions typically require internal controls deficiencies to be identified (½ marks each), explained (½ marks each) and, often, to give a relevant recommendation to address the deficiency (1 mark each). Occasionally, candidates may be asked to identify internal control strengths as well as deficiencies. Candidates continue to perform well on internal control questions. Candidates were able to confidently identify internal controls deficiencies from the scenario, however some candidates did not clearly explain the deficiency in terms of how it affects the business. The scenario in the exam will always contain more issues than required to be discussed and it was therefore encouraging that candidates generally applied effective exam technique and focused on providing well explained answers which identified the required number of issues as noted in the question. A minority of candidates, rather than evaluating internal controls just formed a point of view as to how well the company was controlling it's operations, and, also included more 'social' factors such as 'the motivational effect of having/not having a bonus system in force in a company' which was not required and does not answer the question. Recommendations to address control weaknesses were on the whole well explained. Most candidates were able to provide good recommendations to address the deficiencies. However occasionally some of the recommendations did not clearly address the specific control weakness identified and candidates are again reminded to ensure that their recommendation is specifically tailored to the requirements of the scenario.

150 HUMMINGBIRD *Walk in the footsteps of a top tutor*

Key answer tips

Part (a) requires the control deficiencies within the sales cycle to be identified. Use the specific information in scenario rather than giving deficiencies that could be present in any sales system. There are always more deficiencies than you need so choose the ones you can write well about. Suggest controls the client can implement to address the control deficiency. Be specific about which member of client staff should be responsible for the control and how frequently they should perform the control.

Note the requirement to produce a covering letter for 2 marks. These are easy marks and should not be overlooked. To obtain the marks you need to include an address, an appropriate greeting, a disclaimer and appropriate sign off.

Part (b) asks for substantive procedures to be performed over the revenue figure. A substantive procedure is used to detect material misstatement in the figure. Tests of controls will not score marks. The requirement relates to revenue within the statement of profit or loss. Do not give procedures over receivables as this is not what the question is asking.

(a)   **Board of directors**
        Hummingbird Co
        23 Buzzard Lane
        Peregrine City
        Hawk Country

        4 December 2014

        Dear Sirs,

        Audit of Hummingbird Scents Co (Hummingbird) for the year ended 30 September 2014

        Please find enclosed the report to management on deficiencies in internal controls identified during the audit for the year ended 30 September 2014. The appendix to this report considers deficiencies in the sales system and recommendations to address those deficiencies.

        Please note that this report only addresses the deficiencies identified during the audit and if further testing had been performed, then more deficiencies may have been reported.

        This report is solely for the use of management and if you have any further questions, then please do not hesitate to contact us.

        Yours faithfully

        An audit firm

APPENDIX

Deficiency	Control
Brenda the sales clerk receives customer orders, raises sales invoices and processes payments for hotel customers. This is a lack of segregation of duties and could lead to a risk of fraudulent transactions or errors, as no one checks the work undertaken by this clerk.	Another sales ledger clerk should be involved in the processing of hotel customer transactions so that no one individual undertakes all elements of the sales cycle. The work could be split so that one clerk raises orders and invoices but a second clerk processes the payments.
Hotel customers have contracted sales prices; however, as online trade prices are automatically loaded into the sales invoices, Brenda has to manually amend the invoices. This significantly increases the risk of error, as if Brenda incorrectly increases the sales prices, then this can lead to a loss of customer goodwill and if they are too low, this results in a loss of revenue for Hummingbird.	As hotel customers account for 40% of revenue, consideration should be given to amending the sales system so that each customer's agreed prices are pre-loaded, therefore no manual amendment of invoices would be required. If this is not feasible, then all sales invoices for hotel customers should be double checked by another member of the finance department prior to being sent out.
Credit limits are determined by the finance director when a new trade customer is set up in the system. However, these limits could be out of date, resulting in limits being too high and sales being made to poor credit risks or too low and Hummingbird losing potential revenue.	Customer credit limits should be regularly reviewed by the finance director and updated based on the level of sales transactions and credit risk.
Customer orders and goods despatched notes (GDN) are given a number based on the customer account number and order number. These numbers are not sequential. Without sequential numbers, it is difficult for Hummingbird to identify missing orders and to monitor if all orders are being despatched in a timely manner, leading to a loss of customer goodwill.	Sales orders and goods despatched notes should be sequentially numbered. On a regular basis, a sequence check of orders should be undertaken to identify any missing orders. Upon despatch, the GDN should be matched to the order; a regular review of unmatched orders should be undertaken to identify any unfulfilled orders.
Hummingbird has changed from a reliable national courier company to a cheaper local courier; as a result some orders have been delivered late. There is a risk that orders may be lost resulting in a loss of revenue for Hummingbird or orders arriving later than normal which would lead to a loss of customer goodwill.	The courier company should be set targets with regards to timeliness of despatches. A review should be undertaken of target despatch times and actual times taken by the new courier company. If late delays continue, then consideration should be given to changing back to the original courier company.

Deficiency	Control
Trade customers' sales invoices are automatically generated by the system at the same time that the online order is placed. However, if goods are not despatched straight away, then customers could be invoiced in advance of receipt of their goods. This is likely to lead to a loss of customer goodwill and the early recognition of revenue in the accounting records.	The system should be amended so that it links into the despatch system. Sales invoices should not be raised until after goods have been despatched.
If Hummingbird makes special offers or discounts sales, the master file data for sales prices is amended by a senior sales ledger clerk. There is a risk that these amendments could be made incorrectly resulting in a loss of sales revenue or overcharging of customers.	When special offers or discounted sales occur, the changes to master file data should be made by a supervisor and each change checked by a responsible official to reduce the risk of errors occurring.
In addition, the sales ledger clerk, although senior, is not senior enough to be given access to changing master file data as this could increase the risk of fraud.	Amendments to master file data should be restricted so that only supervisors and above can make changes.
Monthly statements are not sent to trade customers. If statements are not sent regularly, this increases the likelihood of errors and any disputed invoices not being quickly identified and resolved by Hummingbird.	Hummingbird should produce monthly customer statements for both hotel and trade customers and send them out promptly.
The sales ledger control account is only reconciled at the end of September in order to verify the year-end balance. If the sales ledger is only reconciled annually, there is a risk that errors will not be spotted promptly.	The sales ledger control account should be reconciled on a monthly basis to identify any errors. The reconciliations should be reviewed by a responsible official and they should evidence their review.

(b)   Substantive procedures for revenue

- Compare the overall level of revenue against prior years and budget and investigate any significant fluctuations.

- Obtain a schedule of sales for the year broken down into the two categories of hotel and trade customers and compare this to the prior year breakdown and for any unusual movements discuss with management.

- Calculate the gross profit margin for Hummingbird and compare this to the prior year and investigate any significant fluctuations.

- Select a sample of sales invoices for hotel customers and agree the sales prices back to the contracted rates to ensure the accuracy of invoices.

- Select a sample of credit notes raised, trace through to the original invoice and ensure invoice correctly removed from sales.

ACCA marking scheme		
		Marks
(a)	Up to 1 mark each per well explained deficiency and recommendation. If not well explained, then just give ½ marks for each. Overall maximum of 7 deficiencies to be marked.	
	2 marks for presentation: 1 mark for address and intro and 1 mark for conclusion.	
	– Lack of segregation of duties for sales ledger clerk processing hotel customer transactions	
	– Manual override of sales invoices for hotel customers	
	– Credit limits set up when trade customer established, limits not regularly reviewed	
	– Sales orders and goods despatch notes not sequentially numbered	
	– Change to a cheaper courier company to despatch goods increases risk of customer complaints	
	– Trade customers' sales invoices generated on order date, goods may not have been despatched at this stage	
	– Senior sales clerk amends master data file for special offers and discount sales	
	– Monthly statements not sent to trade customers	
	– Sales ledger control account only reconciled at the year end	
	Max	**16**
(b)	Up to 1 mark per well explained procedure.	
	– Analytical review over revenue compared to budget and prior year	
	– Analytical review of two categories of sales compared to prior year	
	– Gross margin review	
	– Agree sales prices for hotel customers to contracted rates	
	– Review credit notes	
	– Follow trade online orders to goods despatched note to sales invoice to sales ledger	
	– Sales cut-off	
	Max	**4**
Total		**20**

Examiner's comments

Part (a) required identification and explanation of deficiencies within the sales system as described and a recommendation for each of these deficiencies. In addition a covering letter was required. This part of the question was answered very well and candidates were able to confidently identify the deficiencies from the scenario. However, some candidates did not always adequately explain what the deficiency meant for Hummingbird. In addition some deficiencies were incorrect, such as 'a failure by couriers to obtain customer signatures' or 'orders being placed without inventory levels being checked'. Deficiencies should be identified directly from the scenario rather than referring to generic points learned for a sales system. The requirement to provide control recommendations was, on the whole, well answered. Most candidates were able to provide good recommendations to address the deficiencies; however some of these recommendations were too brief and did not provide sufficient depth to demonstrate how the control could be implemented. In addition some recommendations failed to address the deficiency identified or were unrealistic. In addition as noted in previous examiner's reports the recommendation of sequence checks was not fully answered. Simply recommending 'that good despatched notes should be sequentially numbered' only scored ½ marks, as the control is to undertake sequence checks, for which the despatch notes need to be sequential. This demonstrated a lack of understanding of this type of control.

A covering letter to the report was required and there were 2 marks available. It was disappointing that some candidates did not provide any letter at all and despite the specific requirement, a significant number of candidates provided their answers as a memo rather than a letter. Not providing a letter or adopting a memo format would have resulted in a failure to maximise marks. Also some candidates provided the beginning of the letter, being a letterhead and an introductory paragraph, but did not complete the letter after the deficiencies and recommendations had been listed. It might have been better to produce the letter in full and then refer to an appendix for the deficiencies and recommendations. It was pleasing that many candidates set their answer out in two columns being deficiency and recommendation as this allows candidates to ensure they have a sufficient number of points and a recommendation for every deficiency identified. Where candidates did not adopt this format the deficiencies and recommendations tended to be repetitive and hence resulted in wasted time.

Part (b) required substantive procedures for revenue. Performance on this question was unsatisfactory. Many candidates provided tests of controls rather than substantive procedures and of those that did provide substantive tests, many provided receivables or cash receipts tests rather than those for revenue. Tests such as reviewing the sales ledger control account or circularising receivables were common but irrelevant. For those candidates who understood what was required their descriptions were often inadequate, such as simply stating 'cut off testing' which is not detailed enough to constitute a substantive procedure as it does not explain how this testing should be performed. Where candidates did explain cut-off testing many chose to examine invoices and rather than despatch notes which demonstrates a lack of judgment and understanding of what triggers transactions to be recorded in the sales system. Many candidates who provided procedures regarding completeness of revenue often did not provide a complete audit trail and often traced their tests to sales ledger rather than sales day book suggesting a lack of understanding over the fundamentals of financial records. Those candidates who scored well provided a range of tests including analytical review against prior year and/or budget, detailed tests on sales invoices and casting of sales day books or invoices.

151 TROMBONE *Walk in the footsteps of a top tutor*

Key answer tips

Part (a) requires repetition of knowledge from the text book of the components of an internal control system. Make sure you explain the components. You do not need to give the full text book definition but make sure some of the key elements are included in your answer.

Part (b) requires the control deficiencies within the payroll cycle to be identified. Use the specific information in scenario rather than giving deficiencies that could be present in any payroll system. There are always more deficiencies than you need so choose the ones you can write well about. Suggest controls the client can implement to address the control deficiency. Be specific about which member of client staff should be responsible for the control and how frequently they should perform the control. Tests of controls are the audit procedures the auditor will perform to obtain evidence to prove the control suggested is in place and working effectively. Be specific about how they would do this.

> Parts (c) and (d) ask for substantive procedures. A substantive procedure is used to detect material misstatement in the figure. Tests of controls will not score marks.

(a) **Internal control components**

ISA 315 *Identifying and Assessing the Risks of Material Misstatement through Understanding the Entity and Its Environment* considers the components of an entity's internal control. It identifies the following components:

Control environment

The control environment includes the governance and management functions and the attitudes, awareness, and actions of those charged with governance and management concerning the entity's internal control and its importance in the entity. The control environment sets the tone of an organisation, influencing the control consciousness of its people.

The control environment has many elements such as communication and enforcement of integrity and ethical values, commitment to competence, participation of those charged with governance, management's philosophy and operating style, organisational structure, assignment of authority and responsibility and human resource policies and practices.

Entity's risk assessment process

For financial reporting purposes, the entity's risk assessment process includes how management identifies business risks relevant to the preparation of financial statements in accordance with the entity's applicable financial reporting framework. It estimates their significance, assesses the likelihood of their occurrence, and decides upon actions to respond to and manage them and the results thereof.

Information system, including the related business processes, relevant to financial reporting, and communication

The information system relevant to financial reporting objectives, which includes the accounting system, consists of the procedures and records designed and established to initiate, record, process, and report entity transactions (as well as events and conditions) and to maintain accountability for the related assets, liabilities, and equity.

Control activities relevant to the audit

Control activities are the policies and procedures which help ensure that management directives are carried out. Control activities, whether within information technology or manual systems, have various objectives and are applied at various organisational and functional levels.

Monitoring of controls

Monitoring of controls is a process to assess the effectiveness of internal control performance over time. It involves assessing the effectiveness of controls on a timely basis and taking necessary remedial actions. Management accomplishes the monitoring of controls through ongoing activities, separate evaluations, or a combination of the two. Ongoing monitoring activities are often built into the normal recurring activities of an entity and include regular management and supervisory activities.

(b) **Trombone Co's payroll system deficiencies, controls and test of controls**

Deficiencies	Controls	Test of controls
The wages calculations are generated by the payroll system and there are no checks performed. Therefore, if system errors occur during the payroll processing, this would not be identified. This could result in wages being over or under calculated, leading to an additional payroll cost or loss of employee goodwill.	A senior member of the payroll team should recalculate the gross to net pay workings for a sample of employees and compare their results to the output from the payroll system. These calculations should be signed as approved before payments are made.	Review a sample of the gross to net pay calculations for evidence that they are undertaken and signed as approved.
Annual wages increases are updated in the payroll system standing data by clerks. Payroll clerks are not senior enough to be making changes to standing data as they could make mistakes leading to incorrect payment of wages. In addition, if they can access standing data, they could make unauthorised changes.	Payroll clerks should not have access to standing data changes within the system. The annual wages increase should be performed by a senior member of the payroll department and this should be checked by another responsible official for errors.	Ask a clerk to attempt to make a change to payroll standing data; the system should reject this attempt. Review the log of standing data amendments to identify whether the wage rate increases were changed by a senior member of payroll.
Overtime worked by employees is not all authorised by the relevant department head, as only overtime in excess of 30% of standard hours requires authorisation. This increases the risk that employees will claim for overtime even though they did not work these additional hours resulting in additional payroll costs for Trombone.	All overtime hours worked should be authorised by the relevant department head. This should be evidenced by signature on the employees' weekly overtime sheets.	Review a sample of employee weekly overtime sheets for evidence of signature by relevant department head.

Deficiencies	Controls	Test of controls
Time taken off as payment for overtime worked should be agreed by payroll clerks to the overtime worked report; however, this has not always occurred.	Payroll clerks should be reminded of the procedures to be undertaken when processing the overtime sheets. They should sign as evidence on the overtime sheets that they have agreed any time taken off to the relevant overtime report.	Select a sample of overtime sheets with time taken off and confirm that there is evidence of a check by the payroll clerk to the overtime worked report.
Employees could be taking unauthorised leave if they take time off but have not worked the required overtime.		
The overtime worked report is emailed to the department heads and they report by exception if there are any errors.	All department heads should report to the payroll department on whether or not the overtime report is correct. The payroll department should follow up on any non-replies and not make payments until agreed by the department head.	For a sample of overtime reports emailed to department heads confirm that a response has been received from each head by reviewing all responses.
If department heads are busy or do not receive the email and do not report to payroll on time, then it will be assumed that the overtime report is correct even though there may be errors. This could result in the payroll department making incorrect overtime payments.		
Department heads are meant to arrange for annual leave cover so that overtime sheets are authorised on a timely basis; however, this has not always happened.	Department heads should be reminded of the procedures with regards to annual leave and arrangement of suitable cover.	Discuss with payroll clerks the process they follow for obtaining authorisation of overtime sheets, in particular during periods of annual leave. Compare this to the process which they should adopt to identify any control exceptions.
If overtime sheets are authorised late, then this can lead to employee dissatisfaction as it will delay payment of the overtime worked.	During annual leave periods, payroll clerks should monitor that overtime sheets are being submitted by department heads on a timely basis and follow up any late sheets.	

Deficiencies	Controls	Test of controls
The finance director reviews the total list of bank transfers with the total to be paid per the payroll records. There could be employees omitted along with fictitious employees added to the payment listing, so that although the total payments list agrees to payroll totals, there could be fraudulent payments being made.	The finance director when authorising the payments should on a sample basis perform checks from payroll records to payment list and vice versa to confirm that payments are complete and only made to *bona fide* employees. The finance director should sign the payments list as evidence that he has undertaken these checks.	Obtain a sample of payments list and review for signature by the finance director as evidence that the control is operating correctly.

(c)   Payroll substantive procedures

- Agree the total wages and salaries expense per the payroll system to the trial balance, investigate any differences.
- Cast a sample of payroll records to confirm completeness and accuracy of the payroll expense.
- For a sample of employees, recalculate the gross and net pay and agree to the payroll records to confirm accuracy.
- Recalculate the statutory deductions to confirm whether correct deductions for this year have been made in the payroll.
- Compare the total payroll expense to the prior year and investigate any significant differences.
- Review monthly payroll charges, compare this to the prior year and budgets and discuss with management for any significant variances.
- Perform a proof in total of total wages and salaries, incorporating joiners and leavers and the annual pay increase. Compare this to the actual wages and salaries in the financial statements and investigate any significant differences.
- Select a sample of joiners and leavers, agree their start/leaving date to supporting documentation, recalculate that their first/last pay packet was accurately calculated and recorded.
- Agree the total net pay per the payroll records to the bank transfer listing of payments and to the cashbook.
- Agree the individual wages and salaries per the payroll to the personnel records for a sample.
- Select a sample of weekly overtime sheets and trace to overtime payment in payroll records to confirm completeness of overtime paid.

(d)   Accrual for income tax payable on employment income

Procedures the auditor should adopt in respect of auditing this accrual include:

- Agree the year-end income tax payable accrual to the payroll records to confirm accuracy.
- Re-perform the calculation of the accrual to confirm accuracy.

- Agree the subsequent payment to the post year-end cash book and bank statements to confirm completeness.

- Review any correspondence with tax authorities to assess whether there are any additional outstanding payments due; if so, agree they are included in the year-end accrual.

- Review any disclosures made of the income tax accrual and assess whether these are in compliance with accounting standards and legislation.

	ACCA marking scheme		Marks
(a)	Up to 1 mark per explained component, being ½ mark for identifying the component and ½ mark for an explanation. Control environment – governance and management function, attitudes awareness and actions of management Control environment – made up of a number of elements (need to list at least 2 to score 1 mark) Entity's risk assessment – process for identifying risk Information system relevant to financial reporting – procedures and records to record an entity's transactions, assets and liabilities and to maintain accountability Control activities – policies and procedures to ensure management directives are carried out Monitoring controls – assess effectiveness of internal controls **Note to markers:** Please award credit for reasonable explanations of internal control components, even if not listed above.		
		Max	5
(b)	Up to 1 mark per well explained deficiency, up to 1 mark for each well explained recommendation and up to 1 mark for each well described test of control. Overall maximum of 5 marks each for deficiencies, controls and tests of control. • Payroll calculations not checked • Payroll clerks update standing data for wages increases • Authorisation of overtime sheets only undertaken if overtime exceeds 30% of standard hours • Time off as payment for overtime not checked to overtime worked report • Review of overtime worked reports by department heads • Authorisation of overtime sheets when department heads on annual leave • Finance director only reviews totals of payroll records and payments list		
		Max	15
(c)	Up to 1 mark per well described substantive procedure. • Agree wages and salaries per payroll to trial balance • Cast payroll records • Recalculate gross and net pay • Recalculate statutory deductions • Compare total payroll to prior year • Review monthly payroll to prior year and budget • Proof in total of payroll and agree to the financial statements • Verify joiners/leavers and recalculate first/last pay • Agree wages and salaries paid per payroll to bank transfer list and cashbook • Agree the individual wages and salaries as per the payroll to the personnel records • Agree sample of weekly overtime sheets to overtime payment in payroll records		
		Max	6

(d)	Up to 1 mark per well described procedure.		
	• Agree to the payroll records to confirm the accuracy of the accrual		
	• Re-perform the calculation of the accrual		
	• Agree the subsequent payment to the post year-end cash book and bank statements		
	• Review any correspondence with tax authorities to assess whether there are any additional outstanding payments due, if so, agree they are included in the year end accrual		
	• Review disclosures and assess whether these are adequate and in compliance		
		Max	**4**
Total			**30**

Examiner's comments

Part (a) asked candidates to identify and briefly explain the components of an entity's internal control. Candidates' performance was mixed on this question with many not even attempting it. There were some candidates who had clearly revised this area and were able to confidently identify the five components and explain what they related to. Some candidates were confused by 'information systems' and incorrectly related this solely to a computer environment. Many candidates were only able to identify the components and either did not provide an explanation or it was incorrect. Also a significant minority of candidates explained the components from the perspective of what this meant for the audit firm rather than the company. In addition a significant minority of candidates did not understand the question requirement, or did not have sufficient technical knowledge of this area and so instead of providing components, such as, control environment and control activities, focused on providing a list of internal controls such as authorisation or segregation of duties controls.

Part (b) required candidates to identify and explain deficiencies in the payroll system, recommend controls to address these deficiencies, and a test of control for each of these recommendations that could be used to assess if it was operating effectively if implemented. The first two parts of this questions were answered satisfactorily by candidates, however the tests of controls proved challenging for many. Candidates were able to comfortably identify deficiencies from the scenario, although a minority of candidates identified deficiencies which were generic to payroll systems rather than specific to the question, such as references to 'clock cards', which were not a component of the system under review. Also some candidates identified points which were not valid deficiencies, such as employees being able to complete their own overtime sheets, being allowed a choice between days off or payment of overtime and overtime sheets being entered by payroll clerks. Although sufficient deficiencies were identified by many candidates, they did not always adequately explain what the deficiency meant to Trombone. For example, candidates identified the deficiency that 'the overtime worked reports are not always checked,' however some failed to explain the implication of this in that it could lead to employees taking days off when they had not worked the overtime hours required. The requirement to provide controls was answered satisfactorily. Most candidates were able to provide good recommendations to address the deficiencies; however in some instances these recommendations were too brief. Candidates have a tendency to state control objectives rather than valid procedures which can be implemented by the client. In addition some recommendations failed to address the deficiency identified, for example where department heads failed to assign a deputy to authorise overtime whilst on annual leave, many candidates simply recommended that this control already existing control be put in place, rather than addressing how the control should be amended to ensure it was followed at all times. The requirement for tests of controls was answered unsatisfactorily. Many candidates are still confusing substantive procedures and test of controls. A significant number of candidates suggested substantive procedures such as 'recalculating gross and net pay calculations', rather than a test of control which might be to 'review evidence of the recalculation of payroll'. Candidates need to review their understanding of these different types of audit procedures and ensure that they appreciate that substantive tests focus on the number within the financial statements whereas test of controls are verifying if client procedures are operating. In many instances candidates focused on re-performing the control rather than testing it had operated. Observation of a control was commonly suggested by candidates, however in many cases this is not an effective way of testing that a control has operated throughout the year. Most candidates presented their answers well, adopting a three column approach with deficiency, the control recommendation and the test of control in separate columns. This approach ensured that all elements of the question were addressed and it was easier to see which recommendations and tests related to which deficiencies.

Part (c) required substantive procedures to confirm the completeness and accuracy of the payroll expense. On the whole candidates performed well in this area. A good proportion of candidates were able to suggest practical payroll procedures such as analytical review of prior year and current year charges or undertaking a proof in total calculation. Other common answers included recalculation of a sample of payroll calculations or statutory deductions. Common mistakes made by candidates were:

- Giving objectives rather than procedures 'ensure that the gross and net pay calculations are correct', this is not a detailed substantive procedure and so would not score any marks.

- Lack of detail in tests such as 'check that the payroll calculations are correct', this would not score any marks as it does not explain what should be checked or how this testing would be carried out.

- Providing tests of controls rather than substantive procedures, such as focusing on authorisation of payroll.

The requirement verb was to 'describe' therefore sufficient detail was required to score the 1 mark available per test. Candidates are reminded yet again that substantive procedures are a core topic area and they must be able to produce relevant detailed procedures and to apply their knowledge to different areas of the financial statements.

Part (d) required substantive procedures in respect of the year end accrual for tax payable on employment income. Where answered, performance on this requirement was disappointing. Candidates were provided with a short scenario to explain how the employment taxes were remitted to the taxation authorities and that at the year-end there would be an accrual for any outstanding amount. The scenario was provided so that candidates could apply their knowledge of accruals to the specific circumstances; however from the answers provided it seems that some did not take notice of detail provided.

Many answers demonstrated that candidates did not know what a tax accrual was and hence suggested procedures focused on 'discussions with management' or 'obtaining written representations'. This accrual was not judgemental and so the above procedures would not have scored many marks. Those candidates that scored well suggested answers such as 'recalculation of the accrual,' 'comparison with prior year or months' and 'verifying the subsequent payment after the year end'.

152 OREGANO *Walk in the footsteps of a top tutor*

(a)   Documenting the sales and despatch system

Tutor's top tips

Part (a) is quite a difficult requirement unless you know the different methods of documenting systems. Therefore if you don't know it, don't waste time in the exam trying to think of something. Move onto the next part of the question and come back to it when you have finished everything you can do on the paper.

There are several methods which can be used by the internal audit department of Oregano Co (Oregano) to document their system.

Narrative notes

Narrative notes consist of a written description of the system; they would detail what occurs in the system at each stage and would include any controls which operate at each stage.

Advantages of this method include:

- They are simple to record; after discussion with staff members of Oregano, these discussions are easily written up as notes.

- They can facilitate understanding by all members of the internal audit team, especially more junior members who might find alternative methods too complex.

Disadvantages of this method include:

- Narrative notes may prove to be too cumbersome, especially if the sales and distribution system is complex.

- This method can make it more difficult to identify missing internal controls as the notes record the detail but do not identify control exceptions clearly.

Questionnaires

Internal control questionnaires (ICQ) or internal control evaluation questionnaires (ICEQ) contain a list of questions; ICQs are used to assess whether controls exist whereas ICEQs test the effectiveness of the controls.

Advantages of this method include:

- Questionnaires are quick to prepare, which means they are a timely method for recording the system.

- They ensure that all controls present within the system are considered and recorded; hence missing controls or deficiencies are clearly highlighted by the internal audit team.

Disadvantages of this method include:

- It can be easy for the staff members of Oregano to overstate the level of the controls present as they are asked a series of questions relating to potential controls.

- A standard list of questions may miss out unusual controls of Oregano.

Flowcharts

Flowcharts are a graphic illustration of the internal control system for the sales and despatch system. Lines usually demonstrate the sequence of events and standard symbols are used to signify controls or documents.

Advantages of this method include:

- It is easy to view the sales system in its entirety as it is all presented together in one diagram.

- Due to the use of standard symbols for controls, they are easy to spot as are any missing controls.

Disadvantages of this method include:

- They can sometimes be difficult to amend, as any amendments may require the whole flowchart to be redrawn.

- There is still the need for narrative notes to accompany the flowchart and hence it can be a time consuming method.

Note: Full marks will be awarded for describing TWO methods for documenting the sales and despatch system and explaining ONE advantage and ONE disadvantage for each method.

(b)   Control objectives for sales and despatch system

Tutor's top tips

Control objectives are the reasons why controls are put in place. They address the risks that could happen in the system. Be careful not to suggest that a control objective is to ensure a control is in place. You need to say the reason why the control should be in place.

- To ensure that orders are only accepted if goods are available to be processed for customers.

- To ensure that all orders are recorded completely and accurately.

- To ensure that goods are not supplied to poor credit risks.

- To ensure that goods are despatched for all orders on a timely basis.

- To ensure that goods are despatched correctly to customers and that they are of an adequate quality.

- To ensure that all goods despatched are correctly invoiced.

- To ensure completeness of income for goods despatched.

- To ensure that sales discounts are only provided to valid customers.

(c)   Deficiencies and controls for Oregano Co's sales and despatch system

Tutor's top tips

Controls deficiencies and recommendations questions are usually quite straightforward, however, you must explain the deficiencies and controls in sufficient detail to score marks. If you are too brief you will only score ½ marks.

Deficiency	*Control*
Inventory availability for telephone orders is not checked at the time the order is placed. The order clerks manually check the availability later and only then inform customers if there is insufficient inventory available.	When telephone orders are placed, the order clerk should check the inventory system whilst the customer is on the phone; they can then give an accurate assessment of the availability of goods and there is no risk of forgetting to inform customers.
There is the risk that where goods are not available, order clerks could forget to contact the customers, leading to unfulfilled orders. This could lead to customer dissatisfaction, and would impact Oregano's reputation.	
Telephone orders are not recorded immediately on the three part pre-printed order forms; these are completed after the telephone call.	All telephone orders should be recorded immediately on the three part pre-printed order forms. The clerk should also double check all the details taken with the customer over the telephone to ensure the accuracy of the order recorded.
There is a risk that incorrect or insufficient details may be recorded by the clerk and this could result in incorrect orders being despatched or orders failing to be despatched at all, resulting in a loss of customer goodwill.	
Telephone orders are not sequentially numbered. Therefore if orders are misplaced whilst in transit to the despatch department, these orders will not be fulfilled, resulting in dissatisfied customers.	The three part pre-printed orders forms should be sequentially numbered and on a regular basis the despatch department should run a sequence check of orders received. Where there are gaps in the sequence, they should be investigated to identify any missing orders.

Deficiency	Control
Customers are able to place online orders which will exceed their agreed credit limit by 10%. This increases the risk of accepting orders from bad credit risks.	Customer credit limits should be reviewed more regularly by a responsible official and should reflect the current spending pattern of customers. If some customers have increased the level of their purchases and are making payments on time, then these customers' credit limits could be increased. The online ordering system should be amended to not allow any orders to be processed which will exceed the customer's credit limit.
A daily pick list is used by the despatch department when sending out customer orders. However, it does not appear that the goods are checked back to the original order; this could result in incorrect goods being sent out.	In addition to the pick list, copies of all the related orders should be printed on a daily basis. When the goods have been picked ready to be despatched, they should be cross checked back to the original order. They should check correct quantities and product descriptions, as well as checking the quality of goods being despatched to ensure they are not damaged.
Additional staff have been drafted in to help the two sales clerks produce the sales invoices. As the extra staff will not be as experienced as the sales clerks, there is an increased risk of mistakes being made in the sales invoices. This could result in customers being under or overcharged.	Only the sales clerks should be able to raise sales invoices. As Oregano is expanding, consideration should be given to recruiting and training more permanent sales clerks who can produce sales invoices.
Discounts given to customers are manually entered onto the sales invoices by sales clerks. This could result in unauthorised sales discounts being given as there does not seem to be any authorisation required.	For customers who are due to receive a discount, the authorised discount levels should be updated to the customer master file. When the sales invoices for these customers are raised, their discounts should automatically appear on the invoice. The invoicing system should be amended to prevent sales clerks from being able to manually enter sales discounts onto invoices.
In addition, a clerk could forget to manually enter the discount or enter an incorrect level of discount for a customer, leading to the sales invoice being overstated and a loss of customer goodwill.	

	ACCA marking scheme	
		Marks
(a)	Up to 1 mark each for a description of a method, up to 1 mark each for an advantage, up to 1 mark each for a disadvantages.	
	– Narrative notes	
	– Questionnaires	
	– Flowcharts	
	Max	**6**
(b)	1 mark for each control objective, overall maximum of 2 points.	
	– To ensure orders are only accepted if goods are available to be processed for customers	
	– To ensure all orders are recorded completely and accurately	
	– To ensure goods are not supplied to poor credit risks	
	– To ensure goods are despatched for all orders on a timely basis	
	– To ensure goods are despatched correctly to customers and are of an adequate quality	
	– To ensure all goods despatched are correctly invoiced	
	– To ensure completeness of income for goods despatched	
	– To ensure sales discounts are only provided to valid customers	
	Max	**2**
(c)	Up to 1 mark per well explained deficiency and up to 1 mark for each control. Overall max of 6 marks for deficiencies and 6 marks for controls.	
	– Inventory not checked when order taken	
	– Orders not completed on pre-printed order forms	
	– Order forms not sequentially numbered	
	– Credit limits being exceeded	
	– Goods despatched not agreed to order to check quantity and quality	
	– Sales invoices being raised by inexperienced staff	
	– Sales discounts manually entered by sales clerks	
	Max	**12**
Total		**20**

Examiner's comments

Part (a) required a description of two methods for documenting the sales and despatch system along with an advantage and disadvantage for each method. Candidates' performance was unsatisfactory on this question, with a number of candidates not even attempting it. A significant proportion of candidates did not understand the question requirement fully, and so instead of suggesting methods such as flowcharts, narrative notes or questionnaires they considered manual and automated/electronic methods for a system. In addition some candidates considered online versus telephone methods for recording sales transactions and others interpreted the question as requiring the documents of a sales system and so considered sales invoices and despatch notes. The question requirement was clear, candidates either did not read it carefully or they lacked the technical knowledge on documentation methods. Those candidates who did correctly interpret the requirement often failed to maximise their marks as they identified the methods but did not describe them. In addition, candidates advantages and disadvantages were far too brief, a describe requirement needs more than a few words and 'easy to understand' is not detailed enough to score the 1 mark available.

Part (b) required two controls objectives for the sales and despatch system. Candidates could have used the scenario to help or answered this question using their technical knowledge, however overall performance was unsatisfactory. A significant proportion of candidates provided controls rather than control objectives, this was not what was required and so would not have scored any marks. This indicates a lack of knowledge as to what a control is rather than a control objective. Objectives have been tested in previous diets, and candidates should endeavour to practice past exam questions when preparing for this exam.

Part (c) required an identification and explanation of deficiencies and a recommendation for each of these deficiencies. This part of the question was answered very well and candidates were able to confidently identify six deficiencies from the scenario. However, candidates did not always adequately explain what the deficiency meant to Oregano. For example, candidates easily identified the deficiency that credit limits were being exceeded by 10% for online orders; however some failed to explain that this could lead to an increase in bad debts. The requirement to provide controls was, on the whole, well answered. Most candidates were able to provide good recommendations to address the deficiencies; however some of these recommendations were too brief. In addition some recommendations failed to address the deficiency, for example for the credit limits being exceeded some candidates suggested 'a review of credit limits by a responsible official', this would not prevent orders from exceeding the limits. The main recommendation where candidates failed to maximise their marks was for sequentially numbered orders. Simply recommending 'that sales orders should be sequentially numbered' only scored ½ mark, as the control is to undertake sequence checks, for which the orders need to be sequential. This demonstrated a lack of understanding of this type of control.

153 FOX INDUSTRIES *Walk in the footsteps of a top tutor*

(a) **(i)** **Importance of reporting to those charged with governance**

In accordance with ISA 260 *Communication with Those Charged with Governance*, it is important for the auditors to report to those charged with governance as it helps in the following ways:

(1) It assists the auditor and those charged with governance in understanding matters related to the audit, and in developing a constructive working relationship. This relationship is developed while maintaining the auditor's independence and objectivity.

(2) It helps the auditor in obtaining, from those charged with governance, information relevant to the audit. For example, those charged with governance may assist the auditor in understanding the entity and its environment, in identifying appropriate sources of audit evidence and in providing information about specific transactions or events.

(3) It helps those charged with governance in fulfilling their responsibility to oversee the financial reporting process, thereby reducing the risks of material misstatement of the financial statements.

(ii) **Matters to be communicated to those charged with governance**

- The auditor's responsibilities with regards to providing an opinion on the financial statements and that they have carried out their work in accordance with International Standards on Auditing.

- The auditor should explain the planned approach to the audit as well as the audit timetable.

- Any key audit risks identified during the planning stage should be communicated.

- In addition, any significant difficulties encountered during the audit should be communicated.

- Key audit matters that would be communicated in accordance with ISA 701.

- Any significant accounting adjustments arising from the audit.

- During the audit any significant deficiencies in the internal control system identified should be communicated in writing or verbally.

- Those charged with governance should be notified of any written representations required by the auditor.

- Other matters arising from the audit that are significant to the oversight of the financial reporting process.

- If any suspected frauds are identified during the audit, these must be communicated.

- If the auditors are intending to make any modifications to the audit opinion, these should be communicated to those charged with governance.

- For listed entities, a confirmation that the auditors have complied with ethical standards and appropriate safeguards have been put in place for any ethical threats identified.

(b)   Report to management

Tutor's top tips

When asked for a covering letter, don't ignore this as there are usually format marks available. Remember to keep your answer anonymous, don't use your own name in the letter, make up a name. Don't forget to include the point that the letter is solely for the use of management and don't forget to sign off the letter appropriately.

Controls deficiencies and recommendations questions are usually quite straightforward, however, you must explain the deficiencies and controls in sufficient detail to score marks. If you are too brief you will only score ½ marks.

Board of directors
Fox Industries Co
15 Dog Street
Cat Town
X Country
6 June 2013

Dear Sirs,

Audit of Fox Industries Co (Fox) for the year ended 30 April 2013

Please find enclosed the report to management on deficiencies in internal controls identified during the audit for the year ended 30 April 2013. The appendix to this report considers deficiencies in the purchasing and payments system, the implications of those deficiencies and recommendations to address those deficiencies.

Please note that this report only addresses the deficiencies identified during the audit and if further testing had been performed, then more deficiencies may have been reported.

This report is solely for the use of management and if you have any further questions, then please do not hesitate to contact us.

Yours faithfully

An audit firm

APPENDIX

Deficiency	Implication	Recommendation
When raising purchase orders, the clerks choose whichever supplier can despatch the goods the fastest.	This could result in Fox ordering goods at a much higher price or a lower quality than they would like, as the only factor considered was speed of delivery.	An approved supplier list should be compiled; this should take into account the price of goods, their quality and also the speed of delivery.
	It is important that goods are despatched promptly, but this is just one of many criteria that should be used in deciding which supplier to use.	Once the list has been produced, all orders should only be placed with suppliers on the approved list.
Purchase orders are not sequentially numbered.	Failing to sequentially number the orders means that Fox's ordering team are unable to monitor if all orders are being fulfilled in a timely manner; this could result in stock outs.	All purchase orders should be sequentially numbered and on a regular basis a sequence check of unfulfilled orders should be performed.
	If the orders are numbered, then a sequence check can be performed for any unfulfilled orders.	
Purchase orders below $5,000 are not authorised and are processed solely by an order clerk.	This can result in goods being purchased which are not required by Fox. In addition, there is an increased fraud risk as an order clerk could place orders for personal goods up to the value of $5,000, which is significant.	All purchase orders should be authorised by a responsible official. Authorised signatories should be established with varying levels of purchase order authorisation.

Deficiency	Implication	Recommendation
Purchase invoices are input daily by the purchase ledger clerk and due to his experience, he does not utilise any application controls.	Without application controls there is a risk that invoices could be input into the system with inaccuracies or they may be missed out entirely. This could result in suppliers being paid incorrectly or not all, leading to a loss of supplier goodwill.	The purchase ledger clerk should input the invoices in batches and apply application controls, such as control totals, to ensure completeness and accuracy over the input of purchase invoices.
The purchase day book automatically updates with the purchase ledger but this ledger is manually posted to the general ledger.	Manually posting the amounts to the general ledger increases the risk of errors occurring. This could result in the payables balance in the financial statements being under or overstated.	The process should be updated so that on a regular basis the purchase ledger automatically updates the general ledger. A responsible official should then confirm through purchase ledger control account reconciliations that the update has occurred correctly.
Fox's saving (deposit) bank accounts are only reconciled every two months.	If these accounts are only reconciled periodically, there is the risk that errors will not be spotted promptly. Also, this increases the risk of employees committing fraud. If they are aware that these accounts are not regularly reviewed, then they could use these cash sums fraudulently.	All bank accounts should be reconciled on a regular basis, and at least monthly, to identify any unusual or missing items. The reconciliations should be reviewed by a responsible official and they should evidence their review.

Deficiency	Implication	Recommendation
Fox has a policy of delaying payments to their suppliers for as long as possible.	Whilst this maximises Fox's bank balance, there is the risk that Fox is missing out on early settlement discounts. Also, this can lead to a loss of supplier goodwill as well as the risk that suppliers may refuse to supply goods to Fox.	Fox should undertake cash flow forecasting/budgeting to maximise bank balances. The policy of delaying payment should be reviewed, and suppliers should be paid in a systematic way, such that supplier goodwill is not lost.

(c)   Application controls

Tutor's top tips

Make sure you give 'application' controls, i.e. those that you would perform at the time of entering the data to ensure it is complete and accurate. General controls will not score marks.

Document counts – the number of invoices to be input are counted, the invoices are then entered one by one, at the end the number of invoices input is checked against the document count. This helps to ensure completeness of input.

Control totals – here the total of all the invoices, such as the gross value, is manually calculated. The invoices are input, the system aggregates the total of the input invoices' gross value and this is compared to the control total. This helps to ensure completeness and accuracy of input.

One for one checking – the invoices entered into the system are manually agreed back one by one to the original purchase invoices. This helps to ensure completeness and accuracy of input.

Review of output to expected value – an independent assessment is made of the value of purchase invoices to be input, this is the expected value. The invoices are input and the total value of invoices is compared to the expected value. This helps to ensure completeness of input.

Check digits – this control helps to reduce the risk of transposition errors. Mathematical calculations are performed by the system on a particular data field, such as supplier number, a mathematical formula is run by the system, this checks that the data entered into the system is accurate. This helps to ensure accuracy of input.

Range checks – a pre-determined maximum is input into the system for gross invoice value, for example, $10,000; when invoices are input if the amount keyed in is incorrectly entered as being above $10,000, the system will reject the invoice. This helps to ensure accuracy of input.

Existence checks – the system is set up so that certain key data must be entered, such as supplier name, otherwise the invoice is rejected. This helps to ensure accuracy of input.

(d) **Substantive procedures over bank and cash balance of Fox Industries Co (Fox)**

- Obtain Fox's current bank account reconciliation and check the additions to ensure arithmetical accuracy.

- Obtain a bank confirmation letter from Fox's bankers for all of its accounts.

- For the current account, agree the balance per the bank statement to an original year-end bank statement and also to the bank confirmation letter.

- Agree the reconciliation's balance per the cash book to the year-end cash book.

- Trace all of the outstanding lodgements to the pre year-end cash book, post year-end bank statement and also to paying-in-book pre year end.

- Trace all un-presented cheques through to a pre year-end cash book and post year-end statement. For any unusual amounts or significant delays obtain explanations from management.

- Examine any old un-presented cheques to assess if they need to be written back into the purchase ledger as they are no longer valid to be presented.

- Agree all balances listed on the bank confirmation letter to Fox's bank reconciliations or the trial balance to ensure completeness of bank balances.

- Review the cash book and bank statements for any unusual items or large transfers around the year end, as this could be evidence of window dressing.

- Examine the bank confirmation letter for details of any security provided by Fox or any legal right of set-off as this may require disclosure.

- For the saving (deposit) bank accounts, review any reconciling items on the year-end bank reconciliations and agree to supporting documentation.

- In respect of material cash balances, count cash balances at the year end and agree to petty cash records, such as the petty cash book.

- Review the financial statements to ensure that the disclosure of cash and bank balances are complete and accurate.

		ACCA marking scheme		
				Marks
(a)	(i)	Up to 1 mark per well explained point		
		• Assists the auditor and those charged with governance in understanding matters related to the audit		
		• Obtains information relevant to the audit		
		• Helps those charged with governance in fulfilling their responsibility to oversee the financial reporting process		
			Max	**2**
	(ii)	Up to 1 mark for each example matter to be communicated to those charged with governance		
			Max	**3**

<table>
<tr><td>(b)</td><td colspan="2">Up to 1 mark per well explained deficiency, implication and recommendation. If not well explained then just give ½ mark for each. Overall maximum of 4 marks each for deficiencies, implications and recommendations.</td></tr>
<tr><td></td><td colspan="2">2 marks for presentation: ½ for a letterhead, ½ for an introductory paragraph, ½ for disclaimers and ½ for a courteous sign off</td></tr>
<tr><td></td><td colspan="2">
• No approved suppliers list
• Purchase orders not sequentially numbered
• Orders below $5,000 are not authorised by a responsible official
• No application controls over input of purchase invoices
• Purchase ledger manually posted to general ledger
• Saving (deposit) bank accounts only reconciled every two months
• Payments to suppliers delayed
• Finance director only reviews the total of the payment list prior to payment authorising
</td></tr>
<tr><td></td><td align="right">Max</td><td align="center">14</td></tr>
<tr><td>(c)</td><td colspan="2">Up to 1 mark per well explained application control</td></tr>
<tr><td></td><td colspan="2">
• Document counts
• Control totals
• One for one checking
• Review of output to expected value
• Check digits
• Range checks
• Existence checks
</td></tr>
<tr><td></td><td align="right">Max</td><td align="center">4</td></tr>
<tr><td>(d)</td><td colspan="2">Up to 1 mark per substantive procedure</td></tr>
<tr><td></td><td colspan="2">
• Check additions of bank reconciliation
• Obtain bank confirmation letter
• Bank balance to statement/bank confirmation
• Cash book balance to cash book
• Outstanding lodgements
Unpresented cheques review
Old cheques write back
Agree all balances on bank confirmation
Unusual items/window dressing
Security/legal right set-off
Review reconciliations for saving (deposit) accounts
Cash counts for significant cash balances
Review disclosure of bank and cash in financial statements
</td></tr>
<tr><td></td><td align="right">Max</td><td align="center">7</td></tr>
<tr><td>**Total**</td><td></td><td align="center">30</td></tr>
</table>

Examiner's comments

Most candidates performed unsatisfactorily on part (ai). They needed to focus on WHY it was important to communicate rather than WHAT needed to be reported as this was the requirement of part (aii). Answers that focused on what was to be communicated would not have gained credit as this was not the question requirement for (ai). In addition some candidates simply restated the requirement, explaining that it was important to communicate, but without answering why. Part (aii) was answered better, with most candidates focusing on the areas of fraud, material misstatement and internal control deficiencies. Some candidates focused on providing details of specific audit issues that would be discussed during the audit as opposed to areas which would be formally reported to TCWG.

Part (b) required a report to management which identifies and explains four deficiencies, the implications and a recommendation for each of these deficiencies; in addition a covering letter was required. This part of the question was answered very well and candidates were able to confidently identify the deficiencies from the scenario. However, candidates did not always adequately explain the implication of the deficiency to the business. For example, for the deficiency of purchase orders not being sequentially numbered, many candidates focused on the difficulties of agreeing invoices to orders, as opposed to the key issue of unfulfilled orders and hence stock outs. In addition many implications were vague such as 'there will be errors if application controls are not applied by the purchase ledger clerk' this answer does not give any examples of what type of errors and where they may occur. Candidates need to think in a practical manner and apply their knowledge when answering these types of questions. The requirement to provide controls was, on the whole, well answered. Most candidates were able to provide good recommendations to address the deficiencies. However some of these recommendations were too brief, for example simply stating 'apply application controls' to address the deficiency of the purchase ledger clerk. The main recommendation where candidates failed to maximise their marks was for sequentially numbered purchase orders. Simply recommending 'that purchase orders should be sequentially numbered' only scored ½ marks, as the control is to undertake sequence checks, for which the orders need to be sequential. This demonstrated a lack of understanding of this type of control.

A covering letter to the report was required and there were 2 marks available. Despite this specific requirement a significant number of candidates provided their answers as a memo rather than as a letter. Adopting a memo format resulted in a failure to maximise marks. The two marks were allocated as ½ for a letterhead, ½ for an introductory paragraph, ½ for disclaimers and ½ for a courteous sign off of the letter, which requires more than just a signature.

Many candidates set their answer out in columns being deficiency, implication and recommendation. However, those who explained all of the deficiencies, the implications and then separately provided all of the recommendations tended to repeat themselves and possibly wasted some time. A significant proportion of candidates provided many more than the number of points required. It was not uncommon to see answers with eight deficiencies. Also in many answers deficiencies were combined such as; 'purchase orders are not sequentially numbered and only orders over $5,000 require authorisation', the implications and recommendations would then also be combined. Providing many more points than required and combining answers leads to unstructured answers that are difficult to mark. Spending too much time on this part of the exam also puts candidates under time pressure for the rest of the paper.

Part (c) required application controls to ensure the completeness and accuracy of the input of purchase invoices. Performance on this question was quite unsatisfactory. Many candidates failed to pick up marks for this question; also this question was left unanswered by some candidates. The requirement was for application controls, these could be computerised or manual, but they needed to address the specific area of INPUT of invoices. Many candidates gave general computer controls such as passwords or provided auditor's substantive tests. In addition candidates listed recommendations from part 1(b) such as 'sequentially numbered orders or regular bank reconciliations'; these have nothing to do with input of invoices. Some answers focused on auditing the purchase cycle, agreeing orders to goods received notes and to invoices. Candidates clearly either have a knowledge gap in this area or failed to read the question requirement carefully.

Part (d) required substantive procedures for bank and cash at the year end. Performance on this question was unsatisfactory. Substantive procedures are a key area of the paper and may feature in each session. Some scripts were with hardly any valid bank and cash procedures. Tests which start with 'to ensure that' are unlikely to gain any marks as these are objectives rather than audit tests. Also some candidates failed to read the question requirement which stated that the audit was of year end cash and bank; these answers focused more on tests of controls over the whole of the year for cash and bank, these did not gain any credit. Some candidates focused on the bank reconciliation and auditing its detail, such as un-presented cheques and outstanding lodgements. Most candidates were able to suggest obtaining a bank confirmation letter and counting petty cash, however this seemed to be the extent of many answers. It was unsatisfactory to see that many candidates did not understand the purpose of the bank reconciliation as a common answer was 'to agree the bank confirmation letter to the financial statements' as opposed to the bank reconciliation. Many provided vague answers such as 'cast the ledger' and a minority misunderstood the question and focused on auditing payables and receivables.

154 LILY WINDOW GLASS *Walk in the footsteps of a top tutor*

(a) Inventory count arrangements

Tutor's top tips

Controls deficiencies and recommendations questions are usually quite straightforward, however, you must explain the deficiencies and controls in sufficient detail to score marks. If you are too brief you will only score ½ marks.

Deficiencies	Recommendations
The warehouse manager is planning to supervise the inventory count. Whilst he is familiar with the inventory, he has overall responsibility for the inventory and so is not independent. He may want to hide inefficiencies and any issues that arise so that his department is not criticised.	An alternative supervisor who is not normally involved with the inventory, such as an internal audit manager, should supervise the inventory count. The warehouse manager and his team should not be involved in the count at all.
There are ten teams of counters, each team having two members of staff. However, there is no clear division of responsibilities within the team. Therefore, both members of staff could count together rather than checking each other's count; and errors in their count may not be identified.	Each team should be informed that both members are required to count their assigned inventory separately. Therefore, one counts and the second member checks that the inventory has been counted correctly.

Deficiencies	*Recommendations*

The internal audit teams are undertaking inventory counts rather than reviewing the controls and performing sample test counts. Their role should be focused on confirming the accuracy of the inventory counting procedures.

The internal audit counters should sample check the counting undertaken by the ten teams to provide an extra control over the completeness and accuracy of the count.

Once areas are counted, the teams are not flagging the aisles as completed. Therefore there is the risk that some areas of the warehouse could be double counted or missed out.

All aisles should be flagged as completed, once the inventory has been counted. In addition, internal audit or the count supervisor should check at the end of the count that all 20 aisles have been flagged as completed.

Inventory not listed on the sheets is to be entered onto separate sheets, which are not sequentially numbered. Therefore the supervisor will be unable to ensure the completeness of all inventory sheets.

Each team should be given a blank sheet for entering any inventory count which is not on their sheets. This blank sheet should be sequentially numbered, any unused sheets should be returned at the end of the count, and the supervisor should check the sequence of all sheets at the end of the count.

The sheets are completed in ink and are sequentially numbered, however, there is no indication that they are signed by the counting team. Therefore if any issues arise with the counting in an aisle, it will be difficult to follow up as the identity of the counting team will not be known.

All inventory sheets should be signed by the relevant team upon completion of an aisle. When the sheets are returned, the supervisor should check that they have been signed.

Damaged goods are not being stored in a central area, and instead the counter is just noting on the inventory sheets the level of damage. However, it will be difficult for the finance team to decide on an appropriate level of write down if they are not able to see the damaged goods. In addition, if these goods are left in the aisles, they could be inadvertently sold to customers or moved to another aisle.

Damaged goods should be clearly flagged by the counting teams and at the end of the count appropriate machinery should be used to move all damaged windows to a central location. This will avoid the risk of selling these goods.

A senior member of the finance team should then inspect these goods to assess the level of any write down or allowance.

Deficiencies

Lily Window Glass Co (Lily) undertakes continuous production and so there will be movements of goods during the count. Inventory records could be under/overstated if goods are missed or double counted due to movements in the warehouse.

Recommendations

It is not practical to stop all inventory movements as the production needs to continue. However, any raw materials required for 31 December should be estimated and put to one side. These will not be included as raw materials and instead will be work-in-progress.

The goods which are manufactured on 31 December should be stored to one side, and at the end of the count should be counted once and included within finished goods.

Any goods received from suppliers should be stored in one location and counted once at the end and included as part of raw materials. Goods to be despatched to customers should be kept to a minimum for the day of the count.

The warehouse manager is to assess the level of work-in-progress and raw materials. In the past, a specialist has undertaken this role. It is unlikely that the warehouse manager has the experience to assess the level of work-in-progress as this is something that the factory manager would be more familiar with.

A specialist should be utilised to assess both work-in-progress and the quantities of raw materials.

In addition, whilst the warehouse manager is familiar with the raw materials, if he makes a mistake in assessing the quantities then inventory could be materially misstated.

With regards to the warehouse manager, he could estimate the raw materials and the specialist could check it. This would give an indication as to whether he is able to accurately assess the quantities for subsequent inventory counts.

(b)   Procedures during the inventory count

Tutor's top tips

During the inventory count the auditor will perform both tests of controls and substantive procedures therefore this gives plenty of scope for answers.

- Observe the counting teams of Lily to confirm whether the inventory count instructions are being followed correctly.

- Select a sample and perform test counts from inventory sheets to warehouse aisle and from warehouse aisle to inventory sheets.

- Confirm the procedures for identifying and segregating damaged goods are operating correctly.

- Select a sample of damaged items as noted on the inventory sheets and inspect these windows to confirm whether the level of damage is correctly noted.

- Observe the procedures for movements of inventory during the count, to confirm that no raw materials or finished goods have been omitted or counted twice.

- Obtain a photocopy of the completed sequentially numbered inventory sheets for follow up testing on the final audit.

- Identify and make a note of the last goods received notes (GRNs) and goods despatched notes (GDNs) for 31 December in order to perform cut-off procedures.

- Observe the procedures carried out by the warehouse manager in assessing the level of work-in-progress and consider the reasonableness of any assumptions used.

- Discuss with the warehouse manager how he has estimated the raw materials quantities. To the extent that it is possible, re-perform the procedures adopted by the warehouse manager.

- Identify and record any inventory held for third parties (if any) and confirm that it is excluded from the count.

(c)   Computer-assisted audit techniques (CAATS)

(i)   Audit procedures using CAATS

- The audit team can use audit software to calculate inventory days for the year-to-date to compare against the prior year to identify whether inventory is turning over slower, as this may be an indication that it is overvalued.

- Audit software can be utilised to produce an aged inventory analysis to identify any slow moving goods, which may require write down or an allowance.

- Cast the inventory listing to confirm the completeness and accuracy of inventory.

- Audit software can be used to select a representative sample of items for testing to confirm net realisable value and/or cost.

- Audit software can be utilised to recalculate cost and net realisable value for a sample of inventory.

- CAATs can be used to verify cut-off by testing whether the dates of the last GRNs and GDNs recorded relate to pre year end; and that any with a date of 1 January 2013 onwards have been excluded from the inventory records.

- CAATs can be used to confirm whether any inventory adjustments noted during the count have been correctly updated into final inventory records.

(ii)   Advantages of using CAATS

- CAATs enable the audit team to test a large volume of inventory data accurately and quickly.

- If CAATs are utilised on the audit of Lily, then as long as they do not change their inventory systems, they can be cost effective after setup.

- CAATs can test program controls within the inventory system as well as general IT controls, such as passwords.

- Allows the team to test the actual inventory system and records rather than printouts from the system which could be incorrect.

- CAATs reduce the level of human error in testing and hence provide a better quality of audit evidence.

- CAATs results can be compared with traditional audit testing; if these two sources agree, then overall audit confidence will increase.

- The use of CAATs frees up audit team members to focus on judgemental and high risk areas, rather than number crunching.

(iii)   Disadvantages of using CAATS

- The cost of using CAATs in this first year will be high as there will be significant set up costs, it will also be a time-consuming process which increases costs.

- As this is the first time that CAATs will be used on Lily's audit, then the team may require training on the specific CAATs to be utilised.

- If Lily's inventory system is likely to change in the foreseeable future, then costly revisions may be required to the designed CAATs.

- The inventory system may not be compatible with the audit firm's CAATs, in which case bespoke CAATs may be required, which will increase the audit costs.

- If testing is performed over the live inventory system, then there is a risk that the data could be corrupted or lost.

- If testing is performed using copy files rather than live data, then there is the risk that these files are not genuine copies of the actual files.

- In order to perform CAATs, there must be adequate systems documentation available. If this is not the case for Lily, then it will be more difficult to devise appropriate CAATs due to a lack of understanding of the inventory system.

ACCA marking scheme		
		Marks
(a) Up to 1 mark per well explained deficiency and up to 1 mark per recommendation. If not well explained then just give ½ mark for each.		
• Warehouse manager supervising the count		
• No division of responsibilities within each counting team		
• Internal audit teams should be checking controls and performing sample counts		
• No flagging of aisles once counting complete		
• Additional inventory listed on sheets which are not sequentially numbered		
• Inventory sheets not signed by counters		
• Damaged goods not moved to central location		
• Movements of inventory during the count		
• Warehouse manager not qualified to assess the level of work-in-progress		
• Warehouse manager not experienced enough to assess the quantities of raw materials		
	Max	12

(b)   Up to 1 mark per well described procedure
- Observe the counters to confirm if inventory count instructions are being followed
- Perform test counts inventory to sheets and sheets to inventory
- Confirm procedures for damaged goods are operating correctly
- Inspect damaged goods to confirm whether the level of damage is correctly noted
- Observe procedures for movements of inventory during the count
- Obtain a photocopy of the completed inventory sheets
- Identify and make a note of the last goods received notes and goods despatched notes
- Observe the procedures carried out by warehouse manager in assessing the level of work-in-progress
- Discuss with the warehouse manager how he has estimated the raw materials quantities
- Identify inventory held for third parties and ensure excluded from count

                                                                              Max   **6**

(c)   (i)   Up to 1 mark per well described procedure, max of 4 procedures
- Calculate inventory days
- Produce an aged inventory analysis to identify any slow moving goods
- Cast the inventory listing
- Select a sample of items for testing to confirm net realisable value (NRV) and/or cost
- Recalculate cost and NRV for sample of inventory
- Computer-assisted audit techniques (CAATs) can be used to confirm cut-off
- CAATs can be used to confirm whether inventory adjustments noted during the count have been updated to inventory records.

                                                                              Max   **4**

        (ii)   Up to 1 mark per well explained advantage
- Test a large volume of inventory data accurately and quickly
- Cost effective after setup
- CAATs can test program controls as well as general IT controls
- Test the actual inventory system and records rather than printouts from the system
- CAATs reduce the level of human error in testing
- CAATs results can be compared with traditional audit testing
- Free up audit team members to focus on judgemental and high risk areas

                                                                              Max   **4**

        (iii)   Up to 1 mark per well explained disadvantage
- Costs of using CAATs in this first year will be high
- Team may require training on the specific CAATs to be utilised
- Changes in the inventory system may require costly revisions to the CAATs
- The inventory system may not be compatible with the audit firm's CAATs
- If testing the live system, there is a risk the data could be corrupted or lost
- If using copy files rather than live data, there is the risk that these files are not genuine copies
- Adequate systems documentation must be available

                                                                              Max   **4**

Total   **30**

Examiner's comments

Part (a) required candidates to identify and explain, for the inventory count arrangements of Lily, deficiencies and suggest a recommendation for each deficiency.

Most candidates performed very well on this part of the question. They were able to confidently identify deficiencies from the scenario. However, some candidates did not address the question requirement fully as they did not 'identify and explain'. Candidates identified, but did not go on to explain why this was a deficiency. For example 'additional inventory sheets are not numbered' would receive ½ mark, however to obtain the other ½ mark they needed to explain how this could cause problems during the inventory count; such as 'the additional sheets could be lost resulting in understated inventory quantities'.

The requirement to provide controls was also well answered. Most candidates were able to provide practical recommendations to address the deficiencies. The main exception to this was with regards to the issue of continued movements of goods during the count. The scenario stated that Lily undertakes continuous production; therefore to suggest 'that production is halted for the inventory count' demonstrated a failure to read and understand the scenario. The scenario is designed to help candidates and so they should not ignore elements of it. Some candidates incorrectly identified deficiencies from the scenario, demonstrating a fundamental lack of understanding of the purpose of an inventory count. For example, a significant minority believed that inventory sheets should contain inventory quantities when in fact this is incorrect, as this would encourage markers to just agree the stated quantities rather than counting properly. In addition candidates felt that counters should not use ink on the count sheets as pencil would be easier for adjustments, again this is incorrect, as if the counts are in pencil then the quantities could be erroneously amended after the count. Also candidates felt that there should be more warehouse staff involved in the count, despite the self-review risk.

Many candidates set their answer out in two columns being deficiency and recommendation. However, those who explained all of the deficiencies and then separately provided all of the recommendations tended to repeat themselves and possibly wasted some time. In addition, it was not uncommon to see candidates provide many more answers than required.

Part (b) required procedures the auditor should undertake during the inventory count of Lily. Performance was unsatisfactory on this part of the question. The requirement stated in capitals that procedures DURING the count were required; however a significant proportion of candidates ignored this word completely and provided procedures both before and after the count. Many answers actually stated 'before the count...', candidates must read the question requirements properly. Those candidates who had read the question properly often struggled to provide an adequate number of well described points. The common answers given were 'to observe the inventory counters' although candidates did not make it clear what they were observing for; or 'undertake test counts' but with no explanation of the direction of the test and whether it was for completeness or existence. Some candidates provided all possible inventory tests, in particular focusing on NRV testing. This demonstrated that candidates had learnt a standard list of inventory tests and rather than applying these to the question set just proceeded to list them all. This approach wastes time and tends not to score well as of the answers provided very few tended to be relevant.

Part (ci) required a description of four audit procedures that could be carried out for inventory using CAATs. Performance on this question was unsatisfactory. Candidates needed to apply their knowledge of CAATs to inventory procedures, many failed to do this. Again lots of candidates did not read the question properly and so despite the requirement to apply their answer to inventory, they proceeded to refer to tests on receivables and payables. Also many candidates appear not to actually understand what CAATs are, who uses them and how they work. Therefore many answers focused on the company using CAATs rather than the auditor, many procedures given were not related to CAATs for example 'discuss inventory valuation with the directors' or 'agree goods received notes to purchase invoices'. Those candidates who scored well tended to mainly focus on analytical review procedures for inventory that could be undertaken as part of audit software tests.

Part (cii) required an explanation of the advantages of using CAATs. This question was on the whole answered well. Candidates were able to identify an adequate number of advantages to score well on this part of the question. The main advantages given related to saving time; reducing costs; improving the accuracy of testing and the ability to test larger samples. A minority of candidates failed to explain their advantages; answers such as 'saves time' were commonly provided, this is not an explanation and so would not have scored well.

Part (ciii) required an explanation of the disadvantages of using CAATs. Again, this part of the question was answered well. Candidates were able to identify an adequate number of points to score well. The main disadvantages given related to increased costs; training requirements and the corruption of client data. It was apparent that candidates had learnt a standard list of points for CAATs

155 PEAR INTERNATIONAL *Walk in the footsteps of a top tutor*

Key answer tips

Part (a) requires repetition of knowledge from the text book. Use subheadings to make it easy for the marker to see that you have answered both advantages and disadvantages of each type of method.

Part (b) Controls deficiencies and recommendations questions are usually quite straightforward, however, you must explain the deficiencies and controls in sufficient detail to score marks. If you are too brief you will only score ½ marks. When suggesting tests of controls remember that you are looking for evidence that the client has implemented the control effectively. Do not suggest the auditor should perform the control as this doesn't prove the client has performed the control. Also be careful not to give substantive procedures as these have a different purpose to a test of control and will not score marks.

(a)   Advantages and Disadvantages of methods of recording the system

Narrative Notes

Advantages

The main advantage of narrative notes is that they are simple to record, after discussion with the company these discussions are easily written up as notes.

Additionally, as the notes are simple to record, this can facilitate understanding by all members of the team, especially more junior members who might find alternative methods too complex.

Disadvantages

Narrative notes may prove to be too cumbersome, especially if the system is complex.

This method can make it more difficult to identify missing internal controls as the notes record the detail but do not identify control exceptions clearly.

Questionnaires

Internal control questionnaires are used to assess whether controls exist which meet specific objectives or prevent or detect errors and omissions.

Advantages

Questionnaires are quick to prepare, which means they are a cost effective method for recording the system.

They ensure that all controls present within the system are considered and recorded; hence missing controls or deficiencies are clearly highlighted.

Questionnaires are simple to complete and therefore any members of the team can complete them and they are easy to use and understand.

Disadvantages

It can be easy for the company to overstate the level of the controls present as they are asked a series of questions relating to potential controls.

Without careful tailoring of the questionnaire to make it company specific, there is a risk that controls may be misunderstood and unusual controls missed.

(b) **Pear International's internal control**

Deficiency	Control	Test of control
Currently the website is not integrated into inventory system. This can result in Pear accepting customer orders when they do not have the goods in inventory. This can cause them to lose sales and customer goodwill.	The website should be updated to include an interface into the inventory system; this should check inventory levels and only process orders if adequate inventory is held. If inventory is out of stock, this should appear on the website with an approximate waiting time.	Test data could be used to attempt to process orders via the website for items which are not currently held in inventory. The orders should be flagged as being out of stock and indicate an approximate waiting time.
For goods despatched by local couriers, customer signatures are not always obtained. This can lead to customers falsely claiming that they have not received their goods. Pear would not be able to prove that they had in fact despatched the goods and may result in goods being despatched twice.	Pear should remind all local couriers that customer signatures must be obtained as proof of despatch and payment will not be made for any despatches with missing signatures.	Select a sample of despatches by couriers and ask Pear for proof of despatch by viewing customer signatures.

Deficiency	Control	Test of control
There have been a number of situations where the sales orders have not been fulfilled in a timely manner. This can lead to a loss of customer goodwill and if it persists will damage the reputation of Pear as a reliable supplier.	Once goods are despatched they should be matched to sales orders and flagged as fulfilled. The system should automatically flag any outstanding sales orders past a predetermined period, such as five days. This report should be reviewed by a responsible official.	Review the report of outstanding sales orders. If significant, discuss with a responsible official to understand why there is still a significant time period between sales order and despatch date. Select a sample of sales orders and compare the date of order to the goods despatch date to ascertain whether this is within the acceptable predetermined period.
Customer credit limits are set by sales ledger clerks. Sales ledger clerks are not sufficiently senior and so may set limits too high, leading to irrecoverable debts, or too low, leading to a loss of sales.	Credit limits should be set by a senior member of the sales ledger department and not by sales ledger clerks. These limits should be regularly reviewed by a responsible official.	For a sample of new customers accepted in the year, review the authorisation of the credit limit, and ensure that this was performed by a responsible official. Enquire of sales ledger clerks as to who can set credit limits.
Sales discounts are set by Pear's sales team. In order to boost their sales, members of the sales team may set the discounts too high, leading to a loss of revenue.	All members of the sales team should be given authority to grant sales discounts up to a set limit. Any sales discounts above these limits should be authorised by sales area managers or the sales director. Regular review of sales discount levels should be undertaken by the sales director, and this review should be evidenced.	Discuss with members of the sales team the process for setting sales discounts. Review the sales discount report for evidence of review by the sales director.

Deficiency	Control	Test of control
Supplier statement reconciliations are no longer performed. This may result in errors in the recording of purchases and payables not being identified in a timely manner.	Supplier statement reconciliations should be performed on a monthly basis for all suppliers and these should be reviewed by a responsible official.	Review the file of reconciliations to ensure that they are being performed on a regular basis and that they have been reviewed by a responsible official.
Changes to supplier details in the purchase ledger master file can be undertaken by purchase ledger clerks. This could lead to key supplier data being accidently amended or fictitious suppliers being set up, which can increase the risk of fraud.	Only purchase ledger supervisors should have the authority to make changes to master file data. This should be controlled via passwords. Regular review of any changes to master file data by a responsible official and this review should be evidenced.	Request a purchase ledger clerk to attempt to access the master file and to make an amendment, the system should not allow this. Review a report of master data changes and review the authority of those making amendments.
Pear has considerable levels of surplus plant and equipment. Surplus unused plant is at risk of theft. In addition, if the surplus plant is not disposed of then the company could lose sundry income.	Regular review of the plant and equipment on the factory floor by senior factory personnel to identify any old or surplus equipment. As part of the capital expenditure process there should be a requirement to confirm the treatment of the equipment being replaced.	Observe the review process by senior factory personnel, identifying the treatment of any old equipment. Review processed capital expenditure forms to ascertain if the treatment of replaced equipment is stated.
Purchase requisitions are authorised by production supervisors. Production supervisors are not sufficiently independent or senior to authorise capital expenditure.	Capital expenditure authorisation levels to be established. Production supervisors should only be able to authorise low value items, any high value items should be authorised by the board.	Review a sample of authorised capital expenditure forms and identify if the correct signatory has authorised them.

(c) **Substantive procedures – Additions and disposals**

Additions

- Obtain a breakdown of additions, cast the list and agree to the non-current asset register to confirm completeness of plant & equipment (P&E).

- Select a sample of additions and agree cost to supplier invoice to confirm valuation.

- Verify rights and obligations by agreeing the addition of plant and equipment to a supplier invoice in the name of Pear.

- Review the list of additions and confirm that they relate to capital expenditure items rather than repairs and maintenance.

- Review board minutes to ensure that significant capital expenditure purchases have been authorised by the board.

- For a sample of additions recorded in P&E physically verify them on the factory floor to confirm existence.

Disposals

- Obtain a breakdown of disposals, cast the list and agree all assets removed from the non-current asset register to confirm existence.

- Select a sample of disposals and agree sale proceeds to supporting documentation such as sundry sales invoices.

- Recalculate the profit/loss on disposal and agree to the income statement.

(d) **Impact on interim and final audit**

Interim audit

Apple & Co could look to rely on any internal control documentation produced by internal audit (IA) as they would need to assess whether the control environment has changed during the year.

If the IA department has performed testing during the year on internal control systems, such as the payroll, sales and purchase systems, then Apple & Co could review and possibly place reliance on this work. This may result in the workload reducing and possibly a decrease in the external audit fee.

During the interim audit, Apple & Co would need to perform a risk assessment to assist in the planning process. It is possible that the IA department may have conducted a risk assessment and so Apple could use this as part of their initial planning process.

Apple & Co would need to consider the risk of fraud and error and non-compliance with law and regulations resulting in misstatements in the financial statements. This is also an area for IA to consider, hence there is scope for Apple & Co to review the work and testing performed by IA to assist in this risk assessment.

Final audit

It is possible that the IA department may assist with year-end inventory counting and controls and so Apple & Co can place some reliance on the work performed by them, however, they would still need to attend the count and perform their own reduced testing.

	ACCA marking scheme		
			Marks
(a)	Up to 1 mark per valid point **Notes:** Simple to understand Facilitate understanding by all team Cumbersome especially if complex system Difficult to identify missing controls **Questionnaires:** Quick to prepare and hence cost effective All internal controls considered and missing controls identified Easy to complete and use Easy to overstate controls Easy to misunderstand controls and miss unusual controls		
		Max	5
(b)	Up to 1 mark per deficiency, up to 1 mark per well explained control and up to 1 mark for each well explained test of control, max of 5 for deficiencies, max of 5 for controls and max of 5 for tests of control. • Website not integrated into inventory system • Customer signatures • Unfulfilled sales orders • Customer credit limits • Sales discounts • Supplier statement reconciliations • Purchase ledger master file • Surplus plant and equipment • Authorisation of capital expenditure		
		Max	15
(c)	Up to 1 mark per substantive procedure **Additions** • Cast list of additions and agree to non-current asset register • Vouch cost to recent supplier invoice • Agree addition to a supplier invoice in the name of Pear to confirm rights and obligations • Review additions and confirm capital expenditure items rather than repairs and maintenance • Review board minutes to ensure authorised by the board • Physically verify them on the factory floor to confirm existence **Disposals** • Cast list of disposals and agree removed from non-current asset register • Vouch sale proceeds to supporting documentation such as sundry sales invoices • Recalculate the profit/loss on disposal		
		Max	6
(d)	Up to 1 mark per well explained point **Interim audit** Systems documentation Testing of systems such as payroll, sales, purchases Risk assessment Fraud and error, non-compliance with law and regulations **Final audit** Inventory count procedures		
		Max	4
Total			30

Examiner's comments

Part (b) required candidates to identify and explain deficiencies, suggest a control for each deficiency and recommend tests of controls to assess if the internal controls of Pear were operating effectively. Most candidates performed well on this part of the question. They were able to confidently identify deficiencies from the scenario. However, many candidates did not address the question requirement fully as they did not 'identify and explain'. Candidates identified, but did not go on to explain why this was a deficiency. For example 'couriers do not always record customer signatures as proof of delivery' would receive ½ mark, however to obtain the other ½ mark they needed to explain how this could cause problems for the company; such as customers could dispute receipt of goods and Pear would need to resend them. The requirement to provide controls was generally well answered. Some candidates gave objectives rather than controls for example 'Pear should ensure that all sales are forwarded to the despatch department' without explaining what the control should be to ensure that this happened. In addition some candidates provided controls which were just too vague to attain the 1 mark available per control. The requirement to provide tests of control was not answered well. Many candidates simply repeated their controls and added 'to check that' or 'to make sure'. These are not tests of control. Also many candidates suggested that the control be tested through observation. For example 'observe the process for authorisation of sales discounts'. This is a weak test as it is likely that if the auditor is present that the control will operate effectively; instead a better test would be 'to review sales invoices for evidence of authorisation of discounts by sales manager.' Many candidates set their answer out in three columns being deficiency, control and test of control. However those who set it out as identification of deficiency, explanation of deficiency and control and then separately addressed the requirement of test of controls tended to miss out some relevant tests of controls. In addition the requirement was for five deficiencies; it was not uncommon to see candidates provide many more than five. Often in one paragraph they would combine two or three points such as authorisation of credit limits and of sales discounts. When points were combined, some candidates did not fully provide controls and tests of controls for each of the given points, therefore failing to maximise their marks.

Part (c) required substantive procedures the auditor should perform on year-end property, plant and equipment (PPE) additions and disposals. Performance was mixed on this part of the question. There were two available marks for addition tests and two marks for disposal tests. Candidates who scored well often did so by providing a number of tests for each area, each test was average and so scored ½ mark each and so they managed to attain full marks in this way. However, some candidates provided detailed procedures and so achieved the 1 mark available per test. This is better utilisation of time. The requirement verb was to 'describe' therefore sufficient detail was required to score 1 mark per test. Candidates are reminded that substantive procedures are a core topic area and they must be able to produce relevant detailed procedures. Many tests given were just too brief. Answers such as 'check accounting records to ensure correct treatment of disposals' are far too vague as it does not explain how we gain comfort that disposals have been recorded correctly. In addition answers such as 'ensure that additions are correctly included' are objectives rather than substantive procedures. Other common mistakes made by candidates were:

- Providing general PPE tests such as for depreciation, rather than just focusing on additions and disposals.
- Giving unrealistic tests such as 'to physically verify on the factory floor that an asset has been disposed of' if it's been disposed of then how can it be physically verified!
- Focusing too much on whether the asset has been disposed of for the best possible price; this is a concern of management and not of the auditor.

Part (d) required candidates to explain the impact on the external auditor's work at the interim and final audits if Pear was to establish an internal audit department. Performance on this question was unsatisfactory. Where the question was attempted, many candidates failed to score more than 1 mark. What was required was an explanation of tasks that internal audit might perform that the external auditor might then look to rely on in either the interim or final audit. For example, they could utilise systems documentation produced by internal audit during the interim audit. Or they could rely on year-end inventory counts undertaken by internal audit as part of their inventory testing at the final audit. Where candidates achieved 1 mark this was usually for a general comment about relying on the work of internal audit and so reducing substantive procedures.

Mistakes made by candidates were:

- Focusing on the role of internal audit in general.
- Giving lengthy answers on factors to consider when placing reliance on internal audit.
- Providing details of what an external auditor does at the interim and final audit stages.

156 GREYSTONE   *Walk in the footsteps of a top tutor*

Key answer tips

Part (a) is a tricky knowledge question. This question demonstrates the need for both breadth and depth of knowledge across the F8 syllabus, including knowing the objectives and key provisions of all of the examinable ISAs. If you don't know this, don't spend time thinking about it, move on to the next part of the question. It is only worth 3 marks so not worth wasting time over.

Part (b) requires control objectives for the purchasing system. Control objectives are the reasons why controls are put in place. They address the risks that could happen in the system. Be careful not to suggest that a control objective is to ensure a control is in place. You need to say the reason why the control should be in place.

Part (c) is a very common style of question and should be practised before sitting the actual exam. Note that the question requires you to link parts (ii) and (iii) to the deficiencies you identified in part (i). For this reason a table format is appropriate for your answer. Your answer to part (c) requires application of knowledge to the specific information given in the question. You cannot 'knowledge dump' in your answer.

Part (d) asks for substantive procedures you could perform on the year-end trade payables balance of Greystone Co. However, as Greystone is a retail entity, the procedures over trade payables will not differ significantly from the standard procedures described in your learning materials.

(a)   **Examples of matters the external auditor should consider in determining whether a deficiency in internal controls is significant**

- The likelihood of the deficiencies leading to material misstatements in the financial statements in the future.
- The susceptibility to loss or fraud of the related asset or liability.
- The subjectivity and complexity of determining estimated amounts.

- The financial statement amounts exposed to the deficiencies.
- The volume of activity that has occurred or could occur in the account balance or class of transactions exposed to the deficiency or deficiencies.
- The importance of the controls to the financial reporting process.
- The cause and frequency of the exceptions detected as a result of the deficiencies in the controls.
- The interaction of the deficiency with other deficiencies in internal control.

Tutor's top tips

Note that the requirement asks for matters which would mean an internal control deficiency is significant, NOT examples of significant internal control deficiencies. Giving examples of deficiencies will not score any marks.

Tutorial note

ISA 265 Communicating Deficiencies in Internal Control to those charged with Governance and Management states that a significant deficiency in internal control is a deficiency or combination of deficiencies in internal control that, in the auditor's professional judgement, is of sufficient importance to merit the attention of those charged with governance.

(b)   Control objectives

- To ensure purchases are completely recorded
- To ensure purchases are accurately recorded
- To ensure purchases are recorded in the period to which they relate
- To ensure purchases are for a valid business use
- To ensure purchases represent value for money

(c)

(i) **Deficiency**	(ii) **Recommendation**	(iii) **Test of control**
The purchasing manager decides on the inventory levels for each store without discussion with store or sales managers. The purchasing manager may not have the appropriate knowledge of the local market for a store.	The purchasing manager should initially hold a meeting with area managers of stores; if meeting all store managers is not practical, he should understand the local markets before agreeing jointly goods to be purchased.	Enquire of the purchasing manager whether meetings are held with store managers. Corroborate this by speaking to some of the store managers. If email communication is available, inspect a sample of emails discussing the quantities to be ordered.
This could result in stores ordering goods that are not likely to sell and hence require heavy discounting. In addition as a fashion chain, if customers perceive that the goods are not meeting the key fashion trends then they may cease to shop at Greystone at all.		

(i) Deficiency

The purchase orders are only reviewed and authorised by a purchasing director in a wholly aggregated manner (by specified regions of countries).

It will be difficult for the purchasing director to assess whether overall the correct buying decisions are being made as the detail of the orders is not being presented and he is the only level of authorisation.

This could result in significant levels of goods being purchased that are not right for particular market sectors.

The store managers are responsible for re-ordering goods through the purchasing manager.

If the store managers forget or order too late, then as the ordering process can take up to four weeks, the store could experience significant stock outs leading to loss of income.

It is not possible for a store to order goods from other local stores for customers who request them. Instead they are told to contact the stores themselves, or use the company website.

Customers are less likely to contact individual stores themselves and this could result in the company losing out on valuable sales.

In addition some goods which are slow moving in one store may be out of stock at another, if goods could be transferred between stores then overall sales may be maximised.

(ii) Recommendation

A purchasing senior manager should review the information prepared for each country and discuss with local purchasing managers the specifics of their orders. These should then be authorised and passed to the purchasing director for final review and sign off.

Automatic re-order levels should be set up in the inventory management systems. As the goods sold reach the re-order levels the purchasing manager should receive an automatic re-order request.

An inter-branch transfer system should be established between stores. This should help stores whose goods are below the re-order level but are awaiting their deliveries from the suppliers.

(iii) Test of control

Confirm with the purchasing senior manager that they discuss the orders with the local purchasing managers and corroborate this by speaking to the local managers.

Inspect a sample of purchase orders for evidence of the purchasing director's signature authorising the purchase.

Using test data, enter a sales order which would reduce inventory to below the re-order level. Inspect the purchasing managers system for an automatic re-order request to ensure the system works effectively.

The auditor could pose as a customer in a store and ask if goods that are not available from that store can be obtained from another store.

(i) **Deficiency**	(ii) **Recommendation**	(iii) **Test of control**
Deliveries from suppliers are accepted without being checked first.	Deliveries from suppliers should only be accepted between designated hours such as the first two hours of the morning when it is quieter. The goods should then be checked on arrival for quantity and quality prior to acceptance from the supplier.	Observe the goods in area at various times of the day to ensure that goods are only accepted during specified hours.
In addition they are then checked by sales assistants to the supplier's delivery note to agree quantities but not quality.		When goods are received, observe to ensure the goods are checked on arrival for quantity and quality.
The stores are receiving goods without checking that these are correct. Hence if a delivery is subsequently disputed there may be little recourse for the company.		If this check is evidenced on the goods received note, inspect as ample of goods received notes for the signature of the person who performed the check.
If the sales assistants are only checking quantities then goods which are not of a saleable condition may be accepted.		
Sales assistants are producing the goods received note (GRN) on receipt of a supplier's delivery note.	A responsible official at each store should produce the GRN from the supplier's delivery information.	Inspect a sample of goods received notes for the signature of the person who prepared it and ensure this is someone of suitable authority such as a store manager.
The assistants may not be adequately experienced to produce the GRN, and this is an important document used in the invoice authorisation process. Errors could lead to under or overpayments.		
Goods are being received without any checks being made against purchase orders.	A copy of the authorised order form should be sent to the store. This should then be checked to the GRN.	Inspect a sample of GRNs for evidence of a signature confirming the GRN has been checked against the authorised order form.
This could result in Greystone receiving and subsequently paying for goods it did not require.	Once checked the order should be sent to head office and logged as completed.	
In addition if no check is made against order then the company may have significant purchase orders which are outstanding, leading to lost sales.	On a regular basis the purchasing clerk should review the order file for any outstanding items.	Enquire of the purchasing clerk how often they review the order file for outstanding items and inspect the file for evidence of a review such as log confirming the check has been performed.

(i) **Deficiency**	(ii) **Recommendation**	(iii) **Test of control**
Purchase invoices are manually matched to a high volume of GRNs from the individual stores. A manual checking process increases the risk of error, resulting in invoices being accepted or rejected erroneously.	The checked GRNs should be logged onto the purchasing system, matched against the relevant order number, then as the invoice is received this should be automatically matched. The purchasing clerk should then review for any unmatched items.	Using test data, enter a purchase invoice and inspect the invoice in the system to see if it has been matched to the relevant GRN and purchase order. Review the level of unmatched items to assess whether the unmatched items are reviewed on a regular basis. A high number of unmatched items may indicate that this check is not carried out as regularly as it should.
The purchase invoice is only logged onto the system as it is being authorised by the purchasing director. If the invoice is misplaced then payables may not be settled on a timely basis. In addition at the year-end the purchase ledger may be understated as invoices relating to the current year have been received but are not in the purchase ledger.	Upon receipt of an invoice this should be logged into a file of unmatched invoices. As it is matched and authorised it should then be moved into the purchase ledger. At the year-end items in the unmatched invoices file should be accrued for, to ensure liabilities are not understated.	Obtain the purchase invoices which have not been logged onto the system. Ensure these are logged into the unmatched invoice file. Enquire of the purchase ledger clerk if there are any other invoices which have not yet been logged into the file or the system.

(d)   Substantive procedures over year-end trade payables

- Obtain a listing of trade payables from the purchase ledger and agree to the general ledger and the financial statements.

- Reconcile the total of purchase ledger accounts with the purchase ledger control account, and cast the list of balances and the purchase ledger control account.

- Review the list of trade payables against prior years to identify any significant omissions.

- Calculate the trade payable days for Greystone and compare to prior years, investigate any significant differences.

- Review after date payments, if they relate to the current year then follow through to the purchase ledger or accrual listing to ensure completeness.

- Review after date invoices and credit notes to ensure no further items need to be accrued.

- Obtain supplier statements and reconcile these to the purchase ledger balances, and investigate any reconciling items.

- Select a sample of payable balances and perform a trade payables' circularisation, follow up any non-replies and any reconciling items between balance confirmed and trade payables' balance.
- Enquire of management their process for identifying goods received but not invoiced or logged in the purchase ledger and ensure that it is reasonable to ensure completeness of payables.
- Select a sample of goods received notes before the year-end and follow through to inclusion in the year-end payables balance, to ensure correct cut-off.
- Review the purchase ledger for any debit balances, for any significant amounts discuss with management and consider reclassification as current assets.
- Review the financial statements to ensure payables are included as current liabilities.

	ACCA marking scheme		
			Marks
(a)	Up to 1 mark per valid point		
	Likelihood of deficiencies leading to errors		
	Risk of fraud		
	Subjectivity and complexity		
	Financial statement amounts		
	Volume of activity		
	Importance of the controls		
	Cause and frequency of exceptions		
	Interaction with other deficiencies		
		Max	**3**
(b)	1 mark for each control objective		
	Ensure purchases are completely recorded		
	Ensure purchases are accurately recorded		
	Ensure purchases are recorded in the correct period		
	Ensure purchases are for a valid business use		
	Ensure purchases represent value for money		
		Max	**3**
(c)	Up to 1 mark per well explained, deficiency, recommendation and test of control. If not well explained then just give ½ mark for each.		
	Purchasing manager orders goods without consulting stores		
	Purchase order reviewed in aggregate by purchasing director		
	Store managers re-order goods		
	No inter-branch transfer system		
	Deliveries accepted without proper checks		
	Sales assistants produce the goods received note		
	Goods received but not checked to purchase orders		
	Manual matching of goods received notes to invoice		
	Purchase invoice logged late		
		Max	**18**
(d)	Up to 1 mark per well explained substantive procedure		
	Agree purchase ledger to general and financial statements		
	Review payable to prior year		
	Calculate trade payables		
	After date payments review		
	After date invoices/credit notes review		
	Supplier statement reviews		
	Payables' circularisation		
	Goods received not invoiced		
	Cut-off testing		
	Debit balances review		
	Disclosure within current liabilities		
		Max	**6**
Total			**30**

157 SHINY HAPPY WINDOWS *Walk in the footsteps of a top tutor*

Key answer tips

Part (a) requires little more than pre-learnt knowledge.

Part (b) is a typical systems review question. You are asked to prepare a management letter of deficiencies to those charged with governance. This is a very common style of question and should be rehearsed before sitting the actual exam. Note that the question requires you to link parts (ii) and (iii) to the deficiencies you identified in part (i). For this reason a table format is appropriate for your answer. Your answer to part (b) requires application of knowledge to the specific information given in the question. You cannot 'knowledge dump' in your answer.

Part (c) asks for tests you could perform on any company's bank balance. You can therefore suggest general tests learnt from your study texts. You do not have to apply your answer to the scenario.

(a)   A control objective is the reason behind needing a control. The objective identifies a risk the company faces. For example there is a risk that purchase orders are placed by employees that are not for a valid business use.

A control procedure is the process or activity designed to mitigate a risk. For example authorisation of purchase orders to ensure they are for a valid business use.

A control procedure is therefore implemented to achieve the control objective.

(b)

Deficiency	Control	Test of Control
A junior clerk opens the post unsupervised. This could result in cash being misappropriated.	A second member of the accounts team or staff independent of the accounts team should assist with the mail, one should open the post and the second should record cash received in the cash log.	Observe the mail opening process, to assess if the control is operating effectively.
Cash and cheques are secured in a small locked box and only banked every few days. A small locked box is not adequate for security of considerable cash receipts, as it can easily be stolen.	Cash and cheques should be ideally banked daily, if not then it should be stored in a fire proof safe, and access to this safe should be restricted to supervised individuals.	Enquire of management where the cash receipts not banked are stored. Inspect the location to ensure cash is suitably secure.

Deficiency	Control	Test of Control
Cash and cheques are only banked every few days and any member of the finance team performs this.	Cash and cheques should be banked every day.	Inspect the paying-in-books to see if cash and cheques have been banked daily or less frequently.
		Review bank statements against the cash received log to confirm all amounts were banked promptly.
Cash should ideally not be held over-night as it is not secure. Also if any member of the team banks cash, then this could result in very junior clerks having access to significant amounts of money.	The cashier should prepare the paying-in-book from the cash received log. Then a separate responsible individual should have responsibility for banking this cash.	Enquire of staff as to who performs the banking process and confirm this person is suitably responsible.
The cashier updates both the cash book and the sales ledger. This is weak segregation of duties, as the cashier could incorrectly enter a receipt and this would impact both the cash book and the sales ledger. In addition weak segregation of duties could increase the risk of a 'teeming and lading' fraud.	The cashier should update the cash book from the cash received log. A member of the sales ledger team should update the sales ledger.	Observe the process for recording cash received into the relevant ledgers and note if the segregation of duties is occurring.
Bank reconciliations are not performed every month and they do not appear to be reviewed by a senior member of the finance department. Errors in the cash cycle may not be promptly identified if reconciliations are performed infrequently.	Bank reconciliations should be performed monthly. A responsible individual should then review them.	Review the file of reconciliations for evidence of regular performance and review by senior finance team members.

(c)   **Substantive procedures over bank balance:**

- Obtain the company's bank reconciliation and cast to ensure arithmetical accuracy.

- Obtain a bank confirmation letter from the company's bankers.

- Verify the balance per the bank statement to an original year end bank statement and also to the bank confirmation letter.

- Verify the reconciliation's balance per the cash book to the year end cash book.

- Trace all of the outstanding lodgements to the pre year end cash book, post year end bank statement and also to paying-in-book pre year end.

- Examine any old unpresented cheques to assess if they need to be written back into the purchase ledger as they are no longer valid to be presented.

- Trace all unpresented cheques through to a pre year end cash book and post year end statement. For any unusual amounts or significant delays obtain explanations from management.

- Agree all balances listed on the bank confirmation letter to the company's bank reconciliations or the trial balance to ensure completeness of bank balances.

- Review the cash book and bank statements for any unusual items or large transfers around the year end, as this could be evidence of window dressing.

- Examine the bank confirmation letter for details of any security provided by the company or any legal right of set-off as this may require disclosure.

	ACCA marking scheme	
		Marks
(a)	Up to 1 mark each for each point	
	− Explanation of control objective	
	− Explanation of control procedure	
	− Control procedure achieves control objective	
	Max	**3**
(b)	Up to 1 mark for each deficiency identified and explained, up to 1 mark for each suitable control and up to 1 mark per test of control.	
	− Junior clerk opens post	
	− Small locked box	
	− Cash not banked daily	
	− Cashier updates cash book and sales ledger	
	− Bank reconciliation not performed monthly	
	Maximum for deficiencies	**4**
	Maximum for controls	**4**
	Maximum for test of controls	**4**
(c)	Up to 1 mark per substantive procedure	
	− Cast bank reconciliation	
	− Obtain bank confirmation letter	
	− Bank balance to statement/bank confirmation	
	− Cash book balance to cash book	
	− Outstanding lodgements	
	− Unpresented cheques review	
	− Old cheques write back	
	− Agree all balances on bank confirmation	
	− Unusual items/window dressing	
	− Security/legal right set-off	
	Max	**5**
Total		**20**

158 MATALAS CO *Walk in the footsteps of a top tutor*

Key answer tips

Tutor's top tips

In part (a) you should apply knowledge of independence of external audit to an internal audit situation.

In part (b) read through the scenario line by line to identify the deficiencies in the petty cash system of Matalas. You must explain why they are deficiencies in order to earn the full mark. When suggesting recommendations, remember they must be commercially sensible and practical.

(a) **Factors limiting independence of internal audit**

Reporting system

The chief internal auditor reports to the finance director. This limits the effectiveness of the internal audit reports as the finance director will also be responsible for some of the financial systems that the internal auditor is reporting on. Similarly, the chief internal auditor may soften or limit criticism in reports to avoid confrontation with the finance director.

To ensure independence, the internal auditor should report to an audit committee.

Scope of work

The scope of work of internal audit is decided by the finance director in discussion with the chief internal auditor. This means that the finance director may try and influence the chief internal auditor regarding the areas that the internal audit department is auditing, possibly directing attention away from any contentious areas that the director does not want auditing.

To ensure independence, the scope of work of the internal audit department should be decided by the chief internal auditor, perhaps with the assistance of an audit committee.

Audit work

The chief internal auditor appears to be auditing the controls which were proposed by that department. This limits independence as the auditor is effectively auditing his own work, and may not therefore identify any mistakes.

To ensure independence, the chief internal auditor should not establish control systems in Matalas. However, where controls have already been established, another member of the internal audit should carry out the audit of petty cash to provide some limited independence.

Length of service of internal audit staff

All internal audit staff at Matalas have been employed for at least five years. This may limit their effectiveness as they will be very familiar with the systems being reviewed and therefore may not be sufficiently objective to identify errors in those systems.

To ensure independence, the existing staff should be rotated into different areas of internal audit work and the chief internal auditor independently review the work carried out.

Appointment of chief internal auditor

The chief internal auditor is appointed by the chief executive officer (CEO) of Matalas. Given that the CEO is responsible for the running of the company, it is possible that there will be bias in the appointment of the chief internal auditor; the CEO may appoint someone who he knows will not criticise his work or the company.

To ensure independence, the chief internal auditor should be appointed by an audit committee or at least the appointment agreed by the whole board.

(b) Internal control deficiencies – petty cash

Deficiency	Suggested control
The petty cash balance is approximately three months expenditure. This is excessive and will increase the possibility of petty cash being stolen or errors not being identified.	The petty cash balance should be $2,000, being about one month's expenditure.
The petty cash box itself is not secure; it is placed on a bookcase where any member of staff could steal it.	When not in use, the petty cash box should be kept in the branch safe, or at least a locked drawer in the accountant's desk.
Petty cash appears to be used for some larger items of expenditure (up to $500). Vouchers are only authorised after expenditure is incurred indicating that some significant expenditure can take place without authorisation.	A maximum expenditure limit (e.g. $50) should be set before which prior authorisation is required.
Petty cash vouchers are only signed by the person incurring the expenditure, indicating a lack of authorisation control for that expenditure.	All vouchers should be signed by an independent official showing that the expenditure has been authorised.
Petty cash only appears to be counted by the accounts clerk, who is also responsible for the petty cash balance. There is no independent check that the petty cash balance is accurate.	The counting of petty cash should be checked by the accountant to ensure that the clerk is not stealing the cash.
When the imprest cheque is signed, only the journal entry for petty cash is reviewed, not the petty cash vouchers. The accountant has no evidence that the journal entry actually relates to the petty cash expenditure incurred.	The petty cash vouchers should be available for review to provide evidence of petty cash expenditure.
Petty cash vouchers are not pre-numbered so it is impossible to check the completeness of vouchers; unauthorised expenditure could be blamed on 'missing' vouchers.	Petty cash vouchers should be pre-numbered and the numbering checked in the petty cash book to confirm completeness of recording of expenditure.

ACCA marking scheme		
		Marks
(a) 2 marks for each independence factor. 1 for explaining the issue and 1 for mitigating that factor.		
– Reporting system		
– Scope of work		
– Actual audit work		
– Length of service of internal audit staff		
– Appointment of chief internal auditor		
– External auditor assistance with internal audit? (additional to answer)		
	Max	8
(b) 2 marks for each control deficiency. 1 for explaining the deficiency and 1 for control over that deficiency.		
– Size of petty cash balance		
– Security of petty cash box		
– High value petty cash expenditure – individual items		
– Authorisation of petty cash expenditure		
– Counting of petty cash		
– No review of petty cash vouchers – signing of imprest cheque		
– Vouchers not pre-numbered		
	Max	12
Total		20

Examiner's comments

To obtain the full two marks per point, answers would normally take the format 'issue 1 could limit independence in Matalas, because..... This issue can be overcome by....' However, as the question requirement did not specify the number of points to make, then any number of valid points could be included in the answer. Most candidates included four fairly well explained points in their answer. A minority of candidates provided limited or no explanation of the points made, limiting the marks awarded.

Common errors and reasons why those errors did not obtain marks included:

- Including points in the answer which were not mentioned in the scenario. A minority of candidates mentioned generic reasons why internal audit may not be independent. These points were not relevant and so no marks could be awarded.

- Including points which although could be relevant to the scenario were not necessarily best practice. For example, in many internal audit departments the chief internal auditor is involved in appointing staff because they can identify the skills required and whether that person is suitable to work within the department. These points were not fundamental flaws limiting the independence of the internal audit department.

- Not explaining the reason for the deficiency. For example, a common comment was the chief internal auditor reports to the finance director. While this was correct in relation to the question, the reason in terms of lack of independence of reporting or the finance director suppressing adverse reports on his department was not explained.

- Stating changes to take place within the company without justifying why that change was necessary. For example, stating an audit committee was needed.

- The method of overcoming deficiencies (an audit committee being one) had to be linked to a deficiency identified in the scenario. Simply stating areas of good corporate governance was normally insufficient as the reason for the suggested change was not clear.

- Mentioning that the internal audit department had only six internal auditors limiting their independence. The number of staff may have limited the department's effectiveness, but not necessarily their independence.

Overall, the candidates answered this question well.

In part (b), to obtain the full two marks per point, answers would normally take the format 'issue 1 is a petty cash deficiency in Matalas, because..... . This deficiency can be overcome by....' However, as the question requirement did not specify the number of points to make, then any number of valid points could be included in the answer. Most candidates included up to six fairly well explained points in their answer. Again, a minority of candidates provided limited or no explanation of the points made, limiting the marks awarded. The most interesting point to mark in this question concerned the location of the petty cash box itself. Almost all candidates recognised that it was inappropriate to maintain the petty cash book in public view on a bookcase, with the reason that the box could be stolen easily. However, controls over this deficiency varied from simply keeping the box in a safe to using CCTV and employing security guards to ensure the box was not stolen. Given the (relatively) small amount of money in the box, some controls did appear excessive. However, they were normally marked as valid as certainly in some jurisdictions the control could well be appropriate. Common errors and reasons why those errors did not obtain marks included:

- Not explaining the reason for deficiencies identified. For example, many candidates noted that petty cash was counted by the cashier – but not the deficiency that the cashier could report incorrect cash balances and steal some of the money.

- Suggesting deficiencies that were not mentioned in the scenario. The most common weakness in this respect was the comment that petty cash should be computerised. To gain full marks, the deficiency had to be clearly related to the information provided in scenario.

- Suggesting many, and sometimes completely impractical procedures for the control of petty cash. For example, suggesting that all petty cash vouchers had to be signed by the senior accountant or that a voucher should be signed by one person, recorded in the petty cash book by another and then a third person dispensed the actual cash. Awarding marks in these situations was limited because the controls were simply not practical or cost effective for any company.

- A significant number of candidates struggled to provide sufficient reasons. The overall standard was satisfactory which was possibly more an indication that candidates were not always familiar with petty cash systems but that they could identify and comment on deficiencies

159 ANDROMEDA *Walk in the footsteps of a top tutor*

Key answer tips

Part (a) is a knowledge question regarding reliability of evidence. This requires text book knowledge. Make sure you provide an explanation.

Part (b) asks for audit procedures before and during an inventory count and in relation to R&D expenditure. Your procedures need to be sufficiently detailed to enable another person to understand the procedure to be performed and the reason it should be performed.

Part (c) asks for the audit reporting implications of an unresolved issue. Work through the information in a logical manner to arrive at the appropriate audit report suggestion. Document each step of the process as this is what earns the marks. You cannot earn all of the marks available if you only state the opinion required.

(a)   Reliability of audit evidence

The following factors or generalisations can be made when assessing the reliability of audit evidence:

- The reliability of audit evidence is increased when it is obtained from independent sources outside the entity.

- The reliability of audit evidence which is generated internally is increased when the related controls imposed by the entity, including those over its preparation and maintenance, are effective.

- Audit evidence obtained directly by the auditor is more reliable than audit evidence obtained indirectly or by inference.

- Audit evidence in documentary form, whether paper, electronic or other medium, is more reliable than evidence obtained orally.

- Audit evidence provided by original documents is more reliable than audit evidence provided by photocopies or facsimiles, the reliability of which may depend on the controls over their preparation and maintenance.

(b)   (i)   Inventory count procedures

Before the count

- Review the prior year audit files to identify whether there were any particular warehouses where significant inventory issues arose last year.

- Discuss with management whether any of the warehouses this year are new, or have experienced significant control issues.

- Decide which of the 12 warehouses the audit team members will attend, basing this on materiality and risk of each site.

- Obtain a copy of the proposed inventory count instructions, review them to identify any control deficiencies and if any are noted, discuss them with management prior to the counts.

During the count

- Observe the counting teams of Andromeda to confirm whether the inventory count instructions are being followed correctly.

- Select a sample of inventory and perform test counts from inventory sheets to warehouse aisle and from warehouse aisle to inventory sheets.

- Confirm the procedures for identifying and segregating damaged goods are operating correctly, and assess inventory for evidence of any damaged or slow moving items.

- Observe the procedures for movements of inventory during the count, to confirm that all movements have ceased.

- Obtain a photocopy of the completed sequentially numbered inventory sheets for follow up testing on the final audit.

- Identify and make a note of the last goods received notes and goods despatched notes for 31 December in order to perform cut-off procedures.

- Discuss with the internal audit supervisor how any raw materials quantities have been estimated. Where possible, reperform the procedures adopted by the supervisor.

(ii)   Research and development

- Obtain and cast a schedule of intangible assets, detailing opening balances, amount capitalised in the current year, amortisation and closing balances.

- Agree the opening balances to the prior year financial statements.

- Agree the closing balances to the general ledger, trial balance and draft financial statements.

- Recalculate the amortisation charge for a sample of intangible assets which have commenced production and confirm it is line with the amortisation policy of straight line over five years.

- For the five new projects, discuss with management the details of each project along with the stage of development and whether it has been capitalised or expensed.

- For those expensed as research, agree the costs incurred to invoices and supporting documentation and to inclusion in profit or loss.

- For those capitalised as development, agree costs incurred to invoices and confirm technically feasible by discussion with development managers or review of feasibility reports.

- Review market research reports to confirm Andromeda has the ability to sell the product once complete and probable future economic benefits will arise.

- Review the disclosures for intangible assets in the draft financial statements are in accordance with IAS 38 *Intangible Assets*.

ANSWERS TO PRACTICE QUESTIONS : SECTION 4

(c) Audit reports

One of the projects Andromeda has developed in the year does not meet the recognition criteria under IAS 38 *Intangible Assets* for capitalisation but has been included within intangible assets. This is contrary to IAS 38, as if the criteria are not met, then this project is research expenditure and should be expensed to profit or loss rather than capitalised.

The error is material as it represents 11.8% of profit before tax (0.98m/8.3m) and hence management should adjust the financial statements by removing this project from intangible assets and charging it to profit or loss instead. The finance director's argument that the balance is immaterial is not correct.

If management refuses to amend this error, then the audit report will need to be modified. As management has not complied with IAS 38 and the error is material but not pervasive, then a qualified opinion would be necessary.

A basis for qualified opinion paragraph would be needed and would explain the material misstatement in relation to the incorrect treatment of research and development and the effect on the financial statements. The opinion paragraph would be qualified 'except for'.

		ACCA marking scheme		Marks
(a)		Up to 1 mark per well explained point, maximum of 4 points.		
		• Reliability increased when it is obtained from independent sources		
		• Internally generated evidence more reliable when the controls are effective		
		• Evidence obtained directly by the auditor is more reliable than evidence obtained indirectly or by inference		
		• Evidence in documentary form is more reliable than evidence obtained orally		
		• Evidence provided by original documents is more reliable than evidence provided by copies		
			Max	**4**
(b)	(i)	Up to 1 mark per well described procedure, overall maximum of 8 marks.		
		Before the count		
		• Review the prior year audit files to identify significant inventory issues from last year		
		• Discuss with management if any new warehouses or any sites have significant control issues		
		• Decide which of the 12 warehouses the audit team members will attend		
		• Review a copy of the proposed inventory count instructions		
		During the count		
		• Observe the counters to confirm if inventory count instructions are being followed		
		• Perform test counts inventory to sheets and sheets to inventory		
		• Confirm procedures for damaged goods are operating correctly		
		• Observe procedures for movements of inventory during the count		
		• Obtain a photocopy of the completed inventory sheets		
		• Identify and make a note of the last GRNs and GDNs		
		• Discuss with the internal audit supervisor how he has estimated the raw materials quantities		
			Max	**8**

(ii)	Up to 1 mark per well described procedure, overall maximum of 4 marks.		
	• Cast the schedule of intangible assets		
	• Agree the opening balances to the prior year financial statements		
	• Agree the closing balances to the general ledger, trial balance and draft financial statements		
	• Recalculate amortisation charged in the year and confirm in line with the policy of straight line over five years		
	• For new projects, discuss with management the stage of development and if capitalised or expensed		
	• For those expensed as research, agree costs to invoices, supporting documentation and to inclusion in profit or loss		
	• For those capitalised as development, agree costs to invoice and confirm technically feasible by discussion with development managers or review of feasibility reports		
	• Review market research reports to confirm Andromeda has the ability to sell the product		
	• Review the disclosures in the financial statements in accordance with IAS 38 Intangible Assets		
		Max	**4**
(c)	Up to 1 mark per valid point, overall maximum of 4 marks.		
	• Discussion of issue		
	• Calculation of materiality		
	• Type of audit report modification required		
	• Impact on audit report		
		Max	**4**
Total			**20**

Examiner's comments

Part (a) Candidates were firstly asked to explain four factors, which influence the reliability of audit evidence. One mark was available for each factor; candidates were required to either fully explain the factor or compare that factor to another source. This question was generally well answered. A minority of candidates did not fully describe each factor e.g. they noted written evidence was reliable but did not explain why it was reliable, or alternatively, did not make a comparison such as written evidence is stronger than oral evidence. It was pleasing that candidates planned their time carefully and generally only described the required number of factors.

Part (b) Candidates were further provided with a short scenario based question and were required to describe audit procedures that would be performed before and during an inventory count (8 marks) and audit procedures in relation to research and development costs (4 marks). As in previous sitting and as noted in previous examiner's reports the provision of audit procedures relevant to particular circumstances was not well attempted by the majority of candidates. Most candidates were able to identify that the count procedures should be obtained before the inventory count, however a significant number did not expand to explain the purpose of obtaining this information or the importance of the auditor reviewing the adequacy of these instructions. Candidates often then listed further details to be obtained e.g. location of count, assembling the audit team, whether to use an expert etc. A number of candidates referred to third party inventory however this was not mentioned in the scenario and therefore any related procedures were not valid. Only the better candidates suggested looking at prior year audit files or, considered the materiality of the sites and control issues at sites. Most candidates did note that during the count the auditor should observe the counters to ensure the instructions were being followed. However a significant number of candidates then proceeded to list the count procedures that the company's counting team should follow thereby straying into management responsibilities rather than the procedures relevant to the auditor. Some candidates correctly suggested undertaking test counts, while only a minority suggested obtaining copies of the completed count sheets. Overall it was disappointing that candidates did not seem familiar with the auditor's role at an inventory count. In relation to research and development costs, some candidates correctly suggested that the auditor needed to ensure compliance with the capitalisation criteria in IAS 38 and also suggested recalculating the amortisation charge, but few candidates identified any other relevant procedures. Many candidates did not score any marks for this requirement. Although many candidates suggested a review of invoices, the procedure described was most often testing valuation or rights and obligations rather than to ensure correct classification.

Part (c) Candidates were required to discuss the implication on the audit report if an issue surrounding research and development costs remained unresolved. This question was well answered. Most candidates stated the issue, being that the project did not meet the capitalisation criteria, however few candidates explained the impact on the financial statements e.g. assets would be overstated and profit understated. The majority of candidates correctly calculated materiality, however a small number of candidates incorrectly calculated materiality based on the size of the project as a percentage of total research and development spend (i.e. 49%), thereby not considering the materiality of the issue to the financial statements as a whole. Overall it was encouraging to note that audit report questions have shown a continued improvement in recent sittings.

160 HAWTHORN *Walk in the footsteps of a top tutor*

Key answer tips

In part (a) make sure you give assertions relevant to transactions and events. Procedures need to be properly described to earn a full mark. Make it clear what the auditor needs to do and what the procedure will achieve.

The scenario for part (b) describes very specific issues that have occurred during the year and your procedures need to focus on these issues rather than the balances in general.

(a) Occurrence

The transactions and events that have been recorded have actually occurred and pertain to the entity.

Substantive procedures

Select a sample of sales transactions recorded in the sales day book; agree the details back to a goods despatched note (GDN) and customer order.

Review the monthly breakdown of sales per key product, compare to the prior year and budget and investigate any significant differences.

Completeness

All transactions and events that should have been recorded have been recorded.

Substantive procedures

Select a sample of GDNs raised during the year; agree to the sales invoice and that they are recorded in the sales day book.

Review the total amount of sales, compare to the prior year and budget and investigate any significant differences.

Accuracy

The amounts and other data relating to recorded transactions and events have been recorded appropriately.

Substantive procedures

Select a sample of sales invoices and recalculate that the totals and calculation of sales tax are correct.

For a sample of sales invoices, confirm the sales price stated agrees to the authorised price list.

Cut-off

Transactions and events have been recorded in the correct accounting period.

Substantive procedures

Select a sample of pre and post year-end GDNs and agree that the sale is recorded in the correct period's sales day books.

Review the post year-end sales returns and agree if they relate to pre year-end sales that the revenue has been correctly removed from the sales day book.

Classification

Transactions and events have been recorded in the proper accounts.

Substantive procedures

Agree for a sample of sales invoices that they have been correctly recorded within revenue nominal account codes and included within revenue in the financial statements.

Presentation

Transactions and events are appropriately aggregated or disaggregated and clearly described, and related disclosures are relevant and understandable in the context of the applicable financial reporting framework.

Substantive procedures

Obtain a breakdown of revenue by account code and cast to ensure accuracy. Agree the breakdown of revenue disclosed in the financial statements to the revenue account codes within the nominal ledger.

(b)   (i)   **Substantive procedures for supplier statement reconciliations**

- Select a representative sample of year-end supplier statements and agree the balance to the purchase ledger of Hawthorn. If the balance agrees, then no further work is required.

- Where differences occur due to invoices in transit, confirm from goods received notes (GRN) whether the receipt of goods was pre year end, if so confirm that this receipt is included in year-end accruals.

- Where differences occur due to cash in transit from Hawthorn to the supplier, confirm from the cashbook and bank statements that the cash was sent pre year end.

- Discuss any further adjusting items with the purchase ledger supervisor to understand the nature of the reconciling item, and whether it has been correctly accounted for.

(ii) Substantive procedures for bank reconciliation

- Obtain Hawthorn's bank account reconciliation and cast to check the additions to ensure arithmetical accuracy.

- Agree the balance per the bank reconciliation to an original year-end bank statement and to the bank confirmation letter.

- Agree the reconciliation's balance per the cash book to the year-end cash book.

- Trace all the outstanding lodgements to the pre year-end cash book, post year-end bank statement and also to paying-in-book pre year end.

- Trace all un-presented cheques through to a pre year-end cash book and post year-end statement. For any unusual amounts or significant delays, obtain explanations from management.

- Examine any old un-presented cheques to assess if they need to be written back into the purchase ledger as they are no longer valid to be presented.

(iii) Substantive procedures for receivables

- Review the aged receivable ledger to identify any slow moving or old receivable balances, discuss the status of these balances with the credit controller to assess whether they are likely to pay.

- Select a significant sample of receivables and review whether there are any after date cash receipts, ensure that a sample of slow moving/old receivable balances is also selected.

- Review customer correspondence to identify any balances which are in dispute or unlikely to be paid.

- Review board minutes to identify whether there are any significant concerns in relation to payments by customers.

- Calculate average receivable days and compare this to prior year, investigate any significant differences.

- Inspect post year-end sales returns/credit notes and consider whether an additional allowance against receivables is required.

- Select a sample of goods despatched notes (GDN) before and just after the year end and follow through to the sales ledger to ensure they are recorded in the correct accounting period.

- Select a sample of year-end receivable balances and agree back to valid supporting documentation of GDN and sales order to ensure existence.

			Marks
	ACCA Marking scheme		

(a)	Up to 1 mark per assertion, 1/2 mark for stating assertion and 1/2 mark for explanation, max of 4 marks; up to 1 mark per relevant revenue substantive procedure, max of 4 marks.		

- Occurrence – explanation and relevant substantive procedure
- Completeness – explanation and relevant substantive procedure
- Accuracy – explanation and relevant substantive procedure
- Cut-off – explanation and relevant substantive procedure
- Classification – explanation and relevant substantive procedure
- Presentation – explanation and relevant substantive procedure

Max 8

(b) Up to 1 mark per well described procedure, overall maximum of 3 marks for supplier statement reconciliations, maximum of 4 marks for bank and maximum of 5 marks for receivables.

(i) Supplier statement reconciliation
- Select a sample of supplier statements and agree the balance to the purchase ledger
- Invoices in transit, confirm via GRN if receipt of goods was pre year end, if so confirm included in year-end accruals
- Cash in transit, confirm from cashbook and bank statements the cash was sent pre year end
- Discuss any further adjusting items with the purchase ledger supervisor to understand the nature of the reconciling item, and whether it has been correctly accounted for

Max 3

(ii) Bank reconciliation
- Check additions of bank reconciliation
- Bank balance to statement/bank confirmation
- Cash book balance to cash book
- Outstanding lodgements
- Un-presented cheques review
- Old cheques write back

Max 4

(iii) Receivables
- Aged receivables report to identify any slow moving balances
- Review the after date cash receipts
- Review customer correspondence to assess whether there are any invoices in dispute
- Review board minutes
- Calculate average receivable days
- Post year-end sales returns/credit notes
- Cut-off testing of GDN
- Agree to GDN and sales order to ensure existence

Max 5

Total			**20**

Examiner's comments

Part (a) comprised of (ai) which required four financial statement assertions relevant to classes of transactions and events and part (aii) which required an example substantive procedure for each assertion identified which would be relevant to the audit of revenue. This question was unrelated to the scenario and was knowledge based, and candidates' performance was unsatisfactory. Financial statement assertions are a key element of the F8 syllabus and so it was very disappointing to see that a significant minority of candidates do not know the assertions relevant to classes of transactions and events. A significant proportion of candidates provided existence and valuation which were irrelevant as these are assertions relevant to account balances. Where candidates did correctly identify the assertions they often failed to explain them adequately or did so with reference to assets and liabilities rather than transactions. Also many explanations were too brief or simply repeated the assertion, such as, 'accuracy ensures the amounts in the financial statements are accurate'. A number of candidates provided example procedures which were not relevant when testing revenue, but instead focused on receivables or purchases. This can only be due to a failure to read the question requirement properly. In addition many procedures were vague or incomplete, such as agreeing goods despatch notes to sales invoices but not then agreeing the invoices to the sales day book. Also many of the procedures were tests of control rather than substantive procedures. The direction of the occurrence and completeness tests were often confused resulting in incorrect procedures. The direction of occurrence tests should generally start at accounting records, whereas completeness procedures should begin at source documents.

The remainder of the question provided candidates with three short scenarios detailing matters that had been brought to attention prior to the audit fieldwork and candidates were expected to produce appropriate substantive procedures relevant to each matter. Part (bi) required substantive procedures in relation to auditing supplier statement reconciliations. Part (bii) required substantive procedures over the bank reconciliation and finally part (biii) required substantive procedures in relation to the existence and valuation of receivables. Performance on this question was unsatisfactory. A significant minority did not attempt all parts of this question. Most candidates were unable to tailor their knowledge of general substantive procedures to the specific issues in the scenario and question requirements. Many candidates spotted the terms payables, bank and receivables and proceeded to list all possible tests for these areas. This is not what was required and this approach scored few or no marks. The scenario was provided so that candidates could apply their knowledge. However it seems that many candidates did not take any notice of the scenario at all. As addressed in previous examiner's reports candidates must strive to understand substantive procedures, learning a generic list of tests will not translate to exam success as they must be responsive to the scenario.

In part (bi) candidates needed to focus on testing supplier statement reconciliations rather than trade payables in general. The most common correct answer awarded credit was 'agree the supplier statements to the payables ledger.' Very few candidates scored more than 1 mark. Incorrect answers focused on calculating trade payables days or undertaking a payables circularisation.

In part (bii) many candidates focused on auditing the cash balance rather than the bank reconciliation. Hence answers such as casting the cash book, requesting a bank confirmation letter or counting the petty cash balance were not awarded any credit. Preparation of bank reconciliations is part of the F3 Financial Accounting syllabus and therefore candidates should have considered the items which are included as part of the bank reconciliation and focused on deriving tests to audit each component. In addition to verify if un-presented cheques and outstanding lodgements were valid reconciling items, audit procedures should have focused on inclusion in the pre year-end cashbook and post year-end bank statements. Very few candidates demonstrated an understanding of this point.

In part (biii) stronger candidates were able to generate tests focusing on analytical review against prior year balances, review of aged receivables listing or discussions with management about an allowance for receivables. However, a significant proportion of candidates incorrectly suggested undertaking receivables circularisation, including the detailed steps required, this was despite the scenario clearly stating that the finance director had requested that a circularisation not be carried out. The requirement verb was to 'describe' therefore sufficient detail was required to score the 1 mark available per test.

Candidates must provide enough tests as they should assume 1 mark per valid procedure. Candidates are reminded yet again that substantive procedures are a core topic area and they must be able to produce relevant detailed procedures.

161   ROSE LEISURE CLUB   *Walk in the footsteps of a top tutor*

Key answer tips

Part (a) should represent easy marks. This requirement is straightforward textbook knowledge. Definitions like this should be committed to memory.

Part (b) of this scenario describes very specific issues that have occurred during the year and your procedures need to focus on these issues rather than the balances in general. For example, in part (i), you are not testing the payables and accruals balance in general but specifically focussing on whether the client has captured all liabilities between 25 October and 31 October. For part (ii) you need to suggest alternative procedures to the circularisation as there have been a number who have not responded, therefore alternative evidence must be obtained.

(a)   Fundamental principles

Integrity – to be straightforward and honest in all professional and business relationships.

Objectivity – to not allow bias, conflict of interest or undue influence of others to override professional or business judgements.

Professional Competence and Due Care – to maintain professional knowledge and skill at the level required to ensure that a client receives competent professional services, and to act diligently and in accordance with applicable technical and professional standards.

Confidentiality – to respect the confidentiality of information acquired as a result of professional and business relationships and, therefore, not to disclose any such information to third parties without proper authority, nor use the information for personal advantage.

Professional Behaviour – to comply with relevant laws and regulations and avoid any action that discredits the profession.

(b)   (i)   Substantive procedures – Trade payables and accruals

- Calculate the trade payable days for Rose Leisure Clubs Co (Rose) and compare to prior years, investigate any significant difference, in particular any decrease for this year.

- Compare the total trade payables and list of accruals against prior year and investigate any significant differences.

- Discuss with management the process they have undertaken to quantify the understatement of trade payables due to the cut-off error and consider the materiality of the error.

- Discuss with management whether any correcting journal entry has been included for the understatement.

- Select a sample of purchase invoices received between the period of 25 October and the year end and follow them through to inclusion within accruals or as part of the trade payables journal adjustment.

- Review after date payments; if they relate to the current year, then follow through to the purchase ledger or accrual listing to ensure they are recorded in the correct period.

- Obtain supplier statements and reconcile these to the purchase ledger balances, and investigate any reconciling items.

- Select a sample of payable balances and perform a trade payables' circularisation, follow up any non-replies and any reconciling items between the balance confirmed and the trade payables' balance.

- Select a sample of goods received notes before the year end and after the year end and follow through to inclusion in the correct period's payables balance, to ensure correct cut-off.

(ii) **Substantive procedures – Receivables**

- For non-responses, with the client's permission, the team should arrange to send a follow up circularisation.

- If the receivable does not respond to the follow up, then with the client's permission, the senior should telephone the customer and ask whether they are able to respond in writing to the circularisation request.

- If there are still non-responses, then the senior should undertake alternative procedures to confirm receivables.

- For responses with differences, the senior should identify any disputed amounts, and identify whether these relate to timing differences or whether there are possible errors in the records of Rose.

- Any differences due to timing, such as cash in transit, should be agreed to post year-end cash receipts in the cash book.

- The receivables ledger should be reviewed to identify any possible mispostings as this could be a reason for a response with a difference.

- If any balances have been flagged as disputed by the receivable, then these should be discussed with management to identify whether a write down is necessary.

(iii) **Reorganisation**

- Review the board minutes where the decision to reorganise the business was taken, ascertain if this decision was made pre year end.

- Review the announcement to shareholders in late October, to confirm that this was announced before the year end.

- Obtain a breakdown of the reorganisation provision and confirm that only direct expenditure from restructuring is included.

- Review the expenditure to confirm that there are no retraining costs included.

- Cast the breakdown of the reorganisation provision to ensure correctly calculated.

- For the costs included within the provision, agree to supporting documentation to confirm validity of items included.

- Obtain a written representation confirming management discussions in relation to the announcement of the reorganisation.

- Review the adequacy of the disclosures of the reorganisation in the financial statements to ensure they are in accordance with IAS 37 Provisions, Contingent Liabilities and Contingent Assets.

	ACCA marking scheme	Marks
(a)	Up to 1 mark per well explained point, being ½ mark for the principle and ½ mark for the explanation. Integrity Objectivity Professional competence and due care Confidentiality Professional behaviour <div align="right">**Max**</div>	<div align="right">5</div>
(b)	Up to 1 mark per well described procedure	
(i)	**Trade payables and accruals** – Calculate trade payable days – Compare total trade payables and list of accruals against prior year – Discuss with management process to quantify understatement of payables – Discuss with management whether any correcting journal adjustment posted – Sample invoices received between 25 October and year end and follow to inclusion in year-end accruals or trade payables correcting journal – Review after date payments – Review supplier statements reconciliations – Perform a trade payables' circularisation – Cut-off testing pre and post year-end GRN <div align="right">**Max**</div>	<div align="right">6</div>
(ii)	**Receivables** – For non-responses arrange to send a follow up circularisation – With the client's permission, telephone the customer and ask for a response – For remaining non-responses, undertake alternative procedures to confirm receivables – For responses with differences, identify any disputed amounts, identify whether these relate to timing differences or whether there are possible errors in the records – Cash in transit should be vouched to post year-end cash receipts in the cash book – Review receivables ledger to identify any possible mispostings – Disputed balances, discuss with management whether a write down is necessary <div align="right">**Max**</div>	<div align="right">5</div>

(iii)	**Reorganisation**	
	– Review the board minutes where decision taken	
	– Review the announcement to shareholders in late October	
	– Obtain a breakdown and confirm that only direct expenditure from restructuring is included	
	– Review expenditure to ensure retraining costs excluded	
	– Cast the breakdown of the reorganisation provision	
	– Agree costs included to supporting documentation	
	– Obtain a written representation	
	– Review the adequacy of the disclosures	
	Max	**4**
Total		**20**

Examiner's comments

Part (bi) required substantive procedures for an issue on trade payables and accruals with regards to an early cut off of the purchase ledger resulting in completeness risk. Performance on this question was unsatisfactory. Candidates were unable to tailor their knowledge of general substantive procedures to the specific issue in the scenario. Most saw that the scenario title was trade payables and accruals and proceeded to list all possible payables tests. This is not what was required and hence did not score well. The scenario was provided so that candidates could apply their knowledge; however it seems that many did not take any notice of the scenario at all. What was required was tests to specifically address the risk of cut off and completeness due to the purchase ledger being closed one week early.

Common mistakes made by candidates were:

- Providing procedures to address assertions such as rights and obligation for example 'review year end purchase invoices to ensure in the company name'.

- Giving objectives rather than procedures 'ensure that cut off is correct', this is not a substantive procedure and so would not score any marks.

- Lack of detail in tests such as 'perform analytical procedures over payables', this would score no marks as the actual analytical review procedure has not been given.

- Thinking that 'obtaining a management representation' is a valid answer for all substantive procedure questions.

- Not providing enough tests, candidates should assume 1 mark per valid procedure.

Part (bii) required substantive procedures for an issue on trade receivables circularisations with regards to non-responses and responses with differences. Performance on this question was also unsatisfactory. As above, candidates failed to identify the specific issue from the scenario and instead provided a general list of receivables tests. Some candidates failed to recognise that analytical review procedures were unlikely to be of any benefit as Rose's receivables had changed significantly on the prior year due to a change in the business model. Also Rose was a leisure club and so provided services rather than goods; however candidates still recommended 'reviewing goods despatch notes for cut off'. This again demonstrates that candidates are learning generic lists of procedures and just writing them into their answers with little thought or application to the scenario. This approach will score very few if any marks at all.

Part (biii) required substantive procedures for an issue on a reorganisation announced just before the year end. Performance on this question was also unsatisfactory; a significant minority did not even attempt this part of the question. Those candidates who scored well focused on gaining evidence of the provision, therefore they provided valid procedures like 'recalculating the provision', 'discussing the basis of the provision with management', 'obtaining a written representation confirming the assumptions and basis of the provision' and 'reviewing the board minutes to confirm management have committed to the reorganisation'. Some candidates failed to read the question properly and assumed that the reorganisation had already occurred as opposed to being announced just before the year end. Therefore many provided answers aimed at confirming that assets had been disposed of and staff had been retrained. In addition some candidates focused on whether the company was making the correct business decisions by reorganising. Many procedures also lacked sufficient detail to score the available 1 mark per test. This commonly occurred with tests such as; 'reviewing board minutes' and 'obtain written representation'. These procedures need to be phrased with sufficient detail to obtain credit, therefore if we consider the following candidates answers:

'Obtain a written representation from management' – this would not have scored any marks as it does not specify what the representation is for.

'Obtain a written representation from management in relation to the provision' – this would have scored ½ marks as it did not specify what element of the provision we wanted confirmation over.

'Obtain a written representation from management confirming the assumptions and basis of the provision'– this would have scored 1 mark as it clearly states what is required from management, and in relation to which balance and for which element. As stated in previous examiner reports, substantive procedures are a core topic area and future candidates must focus on being able to generate specific and detailed tests which are applied to any scenario provided.

162 PINEAPPLE BEACH HOTEL *Walk in the footsteps of a top tutor*

Key answer tips

In part (a) make sure you give assertions relevant to account balances. Procedures need to be properly described to earn a full mark. Make it clear what the auditor needs to do and what the procedure will achieve.

(a) **Financial statement assertions and inventory substantive procedures for balances at the year end.**

(i) **Existence**

Assets, liabilities and equity interests exist.

Substantive procedures

During the inventory count select a sample of assets recorded in the inventory records and agree to the warehouse to confirm the assets exist.

Obtain a sample of pre year-end goods despatch notes and agree that these finished goods are excluded from the inventory records.

(ii) **Rights and obligations**

The entity holds or controls the rights to assets, and liabilities are the obligations of the entity.

Substantive procedures

Confirm during the inventory count that any goods belonging to third parties are excluded from the inventory records and count.

For year-end raw materials and finished goods confirm title belongs to the company by agreeing goods to a recent purchase invoice in the company name.

(iii) **Completeness**

All assets, liabilities and equity interests that should have been recorded have been recorded.

Substantive procedures

Obtain a copy of the inventory listing and agree the total to the general ledger and the financial statements.

During the inventory count select a sample of goods physically present in the warehouse and confirm recorded in the inventory records.

(iv) **Accuracy, valuation and allocation**

Assets, liabilities and equity interests are included in the financial statements at appropriate amounts and any resulting valuation or allocation adjustments are appropriately recorded.

Substantive procedures

Select a sample of goods in inventory at the year end, agree the cost per the records to a recent purchase invoice and ensure that the cost is correctly stated.

Select a sample of year-end goods and review post year-end sales invoices to ascertain if net realisable value is above cost or if an adjustment is required.

(v) **Presentation**

Account balances are appropriately aggregated or disaggregated and clearly described, and related disclosures are relevant and understandable in the context of the applicable financial reporting framework.

Substantive procedures

Agree the breakdown of finished goods, work-in-progress and raw materials disclosed in the financial statements to the account codes within the nominal ledger.

(vi) **Classification/Presentation**

Account balances are appropriately aggregated or disaggregated and clearly described, and related disclosures are relevant and understandable in the context of the applicable financial reporting framework.

Substantive procedures

Agree the breakdown of finished goods, work-in-progress and raw materials disclosed in the financial statements to the account codes within the nominal ledger.

(b)   Substantive procedures

Depreciation

- Review the reasonableness of the depreciation rates applied to the new leisure facilities and compare to industry averages.

- Review the capital expenditure budgets for the next few years to assess whether there are any plans to replace any of the new leisure equipment, as this would indicate that the useful life is less than 10 years.

- Review profits and losses on disposal of assets disposed of in the year, to assess the reasonableness of the depreciation policies.

- Select a sample of leisure equipment and recalculate the depreciation charge to ensure that the non-current asset register is correct.

- Perform a proof in total calculation for the depreciation charged on the equipment, discuss with management if significant fluctuations arise.

- Review the disclosure of the depreciation charges and policies in the draft financial statements.

Food poisoning

- Review the correspondence from the customers claiming food poisoning to assess whether Pineapple has a present obligation as a result of a past event.

- Send an enquiry letter to the lawyers of Pineapple to obtain their view as to the probability of the claim being successful.

- Review board minutes to understand whether the directors believe that the claim will be successful or not.

- Review the post year-end period to assess whether any payments have been made to any of the claimants.

- Discuss with management as to whether they propose to include a contingent liability disclosure or not, consider the reasonableness of this.

- Obtain a written management representation confirming management's view that the lawsuit is unlikely to be successful and hence no provision is required.

- Review the adequacy of any disclosures made in the financial statements.

(c)   Working papers

- Name of client – identifies the client being audited.
- Year-end date – identifies the year end to which the audit working papers relate.
- Subject – identifies the area of the financial statements that is being audited, the topic area of the working paper, such as receivables circularisation.
- Working paper reference – provides a clear reference to identify the number of the working paper, for example, R12 being the 12th working paper in the audit of receivables.

- Preparer – identifies the name of the audit team member who prepared the working paper, so any queries can be directed to the relevant person.

- Date prepared – the date that the audit work was performed by the team member; this helps to identify what was known at the time and what issues may have occurred subsequently.

- Reviewer – the name of the audit team member who reviewed the working paper; this provides evidence that the audit work was reviewed by an appropriate member of the team.

- Date of review – the date the audit work was reviewed by the senior member of the team; this should be prior to the date that the audit report was signed.

- Objective of work/test – the aim of the work being performed, could be the related financial statement assertion; this provides the context for why the audit procedure is being performed.

- Details of work performed – the audit tests performed along with sufficient detail of items selected for testing.

- Results of work performed – whether any exceptions arose in the audit work and if any further work is required.

- Conclusion – the overall conclusion on the audit work performed, whether the area is true and fair.

	ACCA marking scheme	Marks
(a)	Up to 1 mark per assertion, ½ mark for stating assertion and ½ mark for explanation, max of 4 marks; up to 1 mark per relevant inventory substantive procedure, max of 4 marks. Existence – explanation and relevant substantive procedure Rights and obligations – explanation and relevant substantive procedure Completeness – explanation and relevant substantive procedure Valuation and allocation – explanation and relevant substantive procedure Classification – explanation and relevant substantive procedure Presentation – explanation and relevant substantive procedure **Max**	**8**
(b)	Up to 1 mark per relevant substantive procedure, max of 4 marks for each issue. **Depreciation** Review the reasonableness of the depreciation rates and compare to industry averages Review the capital expenditure budgets Review profits and losses on disposal for assets disposed of in year Recalculate the depreciation charge for a sample of assets Perform a proof in total calculation for the depreciation charged on the equipment Review the disclosure of depreciation in the draft financial statements **Food poisoning** Review the correspondence from the customers Send an enquiry to the lawyers as to the probability of the claim being successful Review board minutes Review the post year-end period to assess whether any payments have been made Discuss with management as to whether they propose to include a contingent liability disclosure Obtain a written management representation Review any disclosures made in the financial statements **Max**	**8**

(c)	Up to 1 mark per well explained point, ½ mark only if just identifies item to be included, max of 4 points.		
	Name of client		
	Year-end date		
	Subject		
	Working paper reference		
	Preparer		
	Date prepared		
	Reviewer		
	Date of review		
	Objective of work/test		
	Details of work performed		
	Results of work performed		
	Conclusion		
		Max	4
Total			20

Examiner's comments

This question required substantive procedures for depreciation and a contingent liability for a food poisoning case. Performance on this question was unsatisfactory. A significant minority did not even attempt this part of the question. Candidates' answers for depreciation tended to be weaker than for the food poisoning. On the depreciation many candidates did not focus their answer on the issue identified, which related to the depreciation method adopted for the capital expenditure incurred in the year. In the scenario the issue was headed up as depreciation and so this should have given candidates a clue that they needed to focus just on depreciation. However, a significant proportion of answers were on general PPE tests often without any reference at all to depreciation. In addition many felt that generic tests such as 'get an expert's advice' or 'obtain management representation' were appropriate tests; they are not. The food poisoning issue tended to be answered slightly better; however again tests tended to be too brief, 'read board minutes', 'discuss with management' or 'discuss with the lawyer' did not score any marks as they do not explain what is to be discussed or what we are looking for in the board minutes. In addition a minority of candidates focused on auditing the kitchen and food hygiene procedures with tests such as 'observing the kitchen process' or 'writing to customers to see if they have had food poisoning.' This is not the focus of the auditor and does not provide evidence with regards to the potential contingent liability.

Substantive procedures are a core topic area and future candidates must focus on being able to generate specific and detailed tests.

163 TIRROL *Walk in the footsteps of a top tutor*

Key answer tips

Part (a) requires both repetition and application of basic knowledge regarding the use of CAATs. However, the latter carries the majority of the marks and for this reason candidates must refer to the specific information to obtain good quality marks. Simple repetition of learned facts regarding the drawbacks of CAATs will not obtain good marks for this reason.

For each point of explanation relevant to Tirrol you will be awarded 1 mark. Therefore for part (i) you need to make four points of explanation. For part (ii) you need 5 explained problems and five methods of overcoming those problems.

Part (b) again requires a mix of basic knowledge (i.e. what procedures must be performed before reliance is placed on the documentation produced by the internal audit department) and application to the facts presented in the scenario.

(a) (i) Benefits of using audit software

Standard systems at client

The same computerised systems and programs as used in all 25 branches of Tirrol Co. This means that the same audit software can be used in each location providing significant time savings compared to the situation where client systems are different in each location.

Use actual computer files not copies or printouts

Use of audit software means that the Tirrol Co's actual inventory files can be tested rather than having to rely on printouts or screen images. The latter could be incorrect, by accident or by deliberate mistake. The audit firm will have more confidence that the 'real' files have been tested.

Test more items

Use of software will mean that more inventory records can be tested – it is possible that all product lines could be tested for obsolescence rather than a sample using manual techniques. The auditor will therefore gain more evidence and have greater confidence that inventory is valued correctly.

Cost

The relative cost of using audit software decreases the more years that software is used. Any cost overruns this year could be offset against the audit fees in future years when the actual expense will be less.

(ii) Problems on the audit of Tirrol

Timescale – six week reporting deadline – audit planning

The audit report is due to be signed six weeks after the year end. This means that there will be considerable pressure on the auditor to complete audit work without compromising standards by rushing procedures.

This problem can be overcome by careful planning of the audit, use of experienced staff and ensuring other staff such as second partner reviews are booked well in advance.

Timescale – six week reporting deadline – software issues

The audit report is due to be signed about six weeks after the year end. This means that there is little time to write and test audit software, let alone use the software and evaluate the results of testing.

This problem can be alleviated by careful planning. Access to Tirrol Co's software and data files must be obtained as soon as possible and work commenced on tailoring Cal & Co's software following this. Specialist computer audit staff should be booked as soon as possible to perform this work.

First year audit costs

The relative costs of an audit in the first year at a client tend to be greater due to the additional work of ascertaining client systems. This means that Cal & Co may have a limited budget to document systems including computer systems.

This problem can be alleviated to some extent again by good audit planning. The manager must also monitor the audit process carefully, ensuring that any additional work caused by the client not providing access to systems information including computer systems is identified and added to the total billing cost of the audit.

Staff holidays

Most of the audit work will be carried out in July, which is also the month when many of Cal & Co staff take their annual holiday. This means that there will be a shortage of audit staff, particularly as audit work for Tirrol Co is being booked with little notice.

The problem can be alleviated by booking staff as soon as possible and then identifying any shortages. Where necessary, staff may be borrowed from other offices or even different countries on a secondment basis where shortages are acute.

Non-standard systems

Tirrol Co's computer software is non-standard, having been written specifically for the organisation. This means that more time will be necessary to understand the system than if standard systems were used.

This problem can be alleviated either by obtaining documentation from the client or by approaching the software house (with Tirrol Co's permission) to see if they can assist with provision of information on data structures for the inventory systems. Provision of this information will decrease the time taken to tailor audit software for use in Tirrol Co.

Issues of live testing

Cal & Co has been informed that inventory systems must be tested on a live basis. This increases the risk of accidental amendment or deletion of client data systems compared to testing copy files.

To limit the possibility of damage to client systems, Cal & Co can consider performing inventory testing on days when Tirrol Co is not operating e.g. weekends. At the worst, backups of data files taken from the previous day can be re-installed when Cal & Co's testing is complete.

Computer systems

The client has 25 locations, with each location maintaining its own computer system. It is possible that computer systems are not common across the client due to amendments made at the branch level.

This problem can be overcome to some extent by asking staff at each branch whether systems have been amended and focusing audit work on material branches.

Usefulness of audit software

The use of audit software at Tirrol Co does appear to have significant problems this year. This means that even if the audit software is ready, there may still be some risk of incorrect conclusions being derived due to lack of testing, etc.

This problem can be alleviated by seriously considering the possibility of using a manual audit this year. The manager may need to investigate whether a manual audit is feasible and if so whether it could be completed within the necessary timescale with minimal audit risk.

(b) **Reliance on internal audit documentation**

There are two issues to consider; the ability of internal audit to produce the documentation and the actual accuracy of the documentation itself.

The ability of the internal audit department to produce the documentation can be determined by:

- Ensuring that the department has staff who have appropriate qualifications. Provision of a relevant qualification e.g. membership of a computer related institute would be appropriate.

- Ensuring that this and similar documentation is produced using a recognised plan and that the documentation is tested prior to use. The use of different staff in the internal audit department to produce and test documentation will increase confidence in its accuracy.

- Ensuring that the documentation is actually used during internal audit work and that problems with documentation are noted and investigated as part of that work. Being given access to internal audit reports on the inventory software will provide appropriate evidence.

Regarding the actual documentation:

- Reviewing the documentation to ensure that it appears logical and that terms and symbols are used consistently throughout. This will provide evidence that the flowcharts, etc. should be accurate.

- Comparing the documentation against the 'live' inventory system to ensure it correctly reflects the inventory system. This comparison will include tracing individual transactions through the inventory systems.

- Using part of the documentation to amend Cal & Co's audit software, and then ensuring that the software processes inventory system data accurately. However, this stage may be limited due to the need to use live files at Tirrol Co.

				Marks
ACCA marking scheme				
(a)	(i)	**Benefits of audit software**		
		1 mark per benefit – 0.5 for identifying the benefit and 0.5 for explaining the benefit.		
		• Standard systems		
		• Use actual computer files		
		• Test more items		
		• Cost		
			Max	4
	(ii)	**Problems in the audit of Tirrol**		
		2 marks for each problem. 1 for explaining the problem and 1 for explaining how to alleviate the problem.		
		• Six week reporting deadline		
		• Timescale – software issues		
		• First year audit costs		
		• Staff holidays		
		• Non-standard systems		
		• Live testing		
		• Usefulness of audit software		
			Max	10
(b)		Reliance on internal audit documentation		
		1 mark per point		
		• Appropriate qualifications		
		• Produced according to plan		
		• Problems with use noted		
		• Documentation logical		
		• Compare to live system		
		• Use documentation to amend audit software		
			Max	6
Total				20

Examiner's comments

In part (ai), most candidates demonstrated basic knowledge of the use of audit software. A few candidates made some good links to the scenario, for example, explaining how data could be amalgamated to avoid having to visit the 25 branches in the company.

In part (aii), again most candidates provided a range of valid points and obtained decent marks. However, common deficiencies in this section included:

- Not explaining how to overcome the deficiency either by omitting this comment or by making unrealistic comments. E.g. in terms of potential damage to client systems from the use of test data, suggesting the deficiency would be overcome by 'being careful' or in a handful of answers by simply not accepting the audit engagement.

- Suggesting deficiencies that were not mentioned in the scenario. For example, suggesting that inventory valuation would be difficult as experts on car parts were difficult to find, or that the auditor had to attend all 25 locations simultaneously to prevent the client double counting inventory in more than one location.

- Recommending amendments to the client systems for other perceived deficiencies. For example, stating that a distributed processing system was not appropriate for the client and recommending a centralised system instead. Even if this was a recommendation to the client, it would not affect audit planning now and so was not relevant as a current audit problem.

In part (b) most candidates obtained a marginal result explaining either how the internal audit department itself could be relied on or the documentation; only a minority of answers mentioned both. Marks were generally obtained from:

- Considering the work of internal audit in areas such as experience in computer systems, and quality of documentation provided, and

- Testing the documentation itself for example, in comparison to the actual system using walk-through or similar testing methods, or obtaining advice from external specialists.

There were relatively few less relevant points in this section. The main area of weakness related to candidates spending too much time explaining the appointment and general work of internal audit rather than placing reliance on this function.

AUDIT FRAMEWORK

164 CINNAMON *Walk in the footsteps of a top tutor*

Key answer tips

Parts (a) and (b) deal with acceptance of the engagement. For part (a) think of matters that could cause the firm to reject the client. Remember that firm's should only accept clients and work of acceptable risk. Part (b) asks you to 'state' the matters to be included in the engagement letter therefore no explanation needs to be provided.

Part (c) covers quality control which is new to the syllabus. Any students resitting this paper should make sure they have familiarised themselves with this new syllabus area.

Part (d) is a straightforward ethical threats scenario. Make sure you explain how the thical issue could affect the auditor's behaviour in your explanation.

(a)   (i)   Steps prior to accepting the audit of Cinnamon

ISA 210 requirements

ISA 210 *Agreeing the Terms of Audit Engagements* provides guidance to Salt & Pepper & Co (Salt & Pepper) on the steps they should take in accepting the new audit client, Cinnamon. It sets out a number of processes that the auditor should perform prior to accepting a new engagement, in addition to considering whether preconditions for the audit are in place.

Independence

Salt & Pepper should consider any issues which might arise which could threaten compliance with ACCA's *Code of Ethics and Conduct* or any local legislation, including conflict of interest with existing clients. If issues arise, then their significance must be considered.

Competence

In addition, they should consider whether they are competent to perform the work and whether they would have appropriate resources available, as well as any specialist skills or knowledge required for the audit of Cinnamon.

Integrity of management

Salt & Pepper should consider what they already know about the directors of Cinnamon; they need to consider the reputation and integrity of the directors. If necessary, the firm may want to obtain references if they do not formally know the directors.

Level of risk

Additionally, Salt & Pepper should consider the level of risk attached to the audit of Cinnamon and whether this is acceptable to the firm. As part of this, they should consider whether the expected audit fee is adequate in relation to the risk of auditing Cinnamon.

Communicate with outgoing auditor

Salt & Pepper should communicate with the outgoing auditor of Cinnamon to assess if there are any ethical or professional reasons why they should not accept appointment. They should obtain permission from Cinnamon's management to contact the existing auditor; if this is not given, then the engagement should be refused.

If given permission to respond, the auditors should reply to Salt & Pepper, who should carefully review the response for any issues that could affect acceptance.

(ii)   **Preconditions for the audit**

ISA 210 *Agreeing the Terms of Audit Engagements* requires auditors to only accept a new audit engagement when it has been confirmed that the preconditions for an audit are present.

To assess whether the preconditions for an audit are present, Salt & Pepper must determine whether the financial reporting framework to be applied in the preparation of Cinnamon's financial statements is acceptable. In considering this, the auditor should assess the nature of the entity, the nature and purpose of the financial statements and whether law or regulations prescribes the applicable reporting framework.

In addition, they must obtain the agreement of Cinnamon's management that it acknowledges and understands its responsibility for the following:

*   Preparation of the financial statements in accordance with the applicable financial reporting framework, including where relevant their fair presentation;

*   For such internal control as management determines is necessary to enable the preparation of financial statements which are free from material misstatement, whether due to fraud or error; and

*   To provide Salt & Pepper with access to all relevant information for the preparation of the financial statements, any additional information that the auditor may request from management and unrestricted access to persons within Cinnamon from whom the auditor determines it necessary to obtain audit evidence.

If the preconditions for an audit are not present, Salt & Pepper shall discuss the matter with Cinnamon's management.

Unless required by law or regulation to do so, the auditor shall not accept the proposed audit engagement:

- If the auditor has determined that the financial reporting framework to be applied in the preparation of the financial statements is unacceptable; or

- If management agreement of their responsibilities has not been obtained.

(b)   Engagement letters

Matters to be included in an audit engagement letter:

- The objective and scope of the audit
- The responsibilities of the auditor
- The responsibilities of management
- Identification of the financial reporting framework for the preparation of the financial statements
- Expected form and content of any reports to be issued
- Elaboration of the scope of the audit with reference to legislation
- The form of any other communication of results of the audit engagement
- The fact that some material misstatements may not be detected
- Arrangements regarding the planning and performance of the audit, including the composition of the audit team
- The expectation that management will provide written representations
- The basis on which fees are computed and any billing arrangements
- A request for management to acknowledge receipt of the audit engagement letter and to agree to the terms of the engagement
- Arrangements concerning the involvement of internal auditors and other staff of the entity
- Any obligations to provide audit working papers to other parties
- Any restriction on the auditor's liability
- Arrangements to make available draft financial statements and any other information.

(c)   Quality control

- The audit team should be properly briefed about the client to enable them to obtain an understanding of the client before they start their work.
- Adequate supervision should be given to the audit juniors to ensure they have someone more senior they can refer to in case of any queries.
- Supervision will also enable the progress of the audit to be tracked to ensure the tight reporting deadline can be met.
- More audit staff may need to be assigned to the team to ensure there is sufficient time to complete the audit work without it being rushed. If the work is rushed, misstatements are more likely to go undetected.
- Review of work should be performed more frequently in order to identify issues promptly so they can be raised with the client and resolved quickly.
- An engagement quality control reviewer may be assigned as the engagement is considered high risk.

(d) **Ethical risks and steps to reduce the risks**

Ethical risk	*Steps to reduce the risks*
Salt & Pepper intends to use junior staff for the audit of their new client Cinnamon as the timing of the audit is when the firm is very busy.	Salt & Pepper should review the staffing of Cinnamon and make changes to increase the amount of experienced team members. If this is not possible, they should discuss with the directors of Cinnamon to see whether the timing of the audit could be moved to a point where the firm has adequate staff resources.
As a new engagement, Salt & Pepper has little knowledge of the risks associated with this audit. If they use too junior staff, they will not be competent enough to assess whether they have performed adequate work, and the risk of giving an incorrect audit opinion is increased.	
Salt & Pepper has not contacted Cinnamon's previous auditors.	Salt & Pepper should contact the previous auditors to identify if there are any ethical issues which would prevent them from acting as auditors of Cinnamon.
Contacting the previous auditors is important as the firm needs to understand why Cinnamon has changed their auditors. They may have been acting unethically and their previous auditors therefore refused to continue.	
In addition, it is professional courtesy to contact the previous auditors.	
The firm is not updating engagement letters for existing clients on the basis that they do not change much on a yearly basis.	Salt & Pepper should comply fully with ISA 210 and annually review the need for revising the engagement letters.
This is not in accordance with ISA 210 *Agreeing the Terms of Audit Engagements* as even if engagement letters are not changed, they should still be reviewed to ensure that they are still relevant and up to date.	
An existing client of Salt & Pepper has proposed an audit fee based on a percentage of the client's final pre-tax profit.	Salt & Pepper should politely decline the proposed contingent fee arrangement as it would be a breach of
This is a contingent fee arrangement and is prohibited as it creates a self-interest threat which cannot be reduced to an adequate level.	ACCA's *Code of Ethics and Conduct*. Instead they should inform the client that the fees will be based on the level of work required to obtain sufficient and appropriate audit evidence.

				Marks
		ACCA marking scheme		

ACCA marking scheme

				Marks

(a)   (i)   Up to 1 mark per well described point.
- Compliance with ACCA's Code of Ethics and Conduct
- Competent
- Reputation and integrity of directors
- Level of risk of Cinnamon audit
- Fee adequate to compensate for risk
- Write to outgoing auditor after obtaining permission to contact
- Review response for any issues

                                                              Max   **5**

     (ii)   Up to 1 mark per valid point.
- Determination of acceptable framework
- Agreement of management responsibilities
- Preparation of financial statements with applicable framework
- Internal controls
- Provide auditor with relevant information and access
- If preconditions are not present discuss with management
- Decline if framework unacceptable
- Decline if agreement of responsibilities not obtained

                                                              Max   **3**

(b)   ½ mark per valid point.
- Objective/scope
- Responsibilities of auditor
- Responsibilities of management
- Identification of framework for financial statements
- Form/content reports
- Elaboration of scope
- Form of communications
- Some misstatements may be missed
- Arrangement for audit
- Written representations required
- Fees/billing
- Management acknowledge letter
- Internal auditor arrangements
- Obligations to provide working papers to others
- Restriction on auditor's liability
- Arrangements to make draft financial statements available

                                                              Max   **2**

(c)   Up to 1 mark per explained point
- Briefing of staff
- Supervision – in case of queries
- Supervision – tracking the progress of the audit
- Increase the size of the team to alleviate time pressure
- Frequent review
- Engagement quality control review

                                                              Max   **4**

(d)   Up to 1 mark per well explained ethical risk and up to 1 mark per well explained step to reduce risk, max of 3 marks for risks and max 3 marks for steps to reduce.
- Use of junior staff
- Contact previous auditor of Cinnamon Brothers Co
- Engagement letters not updated
- Contingent fees

                                                              Max   **6**

Total   **20**

Examiner's comments

This question was based on the audit firm Salt & Pepper & Co and tested candidates' knowledge of ethical threats.

Part (ai) required a description of the steps the firm should take prior to accepting a new audit client Cinnamon Brothers Co (Cinnamon). Candidates performed satisfactorily on this part of the question. Many candidates were able to identify a good range of points including ensuring the firm had adequate resources to complete this audit, identifying if any ethical threats arise, understanding the entity and contacting the previous auditors. However some candidates focused solely on obtaining professional clearance from the previous auditors and it was not uncommon to see a whole page on the detailed steps to be taken. The question requirement was steps prior to accepting an audit; it was not the process for obtaining professional clearance. Those that focused solely on this area would not have scored enough marks to pass this part of the question. Candidates are reminded to answer the question actually asked as opposed to the one they wish had been asked. In addition, some candidates provided answers which focused on the engagement letter; this was incorrect as an engagement letter is only produced once an engagement has been accepted as opposed to prior to acceptance.

Part (aii) required the steps the firm should take to confirm whether the preconditions for the audit were in place. Where it was answered, candidates performed unsatisfactorily on this question. Answers tended to be in two camps, those who had studied preconditions and were able to score all three marks and those who had not studied it and so failed to score any marks. This is a knowledge area and has been tested previously. Candidates must practice past exam questions and ensure they study the breadth of the syllabus. Those candidates who did not score well, tended to repeat points that had been made in part (ai) of the question or they included points that should have been in their answer for (ai). Some chose to combine their answers for (ai) and (aii) together, this tended to produce unfocused answers.

Part (d) required identification and explanation of ethical risks which arise from the audit firm's actions and how these risks may be reduced. This question was answered well by most candidates. Candidates were able to identify from the scenario the ethical risks arising from the firm's actions. Some candidates did not explain the risks correctly or in sufficient detail, sometimes just identifying the risk and not explaining correctly how this was an ethical issue. For example, many identified the risk of the audit fee being based on a percentage of the client's pre-tax profit; however this was incorrectly explained as being an issue of fee dependence rather than it being a contingent fee. As the risk was incorrectly explained this resulted in an irrelevant action for reducing the ethical risk. Therefore only the ½ marks for identification would have been awarded. In addition some candidates incorrectly thought that there was an ethical risk because Cinnamon wanted their audit complete by February. The ethical risk was that in order to meet the client's deadline the firm would be using more junior staff and hence increased the risk of giving an incorrect opinion.

The second part of this question required steps for reducing the ethical risks. Candidates' performance was generally satisfactory although some answers tended to be quite brief. For example for the risk of the engagement letters not being updated, the response given by some candidates was 'Update the engagement letters,' this is not a sufficiently detailed explanation.

165   ORANGE FINANCIALS *Walk in the footsteps of a top tutor*

Key answer tips

This is a typical ethical threats question focusing on threats to objectivity. Remember to explain the threat properly, don't just state the name of the threat but explain how it could affect the auditor's behaviour when performing the audit.

(a)   Responsibilities of auditor in relation to fraud and error

- An auditor conducting an audit in accordance with ISA 240 *The Auditor's Responsibilities Relating to Fraud in an Audit of Financial Statements is* responsible for obtaining reasonable assurance that the financial statements taken as a whole are free from material misstatement, whether caused by fraud or error.

- In order to fulfil this responsibility auditors are required to identify and assess the risks of material misstatement of the financial statements due to fraud.

- The auditor will need to obtain sufficient appropriate audit evidence regarding the assessed risks of material misstatement due to fraud, through designing and implementing appropriate responses.

- In addition, the auditor must respond appropriately to fraud or suspected fraud identified during the audit.

- When obtaining reasonable assurance, the auditor is responsible for maintaining professional scepticism throughout the audit, considering the potential for management override of controls and recognising the fact that audit procedures that are effective in detecting error may not be effective in detecting fraud.

- To ensure that the whole engagement team is aware of the risks and responsibilities for fraud and error, ISAs require that a discussion is held within the team. For members not present at the meeting the engagement partner should determine which matters are to be communicated to them.

(b)   Ethical threats and managing these risks

Ethical Threat	*Managing Risk*
Orange Financials Co (Orange) has asked the engagement partner of Currant & Co to attend meetings with potential investors. This represents an advocacy threat as the audit firm may be perceived as promoting investment in Orange and this threatens objectivity.	The engagement partner should politely decline this request from Orange, as it represents too great a threat to independence.

Ethical Threat

Due to the stock exchange listing, Orange has requested that Currant & Co produce the financial statements. This represents a self-review threat. As Orange is currently not a listed company then Currant & Co are permitted to produce the financial statements and also audit them.

However, Orange is seeking a listing and therefore these financial statements will be critical to the potential investors and this increases audit risk.

The assistant finance director of Orange has joined Currant & Co as a partner and has been proposed as the review partner.

This represents a self-review threat, as he was in a position to influence the financial statements whilst working at Orange; if he is the review partner there could be a risk of him reviewing his own work.

Orange has several potential assurance assignments available and Currant & Co wish to be appointed to these. There is a potential self-interest threat as these assurance fees along with the external audit fee could represent a significant proportion of Currant & Co's fee income.

Orange has implied to Currant & Co that they must complete the audit quickly and with minimal questions/issues if they wish to obtain the assurance assignments.

This creates an intimidation threat on the team as they may feel pressure to cut corners and not raise issues, and this could compromise the objectivity of the audit team.

Managing Risk

Ideally, Currant & Co should not undertake the preparation of the financial statements. Due to the imminent listing, this would probably represent too high a risk.

If Currant & Co choose to produce the financial statements then separate teams should undertake each assignment and the audit team should not be part of the accounts preparation process.

This partner must not be involved in the audit of Orange for a period of at least two years. An alternative review partner should be appointed

The firm should assess whether these assignments along with the audit fee would represent more than 15% of gross practice income for two consecutive years. These assurance assignments will only arise if the company obtains its listing and hence will be a public interest company.

If the recurring fees are likely to exceed 15% of annual practice income then additional consideration should be given as to whether these assignments should be sought by the firm.

The engagement partner should politely inform the finance director that the team will undertake the audit in accordance with all relevant ISAs and their own quality control procedures. This means that the audit will take as long as is necessary to obtain sufficient, appropriate evidence to form an opinion. If any residual concerns remain or the intimidation threat continues then Currant & Co may need to consider resigning from the engagement.

Ethical Threat	*Managing Risk*
The finance director has offered the team a free weekend away at a luxury hotel. This represents a self-interest threat as the acceptance of goods and services, unless insignificant in value, is not permitted.	As it is unlikely that a weekend at a luxury hotel for the whole team has an insignificant value, then this offer should be politely declined.
The finance director has offered a senior team member a loan at discounted interest rates.	This loan must not be accepted by the audit senior due to the preferential terms.
Orange does provide loans and hence the provision of a loan is within the normal course of business. However, if the loan is on preferential rates, as this is, then it would represent a self-interest threat.	However, if the terms of the loan are amended so that the interest rate charged is in line with Orange's normal levels, then the provision of the loan is acceptable.

(c) **Benefits of audit committee for Orange Financials Co**

Appointing an audit committee will benefit Orange in the following ways:

- It will help to improve the quality of the financial reporting of Orange; whilst the company already has a finance director, the audit committee will assist by reviewing the financial statements.

- The establishment of an audit committee can help to improve the internal control environment of the company. The audit committee is able to devote more time and attention to areas such as internal controls.

- Orange does not currently have any non-executive directors, hence once appointed, they will bring considerable outside experience to the executive directors as well as challenging their decisions and contributing to an independent judgement.

- The finance director will benefit in that he will be able to raise concerns and discuss accounting issues with the audit committee.

- The audit committee will be responsible for appointing the external auditors and this will strengthen the auditors' independence and contribute to a channel of communication and forum of issues.

- If Orange has an internal audit (IA) department, then establishing an audit committee will also improve the independence of IA.

- The audit committee can also provide advice on risk management to the executive directors. They can create a climate of discipline and control and reduce the opportunity for fraud, and increase the public confidence in the credibility and objectivity of the financial statements.

<table>
<tr><td colspan="3" align="center">**ACCA marking scheme**</td></tr>
<tr><td></td><td></td><td align="right">*Marks*</td></tr>
<tr>
<td>(a)</td>
<td>Up to 1 mark per well explained point
Per ISA 240 – obtain reasonable assurance that the financial statements are free from material misstatement, whether caused by fraud or error
Identify and assess the risks of material misstatement due to fraud
Obtain sufficient appropriate audit evidence
Respond appropriately to fraud or suspected fraud identified during the audit
Maintain professional scepticism throughout the audit
Discussion within the engagement team</td>
<td></td>
</tr>
<tr><td></td><td align="right">**Max**</td><td align="center">**4**</td></tr>
<tr>
<td>(b)</td>
<td>Up to 1 mark per ethical threat and up to 1 mark per managing method, max of 6 for threats and max 6 for methods
Engagement partner attending listing meeting
Preparation of financial statements
Assistant finance director as review partner on audit
Total fee income
Pressure to complete audit quickly and with minimal issues
Weekend away at luxury hotel
Provision of loan at preferential rates</td>
<td></td>
</tr>
<tr><td></td><td align="right">**Max**</td><td align="center">**12**</td></tr>
<tr>
<td>(c)</td>
<td>Up to 1 mark per well explained point
Improve the quality of the financial reporting
Improve the internal control environment of the company
Non-executives will bring outside experience to the executive directors
The finance director will be able to raise concerns with the audit committee
The audit committee will be responsible for appointing the external auditors
Establishing an audit committee will improve the independence of IA
Provide advice on risk management to the executive directors</td>
<td></td>
</tr>
<tr><td></td><td align="right">**Max**</td><td align="center">**4**</td></tr>
<tr><td>**Total**</td><td></td><td align="center">**20**</td></tr>
</table>

Examiner's comments

This question required an explanation of ethical threats from the scenario and a method for reducing each of these threats. This was very well answered with many candidates scoring full marks. Ethics questions are often answered well by candidates and the scenario provided contained many possible threats. Where candidates did not score well this was usually because they only identified rather than explained the ethical threat. In addition some candidates identified the threat but when explaining them they came up with incorrect examples of the type of threat; such as attending the weekend away at a luxury hotel gave rise to a familiarity threat rather than a self-interest threat. The threat which candidates struggled with the most was the intimidation threat caused by management requesting the audit team ask minimal questions. The response given by many candidates was to decline the assurance engagement; this does not address the intimidation threat. Instead candidates needed to stress that this issue needed to be discussed with the finance director and that appropriate audit procedures would be undertaken to ensure the quality of the audit was not compromised. In addition when explaining issues some candidates listed many examples of ethical threats; such as 'the assistant finance director being the review partner gives rise to a familiarity, self-review and self-interest threat.' This scatter gun approach to questions is not recommended as it wastes time.

166 LV FONES CO *Walk in the footsteps of a top tutor*

Key answer tips

Part (a) asks for the five threats to objectivity and examples of each. Be specific with your examples. It is not good enough to say for example, providing non-audit services as an example of a self-review threat. You need to give specific examples of non-audit services which would create such a threat.

Part (b) requires you to apply your knowledge of ethics to the specific circumstances in the scenario. Given that the two elements of the question are linked, a table format is appropriate for your answer.

Part (c) requires steps prior to accepting the audit. These are the considerations that would affect the auditor's decision to accept. A common sense approach can be taken to this question if you don't know the knowledge. Think about what would make you decline the engagement. Remember that the audit firm should only accept clients and engagements of an acceptable level of risk.

(a) Compliance with ACCA's Code of Ethics and Conduct fundamental principles can be threatened by a number of areas. The five categories of threats, which may impact on ethical risk, are:

- Self-interest
- Self-review
- Advocacy
- Familiarity
- Intimidation.

Examples for each category (Only one example required per threat):

Self-interest

- Undue dependence on fee income from one client
- Close personal or business relationships
- Financial interest in a client
- Incentive fee arrangements
- Concern over employment security
- Commercial pressure from outside the employing organisation
- Inappropriate personal use of corporate assets.

Self-review

- Member of assurance team being or recently having been employed by the client in a position to influence the subject matter being reviewed
- Involvement in implementation of financial system and subsequently reporting on the operation of said system
- Same person reviewing decisions or data that prepared them
- An analyst, or member of a board, audit committee or audit firm being in a position to exert a direct or significant influence over the financial reports

- The discovery of a significant error during a re-evaluation of the work undertaken by the member
- Performing a service for a client that directly affects the subject matter of an assurance engagement.

Advocacy

- Acting as an advocate on behalf of a client in litigation or disputes
- Promoting shares in a listed audit client
- Commenting publicly on future events in particular circumstances
- Where information is incomplete or advocating an argument which is unlawful.

Familiarity

- Long association with a client
- Acceptance of gifts or preferential treatment (significant value)
- Over familiarity with management
- Former partner of firm being employed by client
- A person in a position to influence financial or non-financial reporting or business decisions having an immediate or close family member who is in a position to benefit from that influence.

Intimidation

- Threat of litigation
- Threat of removal as assurance firm
- Dominant personality of client director attempting to influence decisions
- Pressure to reduce inappropriately the extent of work performed in order to reduce fees.

(b)

Ethical threat	Managing risk
The audit team has in previous years been offered a staff discount of 10% on purchasing luxury mobile phones.	The audit firm should ascertain whether the discount is to be offered to staff this year.
This is a familiarity threat. It would need to be confirmed if this discount is to be offered to this year's team as well, as only goods of an insignificant value are allowed to be accepted. A discount of 10% may not appear to be significant, but as these are luxury mobile phones then this may still be a significant value.	If it is then the discount should be reviewed for significance. If it is deemed to be of significant value then the offer of discount should be declined.
An audit senior of Jones & Co has been on secondment as the financial controller of LV Fones and is currently part of the audit team.	The firm should clarify exactly what areas the senior assisted the client on. If he worked on areas not related to the financial statements then he may be able to remain in the audit team.
There is a self-review threat if the senior has prepared records or schedules that support the year-end financial statements and he then audits these same documents.	However, it is likely that he has worked on some related schedules and therefore he should be removed from the audit team to ensure that independence is not threatened.

(b)

Ethical threat	**Managing risk**
The total fee income from LV Fones is 16% of the total fees for the audit firm. If the fees for audit and recurring work exceed 15% then there is a self-interest threat.	The firm should assess if the recurring fees will exceed 15%. If this is the case then it might need to consider whether the appearance of independence will still be met if the tax and audit work is retained.
The fees for LV Fones include tax and audit that are assumed to be recurring. However the secondment fees would not recur each year.	No further work should be accepted in the current year from the client, and it might be advisable to perform external quality control reviews. It may also become necessary to consider resigning from either the tax or the audit engagement.
The partner and the finance director know each other socially and have holidayed together. Personal relationships between the client and members of the audit team can create a familiarity or self-interest threat.	The personal relationship should be reviewed in line with Jones's ethical policies.
ACCA's *Code of Ethics and Conduct* does not specifically prohibit friendships between the audit client and the team. However, due to the senior positions held by both parties then there is a risk that independence may be perceived to have been threatened.	Consideration should be given to rotating the partner off this engagement and replacing with an alternative partner.
Last year's audit fee is still outstanding. This amounts to 20% of the total fee and is likely to be a significant value.	Jones & Co should chase the outstanding fees.
A self-interest threat can arise if the fees remain outstanding, as Jones & Co may feel pressure to agree to certain accounting adjustments in order to have the previous year and the current year fee paid.	If they remain outstanding, the firm should discuss with those charged with governance the reasons for the continued non-payment, and ideally agree a payment schedule which will result in the fees being settled before much more work is performed for the current year audit.
In addition outstanding fees could be perceived as a loan to a client, this is strictly prohibited.	

(c)   Prior to accepting

Prior to accepting an audit engagement the firm should consider any issues which might arise which could **threaten compliance with ACCA's** *Code of Ethics and Conduct* or any local legislation. If issues arise then their significance must be considered.

The firm should consider whether they are **competent** to perform the work and whether they would have appropriate resources available, as well as any specialist skills or knowledge.

In addition the audit firm should undertake client screening procedures such as **considering management integrity** and assessing whether any conflict of interest with existing clients would arise.

Further client screening procedures would include **assessing the level of audit risk** of the client and whether the expected engagement fee would be sufficient for the level of anticipated risk.

The prospective firm must **communicate with the outgoing auditor** to assess if there are any ethical or professional reasons why they should not accept appointment.

The **prospective firm must obtain permission** from the client to contact the existing auditor. If this is not given then the engagement should be refused.

The **existing auditor must obtain permission** from the client to respond, if not given then the prospective auditor should refuse the engagement.

If given permission to respond, then the **existing auditor should reply** to the prospective auditor, who should then carefully review the response for any issues that could affect acceptance.

ACCA marking scheme		
		Marks
(a)	½ mark for each threat and ½ per example of a threat	
	Self-interest	
	Self-review	
	Advocacy	
	Familiarity	
	Intimidation	
	Max	**5**
(b)	Up to 1 mark per ethical threat and up to 1 mark per managing method	
	– Staff discount	
	– Secondment	
	– Total fee income	
	– Finance director and partner good friends	
	– Outstanding fees	
	Maximum for threats	**5**
	Maximum for methods	**5**
(c)	Up to 1 mark per step	
	– Compliance with ACCA's Code of Ethics and Conduct	
	– Competent	
	– Consider management integrity	
	– Assess audit risk level	
	– Write outgoing auditor	
	– Permission to contact old auditor	
	– Old auditor permission to respond	
	– Review response	
	– Client screening procedures	
	Max	**5**
Total		**20**

Examiner's comments

Part (a) was unrelated to the scenario and required five threats from the ACCA's Code of Ethics and Conduct along with an example for each threat. This part of the question was very well answered by the vast majority of candidates with most scoring full marks. A significant minority of candidates confused the requirement for threats with that of the fundamental principles and hence provided answers in relation to objectivity, integrity, confidentiality, professional competence and due care and professional behaviour; unfortunately these answers gained no marks. In addition some candidates did not provide an example of each threat, choosing instead to explain the threat in more detail, however this was not what was required.

Part (b) required an explanation of the ethical threats for LV Fones Co along with an explanation of how the threats might be avoided. This question was well answered by most candidates; they were able to clearly identify from the scenario the ethical issues impacting the audit of LV Fones. Some candidates did not explain the threats in sufficient detail, sometimes just identifying the issue and not explaining how this was an ethical threat. For example, many identified that the offer of a staff discount of 10% was an issue, however if they did not then go onto explain that this was a self-interest threat they would have only gained ½ rather than 1 mark. The second part of this question required methods for avoiding the threats, candidates performance here was generally satisfactory. Some answers tended to be quite brief and to include unrealistic steps, such as resigning as auditors to reduce the risk of fee dependence, not allowing the finance director and partner to be friends or suggesting the finance director should resign. In addition many candidates demonstrated that they had not read the scenario properly, as a common suggestion was to not allow the audit senior to undertake the secondment, this was despite the scenario clearly stating that the secondment had already occurred.

Part (c) was well answered by most candidates who were able to identify steps such as contacting the previous auditors as well as various client screening procedures.

167 SAXOPHONE ENTERPRISES *Walk in the footsteps of a top tutor*

Key answer tips

This question focuses on the audit framework and regulation syllabus area. Advantages and disadvantages of outsourcing internal audit should be straightforward in part (a).

Part (b) requires corporate governance weaknesses within the scenario to be explained and a recommendation provided for each. Knowledge of the Corporate Governance Code is required here. Work through on a line by line basis and consider whether the information suggests that the company is being properly managed and controlled in the best interests of the shareholders.

(a)   Advantages/disadvantages of outsourcing internal audit department

Saxophone

Advantages

Staffing

Saxophone Enterprises Co (Saxophone) wishes to expand its internal audit department in terms of size and specialist skills. If they outsource, then there will be no need to spend money in recruiting further staff as Cello & Co (Cello) will provide the staff members.

Immediate solution

As the current internal audit department is small, then outsourcing can provide the number of staff needed straight away.

Skills and experience

Cello is likely to have a large pool of staff available to provide the internal audit service to Saxophone. In addition, the audit firm is likely to have staff with specialist skills already available.

Cost savings

Outsourcing can be an efficient means to control the costs of internal audit as any associated costs such as training will be eliminated as Cello will train its own employees. In addition, the costs for the internal audit service will be agreed in advance. This will ensure that Saxophone can budget accordingly.

Flexibility

If the internal audit department is outsourced, Saxophone will have total flexibility in its internal audit service. Staff can be requested from Cello to suit the company's workloads and requirements. This will ensure that, when required, extra staff is readily available for as long or short a period as needed.

Disadvantages

Existing internal audit department: Saxophone has an existing internal audit department; if they cannot be redeployed elsewhere in the company, then they may need to be made redundant and this could be costly for Saxophone. Staff may oppose the outsourcing if it results in redundancies.

Increased costs: As well as the cost of potential redundancies, the internal audit fee charged by Cello may over a period of time increase, proving to be very expensive.

Knowledge of company: Cello will allocate available staff members to work on the internal audit assignment; this may mean that each visit the staff members are different and hence they may not fully understand the systems of Saxophone. This will decrease the quality of the services provided and increase the time spent by Saxophone's employees in explaining the system to the auditors.

Loss of in-house skills: If the current internal audit team is not deployed elsewhere in the company, valuable internal audit knowledge and experience may be lost. If Saxophone then decided at a future date to bring the service back in-house, this might prove to be too difficult.

Confidentiality: Knowledge of company systems and confidential data will be available to Cello. Although the engagement letter would provide confidentiality clauses, this may not stop breaches of confidentiality.

Control: Saxophone currently has more control over the activities of its internal audit department; however, once outsourced it will need to discuss areas of work and timings well in advance with Cello.

Cello

Advantages

Additional fees for Cello: The audit firm will benefit from the internal audit service being outsourced as this will generate additional fee income. However, the firm will need to monitor the fees to ensure that they do not represent too high a percentage of their total fee income. As a public interest company, fee income should not represent more than 15% of gross practice income for two consecutive years.

Disadvantages

Independence: If Cello provides both external audit and internal audit services, there may be a self-review threat especially where the internal audit work is relied upon by the external auditor team. The firm would need to take steps to ensure that separate teams are put in place as well as additional safeguards.

(b) **Corporate governance weaknesses and recommendations**

(i) **Weakness**	(ii) **Recommendation**
Bill Bassoon is now the chairman; however, until last year he was the chief executive. The chairman is supposed to be an independent non-executive director and hence cannot have previously been the chief executive.	Bill Bassoon should return to his role as chief executive as this will fill the current vacancy and an independent non-executive director should be recruited to fill the role of chairman.
The roles of chairman and chief executive are both very important and carry significant responsibilities; hence this prevents too much power residing in the hands of one individual.	
The board is comprised of five executives and only three non-executive directors.	At least half of the board should be comprised of non-executive directors. Hence the board of Saxophone should consider recruiting and appointing an additional one to two non-executive directors.
There should be an appropriate balance of executives and non-executives, to ensure that the board makes the correct objective decisions, which are in the best interest of the stakeholders of the company, and no individual or group of individuals dominates the board's decision-making.	
Bill Bassoon is considering appointing his close friend as a non-executive director; the friend has experience of running a manufacturing company.	Only independent non-executives with relevant experience and skills should be appointed to the board of Saxophone. The close friend of Bill Bassoon is unlikely to meet these criteria, as he has no experience in the insurance industry, and so should not be appointed.
Non-executives bring valuable experience to a company, but they must also exercise their independent judgment over the whole board. If this director is a close friend of Bill Bassoon, then it is possible that he will not be independent. In addition, other than being a former chief executive, he does not have any relevant experience of the insurance industry and so it is questionable what value he will add to Saxophone.	
The remuneration for directors is set by Jessie Oboe, the finance director. However, no director should be involved in setting their own remuneration as this may result in excessive levels of pay being set.	There should be a fair and transparent policy in place for setting remuneration levels. The non-executive directors should decide on the remuneration of the executives. The finance director or chairman should decide on the pay of the non-executives.

(i) Weakness

All directors' remuneration is in the form of an annual bonus. However, the pay should motivate the directors to focus on the long-term growth of the business. Annual targets can encourage short-term strategies rather than maximising shareholder wealth.

In addition, non-executive directors' pay should not be based on meeting company targets as their pay should be independent of how the company performs.

Saxophone does not currently have an audit committee. Audit committees undertake an important role in that they help the directors to satisfy their responsibility of accountability with regards to maintaining an appropriate relationship with the company's auditor.

A new sales director was appointed nine months ago, however, he has not undergone any board training. All directors should receive induction training when they first join the board so that they are fully aware of their responsibilities.

Saxophone is not planning to hold an annual general meeting (AGM) as the number of shareholders are such that it would be too costly and impractical.

However, the AGM is an important meeting in that it gives the shareholders an opportunity to raise any concerns, receive an answer and vote on important resolutions.

The proposal to send the financial statements and resolutions by email is not appropriate as it does not allow shareholders an opportunity to raise relevant questions.

(ii) Recommendation

The remuneration of executives should be restructured to include a significant proportion aimed at long-term company performance. Perhaps they could be granted share options, as this would help to move the focus to the longer term.

Non-executives should be paid an annual fee for their services, which is unrelated to how Saxophone performs.

Saxophone should appoint an audit committee as soon as possible. The committee should be comprised of at least three independent non-executives, one of whom should have relevant financial experience.

The three current non-executives should be appointed to the audit committee, assuming they meet the requirements of independence.

The new sales director should immediately receive relevant training from Bill Bassoon to ensure that he has a full understanding of his role and responsibilities.

The company should continue to hold the AGM.

Sending information by email in advance of the meeting may be practical and save some costs; however, this should not be seen as a replacement for the AGM.

	ACCA marking scheme		
			Marks
(a)	Up to 1 mark per well explained advantage/disadvantage. Overall maximum of 8 marks for Saxophone and 2 marks for Cello.		
	Saxophone		
	Staffing gaps addressed		
	Immediate solution		
	Skills and experience increased		
	Costs savings		
	Flexibility of service		
	Existing internal audit department staff, cost of potential redundancies		
	Increased costs as fees by Cello & Co may increase over time		
	Knowledge of company and systems reduced		
	Loss of in-house skills		
	Confidentiality issues		
	Control of department reduced		
	Cello		
	Additional fees for Cello & Co		
	Independence issues for audit firm		
		Max	10
(b)	Up to 1 mark per well explained weakness and up to 1 mark per recommendation. Overall maximum of 5 marks for weaknesses and 5 marks for recommendations.		
	Chief executive is now chairman		
	Currently only three of eight directors are non-executive, should be at least half		
	Chairman considering appointing his friend as a non-executive		
	Finance director decides on the remuneration for the directors		
	Remuneration for all directors in form of annual bonus		
	No audit committee at present		
	No induction training for new sales director		
	No AGM planned as felt impractical and too costly		
		Max	10
Total			20

Examiner's comments

Part (a) required advantages and disadvantages for Saxophone and its audit firm, Cello, of outsourcing the internal audit department. Candidates performed well on this question. Many candidates were able to identify a good range of points for both Saxophone and Cello, and the mark allocation of 8 and 2 marks respectively was adhered to. Many answers were well structured with a section for each company with sub headings for advantages and disadvantages; this facilitated the marking of this question. Those candidates who did not score well tended to provide very little detail in their answers, such as for advantages simply stated 'lower costs' or 'more flexibility' these are far too brief to score the 1 mark available per point. The requirement asked candidates to 'explain' their points and this does not provide adequate explanation. Candidates must pay attention to the requirement verb and provide the required level of detail. In addition some candidates included incorrect points such as for advantages the fact that the internal audit work would be quicker as the external auditors knew the company, or that the audit fee would reduce implying that the same team would be used for both tasks or that the work would automatically be relied on which was not appropriate.

Part (b) required an identification and explanation of five corporate governance weaknesses as well as a recommendation for each. Candidates performed well on this question. Most candidates were able to confidently identify weaknesses from the scenario.

However many could not explain the weakness, relying on explanations such as 'this is not good corporate governance'. This was not sufficient to score the extra ½ marks available for each point. Candidates needed to be able to explain how these weaknesses impacted the company. In addition a significant proportion of candidates misread the scenario and thought the chairman and chief executive was the same person. This was not correct; Bill Bassoon had been the chief executive and was now the chairman. Hence answers focused on these key roles being held by the same person rather than the chairman not being independent and failed to score marks as a result. Candidates must read the scenario carefully before they start to write. The recommendations provided were not adequate in many cases and often answers gave corporate governance objectives rather than recommendations, such as, 'the board should be balanced between executive and nonexecutives'. This is an objective; the recommendation should have been to 'appoint additional non-executive directors to ensure a balanced board'.

168 GOOFY *Walk in the footsteps of a top tutor*

Tutor's top tips

Part (a) is a straightforward knowledge based requirement on conflicts of interest and should not pose too many problems.

In part (b) you need to apply your knowledge of outsourcing to the scenario. Don't just list points. Apply them to Goofy.

Part (c) is a typical ethical threats question focusing on threats to objectivity. Remember to explain the threat properly, don't just state the name of the threat but explain how it could affect the auditor's behaviour when performing the audit.

(a) **Safeguards to be adopted to address the conflict of interest of auditing both Goofy Co and Mickey Co:**

- Both Goofy Co and Mickey Co should be notified that NAB & Co would be acting as auditors for each company and, if necessary, consent obtained.
- The use of separate engagement teams, with different engagement partners and team members; once an employee has worked on one audit such as Goofy Co then they would be prevented from being on the audit of Mickey Co for a period of time. This separation of teams is known as building a 'Chinese wall'.
- Procedures to prevent access to information, for example, strict physical separation of both teams, confidential and secure data filing.
- Clear guidelines for members of each engagement team on issues of security and confidentiality. These guidelines could be included within the audit engagement letters.
- Potentially the use of confidentiality agreements signed by employees and partners of the firm.
- Regular monitoring of the application of the above safeguards by a senior individual in NAB & Co not involved in either audit.
- Advising one or both clients to seek additional independent advice.

(b) **Advantages of outsourcing Goofy Co's internal audit department**

Staffing

Goofy Co needs to expand its internal audit department from five employees as it is too small; however, if they outsource then there will be no need to recruit as NAB & Co will provide the staff members and this will be an instant solution.

Skills and experience

NAB & Co is a large firm and so will have a large pool of staff available to provide the internal audit service. In addition, Goofy Co has requested that ad hoc reviews are performed and, depending on the nature of these, it may find that the firm has specialist skills that Goofy Co may not be able to afford if the internal audit department continues to be run internally.

Costs

Any associated costs such as training will be eliminated as NAB & Co will train its own employees. In addition, the costs for the internal audit service will be agreed in advance. This will ensure that Goofy Co can budget accordingly.

As NAB & Co will be performing both the external and internal audit there is a possibility that the fees may be reduced.

Flexibility

If the department is outsourced Goofy Co will have total flexibility in its internal audit service. Staff can be requested from NAB & Co to suit Goofy Co's workloads and requirements. This will ensure that, when required, extra staff can be used to visit a large number of shops and in quieter times there may be no internal audit presence.

Additional fees

NAB & Co will benefit from the internal audit service being outsourced as this will generate additional fee income. However, the firm will need to monitor the fees to ensure that they do not represent too high a percentage of their total fee income.

Disadvantages of outsourcing Goofy Co's internal audit department

Knowledge of systems

NAB & Co will allocate available staff members to work on the internal audit assignment, this may mean that each month the staff members are different and hence they may not understand the systems of Goofy Co. This will decrease the quality of the services provided and increase the time spent by Goofy Co employees explaining the system to the auditors.

Independence

If NAB & Co continues as external auditor as well as providing the internal audit service, there may be a self-review threat, where the internal audit work is relied upon by the external auditors. NAB & Co would need to take steps to ensure that separate teams were put in place as well as additional safeguards.

Existing internal audit department

Goofy Co has an existing internal audit department of five employees. If they cannot be redeployed elsewhere in the company then they may need to be made redundant and this could be costly for the company. Staff may oppose the outsourcing if it results in redundancies.

Cost

As well as the cost of potential redundancies, the internal audit fee charged by NAB & Co may, over a period of time, prove to be very expensive.

Loss of in-house skills

If the current internal audit team is not deployed elsewhere in the company valuable internal audit knowledge and experience may be lost; if Goofy Co then decided at a future date to bring the service back in-house this might prove to be too difficult.

Timing

NAB & Co may find that Goofy Co requires internal audit staff at the busy periods for the audit firm, and hence it might prove difficult to actually provide the required level of resource.

Confidentiality

Knowledge of company systems and confidential data will be available to NAB & Co. Although the engagement letter would provide confidentiality clauses, this may not stop breaches of confidentiality.

Control

Goofy Co will currently have more control over the activities of its internal audit department; however, once outsourced it will need to discuss areas of work and timings well in advance with NAB & Co.

(c) **Ethical threats and managing these risks**

Tutor's top tips

This is a typical ethical threats question focusing on threats to objectivity. Remember to explain the threat properly, don't just state the name of the threat but explain how it could affect the auditor's behaviour when performing the audit.

A familiarity threat arises where an engagement partner is associated with a client for a long period of time. NAB & Co's partner has been involved in the audit of Goofy Co for six years and hence may not maintain her professional scepticism and objectivity.

NAB & Co should monitor the relationship between engagement and client staff, and should consider rotating engagement partners when a long association has occurred. In addition, *ACCA's Code of Ethics and Conduct* recommends that engagement partners rotate off an audit after seven years for listed and public interest entities.

Therefore consideration should be given to appointing an alternative audit partner.

The engagement partner's son has accepted a job as a sales manager at Goofy Co. This could represent a self-interest/familiarity threat if the son was involved in the financial statement process.

It is unlikely that as a sales manager the son would be in a position to influence the financial statements and hence additional safeguards would not be necessary.

A self-interest threat can arise when an audit firm has a financial interest in the company. In this case the partner's son will receive shares as part of his remuneration. As the son is an immediate family member of the partner then if he holds the shares it will be as if the partner holds these shares, and this is prohibited.

In this case as holding shares is prohibited by *ACCA's Code of Ethics and Conduct* the engagement partner should be removed from the audit.

Fees based on the outcome or results of work performed are known as contingent fees and are prohibited by *ACCA's Code of Ethics and Conduct.* Hence Goofy Co's request that 20% of the external audit fee is based on profit after tax would represent a contingent fee.

NAB & Co will not be able to accept contingent fees and should communicate to Goofy Co that the external audit fee needs to be based on the time and level of work performed.

ACCA marking scheme		
		Marks
(a)	Up to 1 mark per well explained safeguard Notify Goofy Co and Mickey Co Separate engagement teams Procedures prevent access to information Clear guidelines on security and confidentiality Confidentiality agreements Monitoring of safeguards Advise seek independent advice	
	Max	**4**
(b)	Up to 1 mark per well explained advantage/disadvantage Staffing gaps addressed immediately Skills and experience increased Costs of training eliminated Possibly reduced fees Flexibility of service Additional fees for NAB & Co Knowledge of systems reduced Independence issues NAB & Co Existing internal audit department staff, cost of potential redundancies Fees by NAB & Co may increase over time Loss of in-house skills Timing of work may not suit NAB & Co Confidentiality issues Control of department reduced	
	Max	**10**
(c)	Up to 1 mark per well explained threat and up to 1 mark for method of managing risk, overall maximum 6 marks Familiarity threat – long association of partner Self-interest threat – son gained employment at client company Self-interest threat – financial interest (shares) in client company Contingent fees	
	Max	**6**
Total		**20**

Examiner's comments

Part (a) required an explanation of the safeguards NAB should implement to manage the potential conflict of interest between their two competing clients. Candidates performed satisfactorily on this part of the question. Most candidates were able to identify safeguards such as separate audit teams and informing both parties and therefore scored half of the available marks. However, many candidates then provided procedures which were a repeat of separate teams, such as separate engagement partners. In addition some candidates' listed general ethical safeguards rather than focusing on the specific requirement of conflicts of interest.

Part (b) required the advantages and disadvantages to both NAB and Goofy Co of outsourcing their internal audit department. Candidates performed well on this question. Most candidates structured their answers to consider advantages and disadvantages for each of the two entities separately and this helped to generate a sufficient number of points. It was pleasing to see that many candidates used the small scenario provided to make their answers relevant, as this was not a general requirement, but one applied to Goofy Co and NAB. Where candidates did not score as well, this was mainly due to a failure to provide sufficient depth to their answers. A common advantage given was 'outsourcing saves costs.' This does not discuss with enough detail how Goofy Co would save costs and hence would not score the 1 mark available. Often candidates then went on to have as a disadvantage 'outsourcing costs more money' again with little explanation of how this can occur. A 'discuss' requirement is relatively detailed and therefore an answer of just a few words will not be sufficient.

Part (c) required an explanation of the ethical threats with respect to the audit of Goofy Co and how these threats may be reduced. This question was answered well by most candidates, and many scored full marks. Candidates were able to clearly identify from the scenario the ethical issues impacting the audit of Goofy Co. Some candidates did not explain the threats in sufficient detail, sometimes just identifying the issue and not explaining how this was an ethical threat. For example, many identified the issue of the engagement partner having been in place for six years, however if they did not then go on to explain that this was a familiarity threat, or they gave an incorrect threat such as self-interest, they would have only gained ½ rather than 1 mark. The second part of this question required methods for reducing the threats. Candidates' performance was generally satisfactory although some answers tended to be quite brief. In addition some candidates confused the issue of contingent fees with undue fee dependence and so focused on ways to reduce the proportion of fees from Goofy Co. In addition many candidates provided more points than were necessary. The requirement was for six marks and had two elements to it: the marking guide awarded 1 mark per threat and 1 per method for reducing risk, hence 3 threats and methods were required for full marks. Yet some candidates listed up to five threats and methods, this then put them under time pressure and led to later questions being impacted.

169 MONTEHODGE CO *Walk in the footsteps of a top tutor*

Key answer tips

Part (a) is a straightforward knowledge question asking for advantages and disadvantages of outsourcing.

Part (b) requires you to work through the scenario to identify reasons why Montehodge would benefit from an internal audit department and reasons why they might not need one. Think of the reasons why a company establishes an internal audit function and apply those to the scenario.

(a)   **Outsourcing internal audit**

Advantages of outsourcing internal audit

Staff recruitment

There will be no need to recruit staff for the internal audit department; the outsourcing company will provide all staff and ensure they are of the appropriate quality.

Skills

The outsourcing company will have a large pool of staff available to provide the internal audit service. This will provide access to specialist skills that the company may not be able to afford if the internal audit department was run internally.

Set up time

The department can be set up in a few weeks rather than taking months to advertise and recruit appropriate staff.

Costs

Costs for the service will be agreed in advance. This makes budgeting easier for the recipient company as the cost and standard of service expected are fixed.

Flexibility (staffing arrangements)

Staff can be hired to suit the workloads and requirements of the recipient company rather than full-time staff being idle for some parts of the year.

Disadvantages of outsourcing internal audit

Staff turnover

The internal audit staff allocated to one company may change frequently; this means that company systems may not always be fully understood, decreasing the quality of the service provided.

External auditors

Where external auditors provide the internal audit service there may be a conflict of interest (self-review threat), where internal audit work is then relied upon by external auditors.

Cost

The cost of the outsourced service may be too high for the company, which means that an internal audit department is not established at all. There may be an assumption that internal provision would be even more expensive.

Confidentiality

Knowledge of company systems and confidential data will be available to a third party. Although the service agreement should provide confidentiality clauses, this may not stop breaches of confidentiality e.g. individuals selling data fraudulently.

Control

Where internal audit is provided in-house, the company will have more control over the activities of the department; there is less need to discuss work patterns or suggest areas of work to the internal audit department.

(b) **For establishing an internal audit department**

Value for money (VFM) audits

MonteHodge has some relatively complex systems such as the stock market monitoring systems. Internal audit may be able to offer VFM services or review potential upgrades to these systems checking again whether value for money is provided.

Accounting system

While not complex, accounting systems must provide accurate information. Internal audit can audit these systems in detail ensuring that fee calculations, for example, are correct.

Computer systems

Maintenance of computer systems is critical to MonteHodge's business. Without computers, the company cannot operate. Internal audit could review the effectiveness of backup and disaster recovery arrangements.

Internal control systems

Internal control systems appear to be limited. Internal audit could check whether basic control systems are needed, recommending implementation of controls where appropriate.

Effect on audit fee

Provision of internal audit may decrease the audit fee where external auditors can place reliance on the work of internal audit. This is unlikely to happen during the first year of internal audit due to lack of experience.

Image to clients

Provision of internal audit will enable MonteHodge Co to provide a better 'image' to its clients. Good controls imply client monies are safe with MonteHodge.

Corporate governance

Although MonteHodge does not need to comply with corporate governance regulations, internal audit could still recommend policies for good corporate governance. For example, suggesting that the chairman and chief executive officer roles are split.

Compliance with regulations

MonteHodge is in the financial services industry. In most jurisdictions, this industry has a significant amount of regulation. An internal audit department could help ensure compliance with those regulations, especially as additional regulations are expected in the future.

Assistance to financial accountant

The financial accountant in MonteHodge is not qualified. Internal audit could therefore provide assistance in compliance with financial reporting standards, etc. as well as recommending control systems.

Against establishing of internal audit department

No statutory requirement

As there is no statutory requirement, the directors may see internal audit as a waste of time and money and therefore not consider establishing the department.

Accounting systems

Many accounting systems are not necessarily complex so the directors may not see the need for another department to review their operations, check integrity, etc.

Family business

MonteHodge is owned by a few shareholders in the same family. There is therefore not the need to provide assurance to other shareholders on the effectiveness of controls, accuracy of financial accounting systems, etc.

Potential cost

There would be a cost of establishing and maintaining the internal audit department. Given that the directors consider focus on profit and trusting employees to be important, then it is unlikely that they would consider the additional cost of establishing internal audit.

Seen as criticism

Some directors may feel challenged by an internal audit department reviewing their work (especially the financial accountant). They are likely therefore not to want to establish an internal audit department.

	ACCA marking scheme		
			Marks
(a)	1 mark for each well explained point.		
	For outsourcing:		
	• Staff recruitment		
	• Skills		
	• Set up time		
	• Costs		
	• Flexibility		
	• Independence		
	Against outsourcing:		
	• Staff turnover		
	• External auditors		
	• Cost		
	• Confidentiality		
	• Control		
	• Independence if provided by external auditor		
		Max	8
(b)	Up to 1 mark per well described point		
	For internal audit		
	• VFM audits		
	• Accounting system		
	• Computer systems		
	• Internal control systems		
	• Effect on audit fee		
	• Image to clients		
	• Corporate governance		
	• Lack of control		
	• Law change		
	• Assistance to financial accountant		
	• Nature of industry (financial services)		
	Against internal audit		
	• No statutory requirement		
	• Family business		
	• Potential cost		
	• Review threat		
		Max	12
Total			20

Examiner's comments

The scenario contained many 'clues' as to why an internal audit department would be useful (or not) and candidates were expected to identify those points and make specific reference to them in their answers.

The requirement verb discuss indicated that some comment was needed to show why the points made were relevant. Many candidates recognised this requirement and provided sufficient well-explained comments to obtain full marks. Other candidates did not relate their comments to the scenario at all, which limited the number of marks obtainable.

Common errors included:

• Not linking the points made to the scenario.

• Not fully explaining the points made. Brief comments such as 'internal audit would be expensive' only attracted ½ of a mark.

REVIEW AND REPORTING

170 CHESTNUT & CO *Walk in the footsteps of a top tutor*

Key answer tips

This question covers audit reports, the output of the audit.

Part (a) requires five elements of an unmodified audit report. These are the sections that are included in the audit report, irrespective of the type of opinion to be issued. Remember to explain **why** these sections are included in the report.

Part (b) requires you to assess the materiality of the issues described as unless they are material, they will not affect the audit report. You also need to discuss the issues in terms of why they pose problems for the audit report. The question also asks for procedures. You must give procedures that would be performed at this stage of the audit. You will not be given marks for stating work that has already been performed. Finally, give the implication for the audit report. Don't waste time stating the reporting implications if the issues get resolved as the requirement makes it clear that the answer should only consider implications if the issues are not resolved.

(a)   Audit report elements and why included

The following elements should be included within an auditor's report along with why:

Title – The auditor's report shall have a title which clearly indicates that it is the report of an independent auditor, this distinguishes this report from any other.

Addressee – The auditor's report shall be addressed as required by the circumstances of the engagement, this is determined by law or regulation but is usually to the shareholders. This clarifies who may rely on the opinion and who may not, such as third parties.

Opinion paragraph – When expressing an unmodified opinion, the auditor's opinion shall either state that the financial statements 'present fairly' or 'give a true and fair view' in accordance with the applicable financial reporting framework. This paragraph details whether the financial statements are true and fair or not.

Basis for opinion - Provides a description of the professional standards applied during the audit to provide confidence to users that the report can be relied upon.

Key audit matters (Compulsory for listed entities. May be included in audit reports of non-listed entities) - To draw attention to any other significant matters of which the users should be aware to aid their understanding of the entity.

Other information – This section explains the auditor's responsibilities for the other information included in the annual report. Here the auditor will explain that they are required to read the other information to identify any inconsistencies with the financial statements or their knowledge obtained during the audit. If any inconsistencies have been identified they will be described in this section.

Management's responsibility for the financial statements – This section of the auditor's report describes the responsibilities of those in the organisation who are responsible for the preparation of the financial statements. This paragraph along with that of the auditor's responsibilities looks to make clear what the role of management is, as well as what the role of the auditor is. It seeks to reduce the expectation gap.

Auditor's responsibility – The auditor's report shall state that the responsibility of the auditor is to express an opinion on the financial statements based on the audit and that the audit was conducted in accordance with International Standards on Auditing and ethical requirements and that the auditor plans and performs the audit to obtain reasonable assurance about whether the financial statements are free from material misstatement. Along with the management's responsibility paragraph, it seeks to make clear the role of the auditor and also what management's role is. Also this paragraph seeks to explain what an audit involves and that only material misstatements are considered, as opposed to all errors.

Other reporting responsibilities – If the auditor addresses other reporting responsibilities in the auditor's report, these shall be addressed in a separate section in the auditor's report titled 'Report on Other Legal and Regulatory Requirements'. This is important where there is local legislation which requires reporting on; this needs to be clearly identified in the report as this is in addition to the requirement of the ISAs.

Signature of the auditor – The auditor's report must be signed, this can be either the personal name of the auditor or, the signature is on behalf of the firm, depending on the jurisdiction in which the auditor is operating. This clarifies which firm or auditor has performed the audit engagement.

Date of the auditor's report – The auditor's report shall be dated no earlier than the date on which the auditor has obtained sufficient appropriate audit evidence on which to base the auditor's opinion on the financial statements. The date of the audit report is important in the case of subsequent events which impact the financial statements; the auditor's role is different depending on whether the audit report was signed or not when the subsequent event came to light.

Auditor's address – The auditor's report shall name the location where the auditor practises. This is useful in case shareholders need to contact the auditors.

(b) Three issues

Palm Industries Co (Palm)

(i) A customer of Palm's owing $350,000 at the year end has not made any post year-end payments as they are disputing the quality of goods received. No allowance for receivables has been made against this balance. As the balance is being disputed, there is a risk of incorrect valuation as some or all of the receivable balance is overstated, as it may not be paid.

This $350,000 receivables balance represents 1.2% (0.35/28.2m) of revenue, 6.3% (0.35/5.6m) of receivables and 7.3% (0.35/4.8m) of profit before tax; hence this is a material issue.

(ii)   A procedure to adopt includes:

- Review whether any payments have subsequently been made by this customer since the audit fieldwork was completed.

- Discuss with management whether the issue of quality of goods sold to the customer has been resolved, or whether it is still in dispute.

- Review the latest customer correspondence with regards to an assessment of the likelihood of the customer making payment.

(iii)   If management refuses to provide against this receivable, the audit report will need to be modified as receivables are overstated.

The error is material but not pervasive therefore a qualified opinion would be necessary. The opinion paragraph would be qualified 'except for'.

The basis for qualified opinion paragraph would include an explanation of the material misstatement in relation to the valuation of receivables and the effect on the financial statements.

Ash Trading Co (Ash)

(i)   Chestnut & Co was only appointed as auditors subsequent to Ash's year end and hence did not attend the year-end inventory count. Therefore, they have not been able to gather sufficient and appropriate audit evidence with regards to the completeness and existence of inventory.

Inventory is a material amount as it represents 21.3% (0.51/2.4m) of profit before tax and 5% (0.51/10.1m) of revenue; hence this is a material issue.

(ii)   A procedure to adopt includes:

- Review the internal audit reports of the inventory count to identify the level of adjustments to the records to assess the reasonableness of relying on the inventory records.

- Undertake a sample check of inventory in the warehouse and compare to the inventory records and then from inventory records to the warehouse, to assess the reasonableness of the inventory records maintained by Ash.

(iii) The auditors will need to modify the audit report as they are unable to obtain sufficient appropriate evidence in relation to inventory.

The issue is material but not pervasive. Therefore a qualified opinion will be required. The opinion paragraph will be qualified 'except for'.

A basis for qualified opinion paragraph will explain the limitation in relation to the lack of evidence over inventory.

Bullfinch.com (Bullfinch)

(i)   A key customer of Bullfinch.com has just notified the company that they are experiencing cash flow difficulties and are unlikely to make any payments for the foreseeable future. This information was received after the year end but provides further evidence of the recoverability of the receivable balance at the year end. If the customer is experiencing cash flow difficulties just a few months after the year end, then it is highly unlikely that the year-end receivable was recoverable as at 31 October and hence is an adjusting event.

The receivables balance is overstated and consideration should be given to adjusting this balance, if material, through the use of an allowance for receivables or by being written off. The total amount outstanding at the year end was $283,000 and is material as it represents 7.4% (0.283/3.8m) of profit before tax and 2.5% (0.283/11.2m) of revenue. Hence, the directors should amend the 2015 financial statements by writing down or writing off the receivable balance.

(ii) A procedure to adopt includes:

- The correspondence with the customer should be reviewed to assess whether there is any likelihood of payment.

- Discuss with management as to why they feel an adjustment is not required in the 2015 financial statements.

- Review the post year-end period to see if any payments have been received from the customer.

(iii) If management refuses to provide against this receivable, the audit report will need to be modified, as receivables are overstated.

The error is material but not pervasive therefore a qualified opinion would be necessary. The opinion paragraph would be qualified 'except for'

The basis for qualified opinion paragraph would include an explanation of the material misstatement in relation to the valuation of receivables and the effect on the financial statements.

ACCA marking scheme		
		Marks
(a) Up to 1 mark per well described element and explanation of why included.		
– Title		
– Addressee		
– Opinion		
– Basis for opinion		
– Key audit matters (Listed entities)		
– Other information		
– Management responsibility		
– Auditor's responsibility		
– Other reporting responsibilities		
– Signature of the auditor		
– Date of the auditor's report		
– Auditor's address		
	Max	5
(b) Up to 1 mark per valid point. Max of 5 marks for each issue.		
Palm		
Overstatement of receivables		
Calculation of materiality		
ONE procedure		
Qualified opinion – except for		
Basis for qualified opinion		
Ash		
Unable to obtain sufficient appropriate evidence		
Calculation of materiality		
ONE procedure		
Qualified opinion – except for		
Basis for qualified opinion		

Bullfinch			
Provides evidence of conditions at the year end			
Adjusting event			
Calculation of materiality			
ONE procedure			
Qualified opinion – except for			
Basis for qualified opinion			
		Max	15
Total			20

Examiner's comments

Part (a) required a description of the elements of an unmodified audit report and an explanation of why they are included. Performance on this part of the question was mixed. Many candidates were able to correctly identify a good number of the elements included in an unmodified audit report. However, it was common to see answers where a heading such as 'auditor's responsibility' was provided without any description of what would be included in this element. The requirement was to describe and not to state or list, hence where an element was identified but not described, this did not score any marks. Candidates are again reminded to take note of the verb used in the requirement to ensure that they appreciate the level of depth that is required to score the marks available. The second part of the requirement was to explain why the element was included; it was disappointing to see that the majority of candidates were not able to do this. Perhaps it was due to a failure to read the question properly, or due to a lack of understanding of audit reports. Where candidates did attempt this part of the question, they often used circular answers, such as 'management responsibilities are included in the audit report to explain the responsibilities of management' instead of explaining that the responsibilities paragraphs are included to try and reduce the expectations gap and to clarify for the user the division of responsibility between management and auditor. In addition a minority of candidates misunderstood the requirement and instead of describing the elements, they explained the different types of audit opinions available, such as adverse or qualified. Some candidates explained the elements of an assurance engagement, rather than answering the question actually set.

Part (b) informed candidates about issues that had been identified during a review of the files for three existing clients. Candidates were required to make an assessment of the materiality of each issue, provide a procedure to resolve each issue and discuss the impact on the audit report if each issue remained unresolved. Performance was satisfactory on this question, with an improvement in candidates' performance compared to the last time this style of question was examined. The majority of candidates were able to identify and discuss the matters appropriately. In addition most candidates correctly identified and calculated that each issue was material. Some candidates launched straight into assessing materiality without discussing the issue and hence missed out on the available discussion marks for each issue. With regards to procedures to undertake to resolve each issue, candidates seemed to especially struggle with Ash. The scenario stated that it was not possible to undertake another full inventory count, however many candidates ignored this and still suggested 'the company should be told to undertake an inventory count'. This seems to indicate a failure by candidates to read the scenario. Other incorrect procedures involved 'contacting the previous auditors' or 'reviewing the competence of internal audit' rather than reviewing the results of the attendance by internal audit at the inventory count. Candidates performed better on auditing Palm; however some candidates incorrectly suggested 'obtaining management written representations' or 'contacting the customer directly to ask if they will pay'. With respect to the audit of Bullfinch, candidates were generally able to identify that the financial statements required amendment, as the error was material and constituted an adjusting event in line with IAS 10 *Events after the Reporting Period*. Fewer candidates were able to fully explain why the amendment was required, with many just stating this was an adjusting event, rather than why it was adjusting.

Performance on the impact on the audit report if each issue remained unresolved was better than in previous exam diets. Many candidates were able to identify the type of audit report modification required and attempt to describe the impact on the audit report. The most common omission was the need for a basis for qualified opinion paragraph. Additionally a minority of candidates ignored the question requirement to only consider the audit report impact if the issue was unresolved. Lots of answers started with 'if resolved the audit report .....' this was not required and no marks were available for this assessment.

171 CLARINET *Walk in the footsteps of a top tutor*

Key answer tips

Going concern is the assumption that the company will continue to trade for the foreseeable future.

Part (a) asks for procedures to address the uncorrected misstatement. The auditor will always try and resolve misstatements with the client to avoid issuing a modified report. You need to give suitable procedures that could be used at this stage of the audit.

Part (b) asks for indicators that the company is not a going concern i.e. will not be able to continue to trade. Look for indicators that the company will not have enough cash to settle its debts when they fall due as cash flow is the main contributor to going concern problems.

Part (c) asks for procedures you would perform during the audit in respect of going concern. A company will remain a going concern if it has sufficient cash to meet its debts when they fall due. Procedures therefore need to focus on gathering evidence that the company will be able to do this.

Part (d) asks for the impact on the audit report if the auditor believes the company is a going concern but a material uncertainty exists. State whether the report and opinion will be modified and if so, how. State the name of the opinion as well as the key words of that opinion to earn the marks available.

(a)   Procedures to undertake in relation to the uncorrected misstatement

- The extent of the potential misstatement should be considered and therefore a large sample of inventory items should be tested to identify the possible size of the misstatement.

- The potential misstatement should be discussed with Clarinet Co's management in order to understand why these inventory differences are occurring.

- The misstatement should be compared to materiality to assess if the error is material individually.

- If not, then it should be added to other errors noted during the audit to assess if in aggregate the uncorrected errors are now material.

- If material, the auditors should ask the directors to adjust the inventory balances to correct the misstatements identified in the 2014 year end.

- Request a written representation from the directors about the uncorrected misstatements including the inventory errors.

- Consider the implication for the audit report if the inventory errors are material and the directors refuses to make adjustments.

(b)   Going concern indicators

Competition

A new competitor, Drums Design Co (Drums), has entered the market and gained considerable market share from Clarinet through competitive pricing. There is a risk that if Clarinet continues to lose market share this will impact on future cash flows. In addition, there may be pressure on Clarinet to drop their prices in order to compete, which will impact profits and cash flows.

Loss of major customer

A significant customer has stopped trading with Clarinet and moved its business to Drums. This could result in a significant loss of future revenues and profit, and unless this customer can be replaced, there will be a reduction of future cash flows.

Loss of specialist staff

A number of Clarinet's specialist developers have left the company and joined Drums and the company has found it difficult to replace these employees due to their experience and skills. The company is looking to develop new products and in order to do this, it needs sufficiently trained staff. If it cannot recruit enough staff, then it could hold up the product development and stop the company from increasing revenue.

Loss of major supplier

Clarinet's main supplier who provides specialist equipment has just stopped trading. If the equipment is highly specialised, there is a risk that Clarinet may not be able to obtain these products from other suppliers which would impact on their ability to trade. More likely, there are other suppliers available but they may be more expensive which will increase the outflows of Clarinet and worsen the cash flow forecast.

Shareholders unwilling to provide further finance

Clarinet needs to raise finance to develop new products in order to gain market share; they approached their shareholders for further finance but they declined to invest further. If Clarinet is unable to obtain suitable finance, then it may be that the shareholders deem Clarinet to be too risky to invest in further. They may be concerned that Clarinet will not be able to offer them a suitable return on their investment, suggesting cash flow problems. In addition, if Clarinet cannot obtain alternative finance, then it will not be able to develop the products it needs to.

Overdraft

Clarinet's overdraft has grown significantly during the year. If the bank does not renew the overdraft and the company is unable to obtain alternative finance, then it may not be able to continue to trade.

Cash flow forecast

Clarinet's cash flow forecast shows a significantly worsening position for the coming 12 months. If the company continues to have cash outflows, then it will increase its overdraft further and will start to run out of available cash.

Claim from customer

One of Clarinet's customers is planning to sue the company for loss of revenue due to hardware being installed by Clarinet in the customer's online ordering system not operating correctly. If the customer is successful, then Clarinet may have to pay a significant settlement which will put further pressure on cash flows. In addition, it is unlikely that this customer will continue to trade with Clarinet and if the problems become known to other customers, this may lead to a further loss of revenue and cash flows as well as impact on Clarinet's reputation.

(c) **Going concern procedures**

- Obtain the company's cash flow forecast and review the cash in and outflows. Assess the assumptions for reasonableness and discuss the findings with management to understand if the company will have sufficient cash flows.

- Perform a sensitivity analysis on the cash flows to understand the margin of safety the company has in terms of its net cash in/outflow.

- Discuss with the finance director whether any new customers have been obtained to replace the one lost.

- Review the company's post year-end sales and order book to assess if the levels of trade are likely to increase in light of the increased competition from Drum and if the revenue figures in the cash flow forecast are reasonable.

- Discuss with the directors whether replacement specialist developers have been recruited to replace those lost to Drum.

- Review any agreements with the bank to determine whether any covenants have been breached, especially in relation to the overdraft.

- Review any bank correspondence to assess the likelihood of the bank renewing the overdraft facility.

- Review the correspondence with shareholders to assess whether any of these are likely to reconsider increasing their investment in the company.

- Discuss with the directors whether they have contacted any banks for finance to help with the new product development.

- Enquire of the lawyers of Clarinet as to the existence of any additional litigation and request their assessment of the likelihood of Clarinet having to make payment to their customer who intends to sue for loss of revenue.

- Perform audit tests in relation to subsequent events to identify any items which might indicate or mitigate the risk of going concern not being appropriate.

- Review the post year-end board minutes to identify any other issues which might indicate further financial difficulties for the company.

- Review post year-end management accounts to assess if in line with cash flow forecast.

- Obtain a written representation confirming the directors' view that Clarinet is a going concern.

(d) **Audit report**

The directors of Clarinet have agreed to make going concern disclosures; however, the impact on the audit report will be dependent on the adequacy of these disclosures.

If the disclosures are adequate, then the audit report will be modified. A section headed 'Material Uncertainty Related to Going Concern would be required.

This paragraph will state that the audit opinion is not modified, indicate that there is a material uncertainty and will cross reference to the disclosure note made by management. It would be included immediately after the opinion paragraph.

If the disclosures made by management are not adequate, the audit opinion will need to be modified as there is a material misstatement.

Depending on the materiality of the issue, this will be either qualified or an adverse opinion. The opinion paragraph will be amended to state 'except for' or the financial statements are not fairly presented.

The basis for qualified or adverse opinion will describe the matter giving rise to the modification and clearly identify the lack of disclosure over the going concern uncertainty.

	ACCA marking scheme		
			Marks
(a)	Up to 1 mark per well described procedure.		
	Test inventory to assess extent of error		
	Discuss with management to understand why errors occurring		
	Compare misstatement to materiality – see if material		
	If not material, add to unadjusted errors schedule, to assess if material in aggregate		
	If material, request directors to amend financial statements		
	Written representation		
	Consider implications for audit report		
		Max	4
(b)	Up to 1 mark per explanation of why this could indicate going concern problems, if just identify indicator then max of ½ mark, overall maximum of 6 indicators.		
	New competitor taking market share from Clarinet		
	Loss of large customer		
	Loss of specialist staff		
	Main supplier ceased to trade		
	Shareholders refused to provide further finance for product development		
	Overdraft facility due for renewal and increased significantly		
	Cash flow shows worsening position		
	Customer potentially suing for loss of revenue		
		Max	6
(c)	Up to 1 mark per well described procedure.		
	Review cash flow forecasts		
	Sensitivity analysis		
	Discuss if new customers obtained		
	Review post year-end sales and order book		
	Discuss if replacement specialist developers recruited		
	Review bank agreements, breach of covenants		
	Review bank correspondence likelihood of overdraft renewal		
	Review shareholders' correspondence		
	Discuss if alternative finance obtained		
	Enquire of lawyers any further litigation and likelihood of Clarinet making payment to customer who may sue		
	Subsequent events		
	Board minutes		
	Management accounts		
	Written representation		
		Max	6

(d)	Up to 1 mark per well described point.			
	Depends on adequacy of disclosures			
	Adequately disclosed – modified report			
	Material uncertainty related to going concern – opinion unmodified			
	Not adequately disclosed – modified opinion as material misstatement			
	Depending on materiality either qualified or adverse opinion.			
	Basis for qualified or adverse opinion			
			Max	4
Total				20

Examiner's comments

Part (a) required a description of the procedures the auditor of Clarinet should undertake in relation to the uncorrected inventory misstatement. This question, where answered, was disappointing. Many candidates entered into lengthy discussions as to whether the write down to inventory was an adjusting or non-adjusting event (and frequently came up with the wrong conclusion). Relatively few considered how critical it was to determine the materiality of the misstatement or to perform further substantive procedures to determine the size of the misstatement. Many also wrote at length about every possible impact on the audit report as well as providing detailed inventory count procedures. It was apparent that there were significant gaps in candidates' technical knowledge in this area.

Part (b) required an explanation of going concern indicators. Candidates performed well on this question. Most candidates were able to identify the required number of indicators from the scenario; this resulted in them achieving full marks. However in order to gain the full marks, candidates were required to explain why this indicator could impact the going concern of Clarinet. Many did not do this, or the explanations provided did not give sufficient depth often simply stating 'this could impact the going concern status'. This would not have scored marks as it does not make clear how the going concern status could be impacted. The requirement verb was to 'explain' therefore sufficient detail was required to score the 1 mark available per point. Once again candidates are reminded to look carefully at the verb at the beginning of the question requirement, as this should help them to understand the level of detail required for their answers. A small minority of candidates misread the requirement and provided indicators from the scenario that Clarinet was a going concern, rather than was not. This can only be due to a failure to read the question requirement properly.

Part (c) required a description of going concern procedures. Candidates' performance was mixed in this area. Those candidates who failed to score well produced vague procedures such as 'obtain the cash flow forecast,' 'review board minutes' and 'discuss with management'. These examples lack the detail of what the actual procedure involves and therefore limit the amount of credit that can be awarded. In addition some procedures were unrealistic such as asking the bank to confirm whether it will renew the overdraft facility when the scenario made it clear that the bank would only make such a decision after seeing the audit report. Candidates must use the scenario and be practical when generating audit procedures.

Part (d) required a description of the impact on the audit report if the auditor believes the company is a going concern but is subject to a material uncertainty. Candidates performed disappointingly on this question. Unfortunately many candidates approached this requirement by suggesting every possible impact on the audit report. Very few candidates seemed to realise that the key issue was whether the disclosures given by the directors were adequate or not and so did not approach the answer in a methodical way. It appears that there is a lack of knowledge in relation to the differences between a modified report and a modified opinion. Once again future candidates are reminded that audit reports is a key element of the syllabus and hence an understanding of how an audit report can be modified and in which circumstances, is considered very important for this exam.

172 PAPRIKA *Walk in the footsteps of a top tutor*

Key answer tips

This was an unusual requirement asking for the amendments needed to the draft audit report. Use your knowledge of audit reports to identify the wording that needs to be amended. You must explain why the statements are wrong and hence why the amendment is needed to earn all of the marks.

(a)   (i)   Pervasive

Pervasive in the context of the audit report means the financial statements are materially misstated to such an extent that they are unreliable as a whole.

This may be where there are multiple material misstatements and is therefore not isolated to just one area of the financial statements.

Material misstatements may be isolated to one balance but they represent a substantial proportion of the financial statements that the effect is pervasive.

In relation to disclosures, the effect will be pervasive if a disclosure is fundamental to the users understanding of the financial statements.

(ii)   Modified opinions

Adverse

An adverse opinion is used where the financial statements are so materially misstated that they do not give a true and fair view.

For example if the going concern basis of preparation had been used when the company was not a going concern.

Disclaimer of opinion

A disclaimer of opinion is used where the auditor has been unable to obtain sufficient appropriate evidence for a substantial proportion of the financial statements. Without sufficient appropriate evidence, the auditor cannot conclude on whether the financial statements are materially misstated. In this situation the auditor will not express an opinion.

For example if the majority of the client's accounting records had been destroyed and no back-ups were available.

(b) **Reliance on the work of an expert**

ISA 620 *Using the Work of an Auditor's Expert* provides guidance to the auditor on factors to consider and steps to take in order to place reliance on the work of an expert.

Brown & Co is required to consider whether the expert has the necessary competence, capabilities including expertise.

They should consider the nature, scope and objective of the inventory expert's work, such as whether they have relevant technical knowledge.

The expert's independence should be ascertained, with potential threats such as undue reliance on Paprika Co or a self-interest threat such as share ownership considered.

In addition, the auditor should meet with the expert and discuss with them their relevant expertise in order to understand their field of expertise; in particular whether they have assessed similar inventory to Paprika Co in the past.

The expert's inventory quantities should be evaluated. Any assumptions used should be carefully reviewed and compared to previous inventory counts. Also the relevance, completeness and accuracy of any source data used should be verified.

(c) **Audit report elements**

Extract 1

'Our responsibility is to express an opinion on all pages of the financial statements.'

This is incomplete as the auditor is required to list the components of the financial statements which have been audited, being: statement of financial position, statement of profit or loss (income statement), statement of cash flows, summary of significant accounting policies and other explanatory information detailed in the notes to the financial statements.

Extract 2

'We conducted our audit in accordance with most of the International Standards on Auditing (ISAs).'

An auditor is required to perform their audit in accordance with all ISAs and cannot just choose to apply some. They must state that they follow all ISAs.

Extract 3

'Obtain maximum assurance as to whether the financial statements are free from all misstatements.'

The auditor is not able to obtain maximum assurance and they cannot confirm that the financial statements contain no errors. This is because they do not test every transaction or balance as it is not practical. They only test a sample of transactions and may only consider material balances. Hence auditors give reasonable assurance that financial statements are free from material misstatements.

Extract 4

'We have a responsibility to prevent fraud and error.'

This is not correct as it is in fact management's and not the auditor's responsibility to prevent and detect fraud and error. The auditor only has a responsibility to detect material misstatements whether caused by fraud or error.

'We prepare the financial statements.'

Again this is a responsibility of management, as they prepare the financial statements. The auditor provides an opinion on the truth and fairness of the financial statements.

Extract 5

'The procedures selected depend on the availability and experience of audit team members.'

The auditor is required to obtain sufficient and appropriate evidence and therefore should carry out any necessary procedures. Availability and experience of team members should not dictate the level of testing performed.

Extract 6

'We express an opinion on the effectiveness of these internal controls.'

The audit report is produced for the shareholders of Paprika Co and the auditor provides an opinion on the truth and fairness of the financial statements. Brown & Co will review the effectiveness of the internal controls and they will report on any key deficiencies identified during the course of the audit to management.

Extract 7

'We did not evaluate the overall presentation of the financial statements as this is management's responsibility.'

Management is responsible for producing the financial statements and so will consider the overall presentation as part of this. However, the auditors also have a responsibility to review the overall presentation to ensure that it is in accordance with relevant accounting standards and in line with their audit findings.

Extract 8

'We considered the reasonableness of any new accounting estimates.'

The auditor is required to consider all material accounting estimates made by management, whether these are brought forward from prior years or are new. Estimates from prior years, such as provisions, need to be considered annually as they may require amendment or may no longer be required.

'We did not review the appropriateness of accounting policies as these are the same as last year.'

Accounting policies must be reviewed annually as there could be a change in Paprika's circumstances which means a change in accounting policy may be required. In addition, new accounting standards may have been issued which require accounting policies to change.

Extract 9

'We relied on the work undertaken by an independent expert.'

Auditors are not expected to have knowledge of all elements of a company and hence it is acceptable to rely on the work of an independent expert. However, it is not acceptable for Brown & Co to refer to this in their audit report, as this implies that they are passing responsibility for this account balance to a third party. The auditor is ultimately responsible for the true and fair opinion and so cannot refer in their report to reliance on any third parties.

ACCA marking scheme				
				Marks
(a)	(i)	Up to 1 mark per point		
		• Renders FS as a whole unreliable		
		• Not isolated		
		• If isolated, substantial proportion of FS		
		• Disclosures which are fundamental to users understanding		
			Max	**2**
	(ii)	Up to 1 mark per well described point		
		• Adverse		
		• Disclaimer		
			Max	**2**
(b)		Up to 1 mark per valid point.		
		• Consider if expert has necessary competence, capabilities		
		• Consider nature, scope and objective of their work		
		• Assess independence		
		• Assess whether relevant expertise		
		• Evaluate inventory assessment including assumptions and source data used		
			Max	**4**
(c)		Up to 1 mark for each element identified and up to 1 mark per explanation, overall maximum of 6 marks for identification and 6 marks for explanation of elements.		
		• Opinion on all pages		
		• Audit in accordance with most International Standards on Auditing		
		• Maximum assurance, free from all misstatements		
		• Responsibility to prevent and detect fraud and error		
		• We prepare financial statements		
		• Procedures depend on availability and experience of team members		
		• We express opinion on effectiveness of internal controls		
		• Did not evaluate overall presentation of financial statements		
		• Considered reasonableness of new accounting estimates		
		• Did not review accounting policies		
		• Relied on work of independent expert		
			Max	**12**
Total				**20**

Examiner's comments

This question required an identification and explanation of elements of the draft audit report provided which required amendment. Candidates' performance was mixed on this question. Reviewing a draft audit report and identifying areas that require amendment was a different style of audit report question than in previous diets. However, many candidates answered this question satisfactorily. These recognised that there were two parts to the requirement, a need to identify the element from the scenario and then a need to explain why this sentence needed amending. Those candidates who scored well also tended to use a two column approach of identify and explain. This resulted in them maximising their marks as they easily identified the elements from the scenario and then for each explained why there was a problem. Those candidates who did not score as well tended to ignore the 'identify' requirement and jumped straight into the explanation. This is not what the question wanted as there were clearly two requirements 'identify' and 'explain' and both needed to be addressed to score well. In addition many candidates focused on redrafting the audit report extracts even though this was specifically excluded from the question requirement.

In this question it was also common to see many more points being provided. All points made are reviewed but marks are only allocated to the best points up to the maximum specified. Candidates would do better if they focused on the quality of points made rather than the quantity.

173 PANDA *Walk in the footsteps of a top tutor*

Key answer tips

Subsequent events are often misunderstood by students as they confuse the accounting treatment with the auditors' responsibilities resulting in very jumbled answers. Keep in mind that the client should prepare the financial statements in accordance with IAS 10. The auditor then performs audit procedures to obtain evidence to see if IAS 10 has been complied with.

(a) **Elements of an assurance engagement**

Three separate parties:

- The intended user who is the person who requires the assurance report.
- The responsible party, which is the organisation responsible for preparing the subject matter to be reviewed.
- The practitioner (i.e. an accountant) who is the professional who will review the subject matter and provide the assurance.

Subject matter

The subject matter is the data that the responsible party has prepared and which requires verification.

Suitable criteria

The subject matter is compared to the criteria in order for it to be assessed and an opinion provided.

Sufficient appropriate evidence

Sufficient appropriate evidence has to be obtained by the practitioner in order to give the required level of assurance.

Written assurance report

An assurance report contains the opinion that is given by the practitioner to the intended user and the responsible party.

(b) **Subsequent events**

Event 1 – Defective chemicals

Panda Co's (Panda) quality control procedures have identified that inventory with a cost of $0·85 million is defective; the scrap value of this inventory is $0·1 million. This information was obtained after the year end but provides further evidence of the net realisable value of inventory at the year end and hence is an adjusting event.

IAS 2 *Inventories* requires that inventory is valued at the lower of cost and net realisable value. The inventory of $0·85 million must be written down to its net realisable value of $0·1 million. The write down of $0·75 million (0·85 − 0·1) is material as it represents 13·4% (0·75/5·6) of profit before tax and 1·4% (0·75/55) of revenue. Hence, the directors should amend the financial statements by writing down the inventory to $0·1 million.

The following audit procedures should be applied to form a conclusion on the adjustment:

- Review the board minutes/quality control reports to assess whether this event was the only case of defective inventory as there could potentially be other inventory which requires writing down.

- Discuss the matter with the directors, checking whether the company has sufficient inventory to continue trading in the short term.

- Obtain a written representation confirming that the company's going concern status is not impacted.

- Obtain a schedule showing the defective inventory and agree to supporting production documentation that it was produced prior to 30 April, as otherwise it would not require a write down at the year end.

- Discuss with management how they have assessed the scrap value of $0·1 million and agree this amount to any supporting documentation to confirm the value.

Event 2 – Explosion

An explosion has occurred in one of the offsite storage locations and property, plant and equipment and inventory valued at $0·9 million have been damaged and now have no scrap value. The directors do not believe they are likely to be able to claim insurance for the damaged assets. This event occurred after the year end and the explosion would not have been in existence at 30 April, and hence this event indicates a non-adjusting event.

The damaged assets of $0·9 million are material as they represent 16·1% (0·9/5·6) of profit before tax and 1·6% (0·9/55) of revenue. As a material non-adjusting event, the assets should not be written down to zero; however, the directors should consider including a disclosure note detailing the explosion and the value of assets impacted.

The following audit procedures should be applied to form a conclusion on any amendment:

- Obtain a schedule showing the damaged property, plant and equipment and agree the net book value to the non-current assets register to confirm what the value of damaged assets was.

- Obtain the latest inventory records for this storage location to ascertain the likely level of inventory at the time of the explosion.

- Discuss with the directors whether they will disclose the effect of the explosion in the financial statements.

- Discuss with the directors why they do not believe that they are able to claim on their insurance; if a claim was to be made, then only uninsured losses would require disclosure, and this may be an immaterial amount.

(c) **Audit report**

The explosion is a non-adjusting post year-end event and the level of damaged assets are material. Hence a disclosure note should be included in the 2013 financial statements and the write down of assets would be included in the 2014 financial statements.

If the directors refuse to make the subsequent event disclosures, then the financial statements are materially misstated.

The lack of disclosure is material but not pervasive, therefore the audit report will be modified and a qualified opinion will be necessary. The opinion paragraph would be qualified 'except for'.

The basis for qualified opinion paragraph would explain the misstatement in relation to the lack of subsequent events disclosure and the effect on the financial statements.

Tutor's top tips

Note that for part (b) the requirement asks for audit reporting implications 'should this issue remain unresolved'. There is no point wasting time writing an answer considering if the issue is resolved.

ACCA marking scheme		
		Marks
(a) Up to 1 mark per well explained element		
• Intended user, responsible party, practitioner		
• Subject matter		
• Suitable criteria		
• Appropriate evidence		
• Assurance report		
	Max	5
(b) Up to 1 mark per valid point, overall maximum of 6 marks per event		
Event 1 – Defective chemicals		
• Provides evidence of conditions at the year end		
• Inventory to be adjusted to lower of cost and net realisable value		
• Calculation of materiality		
• Review board minutes/quality control reports		
• Discuss with the directors, adequate inventory to continue to trade		
• Obtain written representation re going concern		
• Obtain schedule of defective inventory, agree to supporting documentation		
• Discuss with directors basis of the scrap value		
	Max	6
Event 2 – Explosion		
• Provides evidence of conditions that arose subsequent to the year end		
• Non-adjusting event, requires disclosure if material		
• Calculation of materiality		
• Obtain schedule of damaged property, plant and equipment and agree values to asset register		
• Obtain latest inventory records to confirm damaged inventory levels		
• Discuss with the directors if they will make disclosures		
• Discuss with directors why no insurance claim will be made		
	Max	6

(c)	Up to 1 mark per well explained valid point		
	• Disclosure required in 2013 financial statements and adjustment to the assets in 2014 financial statements		
	• Material but not pervasive misstatement, modified audit report, qualified opinion		
	• Opinion paragraph – except for		
	• Basis for qualified opinion		
		Max	3
Total			20

Examiner's comments

Part (a) required an explanation of the five elements of an assurance engagement. This question was unrelated to the scenario and was knowledge based. Performance was mixed on this question, in that many candidates either scored full marks or no marks. Those candidates who were able to identify the elements occasionally failed to score full marks due to a failure to fully explain the element, for example stating 'suitable criteria' and then giving an example of accounting standards, rather than explaining that the suitable criteria are the benchmark for comparing the subject matter against. Some candidates did not understand what was required and focused on the different opinions and positive/negative assurance or on the content of an audit report.

Part (b) required an explanation of whether the financial statements should be amended and audit procedures that should be performed by the auditor to form a conclusion on any required amendment. Performance was mixed on this question. Many candidates were able to correctly identify whether the events were adjusting or non-adjusting. However the justification for this was not always correct; for example stating that 'the explosion was non-adjusting as it occurred after the year end'. Many candidates were able to calculate the materiality of the potential error, using the numbers provided, although some incorrectly calculated the materiality for event 1 using the total cost of inventory of $0.85m rather than the write down of $0.75m. The decision as to whether the financial statements required amendment was answered well for event 1, but less so for event 2 as many candidates did not seem to realise that adding a disclosure note is an amendment. With regards to procedures to undertake to form a conclusion on any required amendment, candidates seemed to struggle with this. Many procedures lacked sufficient detail to score the available 1 mark per test. This commonly occurred with tests such as; 'reviewing board minutes' and 'obtain written representation'. These procedures need to be phrased with sufficient detail to obtain credit and must be tailored to the scenario. In addition a significant minority of candidates wanted to contact Panda's insurance company; this is not a realistic procedure. In addition some candidates wasted time by discussing the impact on the audit report for each event; this was not part of the question requirement for part (b) and so would not have generated any marks. Candidates once again are reminded to only answer the question set.

Part (c) required the impact on the audit report should the issue for event 2, the explosion, remain unresolved. Performance on this question was unsatisfactory. Candidates still continue to recommend an emphasis of matter paragraph for all audit report questions, this is not the case and it was not relevant for this issue. Candidates need to understand what an emphasis of matter paragraph is and why it is used. In addition some candidates are confused with regards to audit report terms and used phrases such as 'qualify the report' rather than modify the report and 'modified opinion' rather than qualified opinion. A significant number of candidates were unable to identify the correct audit report modification, giving multiple options and some candidates seemed to believe that the opinion did not require qualification as it was only the disclosure, as opposed to any numbers that were incorrect. Also some answers contradicted themselves such as 'the issue is material therefore an unqualified opinion can be given'. Additionally many candidates ignored the question requirement to only consider the audit report impact if the issue was unresolved. Lots of answers started with 'if resolved the audit report .....' this was not required. Once again future candidates are reminded that audit reports are the only output of a statutory audit and hence an understanding of how an audit report can be modified and in which circumstances, is considered very important for this exam.

174   VIOLET & CO *Walk in the footsteps of a top tutor*

Key answer tips

Parts (a) and (b) examine written representations. These are only an acceptable form of evidence in certain circumstances. If better evidence is available, that should be obtained.

Part (c) is a straightforward audit reporting question and the requirement gives you an approach to use. Discuss the issue, consider if it is material, recommend further procedures and describe the impact on the audit report. When discussing the impact on the audit report, remember that the opinion is only one element of the report. Consider whether there is a need for any further modifications such as a 'basis for' paragraph if you are suggesting the opinion should be modified or an emphasis of matter paragraph if there are material uncertainties which have been adequately disclosed by the client.

(a)   Written representations

Written representations are necessary information that the auditor requires in connection with the audit of the entity's financial statements. Accordingly, similar to responses to inquiries, written representations are audit evidence.

The auditor needs to obtain written representations from management and, where appropriate, those charged with governance that they believe they have fulfilled their responsibility for the preparation of the financial statements and for the completeness of the information provided to the auditor.

Written representations are needed to support other audit evidence relevant to the financial statements or specific assertions in the financial statements, if determined necessary by the auditor or required by other International Standards on Auditing. This may be necessary for judgemental areas where the auditor has to rely on management explanations.

Written representations can be used to confirm that management have communicated to the auditor all deficiencies in internal controls of which management are aware.

Written representations are normally in the form of a letter, written by the company's management and addressed to the auditor. The letter is usually requested from management but can also be requested from the chief operating officer or chief financial officer. Throughout the fieldwork, the audit team will note any areas where representations may be required.

During the final review stage, the auditors will produce a draft representation letter. The directors will review this and then produce it on their letterhead.

It will be signed by the directors and dated as at the date the audit report is signed, but not after.

(b) **Oral representation**

A representation from management confirming that overdrafts are complete would be relevant evidence. Overdrafts are liabilities and therefore the main focus for the auditor is completeness.

With regards to reliability, the evidence is oral rather than written and so this reduces its reliability. The directors could in the future deny having given this representation, and the auditors would have no documentary evidence to prove what the directors had said.

This evidence is obtained from management rather than being auditor generated, and is therefore less reliable. Management may wish to provide biased evidence in order to reduce the amount of liabilities in the financial statements. The auditors are unbiased and so evidence generated directly by them will be better.

External evidence obtained from the company's banks could be used to confirm the bank overdraft balances and this would be more independent than relying on management's internal confirmations.

(c) **Daisy Designs Co (Daisy)**

(i) Daisy's sales ledger has been corrupted by a computer virus; hence no detailed testing has been performed on revenue and receivables. The audit team will need to see if they can confirm revenue and receivables in an alternative manner. If they are unable to do this, then two significant balances in the financial statements will not have been confirmed. Revenue and receivables are both higher than the total profit before tax (PBT) of $2m; receivables are 170% of PBT and revenue is nearly eight times the PBT; hence this is a very material issue.

(ii) Procedures to be adopted include:

- Discuss with management whether they have any alternative records which detail revenue and receivables for the year.

- Attempt to perform analytical procedures, such as proof in total or monthly comparison to last year, to gain comfort in total for revenue and for receivables.

(iii) The auditors will need to modify the audit report as they are unable to obtain sufficient appropriate evidence in relation to two material and pervasive areas, being receivables and revenue.

The opinion paragraph will be a disclaimer of opinion and will state that we are unable to form an opinion on the financial statements.

A basis for disclaimer of opinion paragraph will explain the limitation in relation to the lack of evidence over revenue and receivables.

Fuchsia Enterprises Co (Fuchsia)

(i) Fuchsia is facing going concern problems as it has experienced difficult trading conditions and it has a negative cash outflow. However, the financial statements have been prepared on a going concern basis, even though it is possible that the company is not a going concern. The prior year financial statements showed a profit of $1.2m and the current financial statements show a loss before tax of $4.4m, the net cash outflow of $3.2m represents 73% of this loss (3.2/4.4m) and hence is a material issue.

(ii) Management are confident that further funding can be obtained; however, the team is sceptical and so the following procedures should be adopted:

- Discuss with management whether any finance has now been secured.

- Review the correspondence with the finance provider to confirm the level of funding that is to be provided and this should be compared to the net cash outflow of $3.2m.

- Review the most recent board minutes to understand whether management's view on Fuchsia's going concern has altered.

- Review the cash flow forecasts for the year and assess the reasonableness of the assumptions adopted.

(iii) If management refuse to amend the going concern basis of the financial statements or at the very least make adequate going concern disclosures, then the audit report will need to be modified. As the going concern basis is probably incorrect and the error is material and pervasive, then an adverse opinion would be necessary.

The opinion paragraph will be an adverse opinion and will state that the financial statements do not give a true and fair view.

A basis for adverse opinion paragraph will explain the inappropriate use of the going concern assumption.

	ACCA marking scheme		
			Marks
(a)	Up to 1 mark per well explained point		
	Written representations are necessary information the auditor needs in connection with the audit of the entity's financial statements		
	Required to confirm directors' responsibilities		
	Required to support other evidence or required by other ISAs		
	Required to confirm management have communicated all deficiencies in internal controls		
	Normally in the form of a letter, written by the company's directors and addressed to the auditor		
	Throughout the fieldwork, note any areas where representations may be required		
	Auditors produce a draft representation letter, directors review and then produce it on their letterhead		
	Signed by the directors and dated just before the date the audit report is signed		
		Max	5
(b)	Up to 1 mark per well described point		
	Relevance		
	Reliability – oral v written		
	Reliability – client v auditor generated		
	Reliability – better external evidence could be obtained		
		Max	3

(c)	Up to 1 mark per valid point, overall maximum of 6 marks PER ISSUE		
	Discussion of issue		
	Calculation of materiality		
	Procedures at completion stage		
	Type of audit report modification required		
	Impact on audit report		
		Max	12
Total			20

Examiner's comments

Part (a) required an explanation of the purpose and procedures for obtaining written representations. This question was unrelated to the scenario and was knowledge based. Performance was unsatisfactory on this question. A majority of candidates were able to provide answers on the purpose of a written representation. However a significant minority strayed from the question requirement and focused on what the audit report implications were if management refused to provide a representation; this was not required and scored no marks. Candidates seemed to confuse written representations with third party confirmations such as bank letters and receivables circularisations. Therefore when discussing the procedures for obtaining a representation these candidates were unable to provide valid answers.

Part (b) required a description of the relevance and reliability of an oral representation given by management for the completeness of the bank overdraft balance. Performance was unsatisfactory on this question. Many candidates were able to apply their knowledge of relevance and reliability of evidence to the specific example given. Many of these easily scored two marks by discussing oral versus written evidence and client generated Vs third party or auditor generated evidence. However, very few adequately considered whether a representation on completeness would be relevant for a liability balance. Some candidates ignored the requirement to focus on relevance and reliability and so provided general points on representations, despite having already done this in part (a).

Part (c) required a discussion of two issues; an assessment of the materiality of each; procedures to resolve each issue and the impact on the audit report if each issue remained unresolved. Performance was mixed on this question. There were a significant minority of candidates who did not devote sufficient time and effort to this question bearing in mind it was worth 12 marks. The requirement to discuss the two issues of Daisy's corrupted sales ledger and Fuchsia's going concern problem was on whole, answered well by most candidates. In addition many candidates correctly identified that each issue was clearly material. A significant minority seemed to believe the corruption of the sales ledger was an adjusting event and so incorrectly proceeded to focus on subsequent events. With regards to procedures to undertake at the completion stage, candidates seemed to struggle with Daisy. Given that the sales ledger had been corrupted procedures such as 'agree goods despatch notes to sales invoices to the sales ledger' or 'reconcile the sales ledger to the general ledger' were unlikely to be possible. Most candidates correctly identified relevant analytical review procedures and a receivables circularisation. Candidates performed better on auditing the going concern of Fuchsia, however some candidates wasted time by providing a long list of going concern tests when only two or three were needed. Performance on the impact on the audit report if each issue remained unresolved was unsatisfactory. Candidates still continue to recommend an emphasis of matter paragraph for all audit report questions, this is not the case and it was not relevant for either issue. Candidates need to understand what an emphasis of matter paragraph is and why it is used. A significant number of candidates were unable to identify the correct audit report modification, suggesting that Daisy's should be qualified or adverse, as opposed to disclaimer of opinion. Also some answers contradicted themselves with answers of 'the issue is not material therefore qualify the opinion'. Additionally many candidates ignored the question requirement to only consider the audit report impact if the issue was unresolved. Lots of answers started with 'if resolved the audit report .....' this was not required. In relation to the impact on the audit report, many candidates were unable to describe how the opinion paragraph would change and so failed to maximise their marks. Once again future candidates are reminded that audit reports are the only output of a statutory audit and hence an understanding of how an audit report can be modified and in which circumstances, is considered very important for this exam.

175 MINNIE *Walk in the footsteps of a top tutor*

Key answer tips

Part (a) is quite tricky but easy marks can be earned by taking a logical and common sense approach. Think about what happens when the auditor identifies misstatements and what they have to do to try and get them resolved.

Part (c) is a straightforward audit reporting requirement. When discussing the impact on the audit report, remember that the opinion is only one element of the report. Consider whether there is a need for any further modifications such as a 'basis for' paragraph if you are suggesting the opinion should be modified.

(a)   Misstatements

ISA 450 *Evaluation of Misstatements Identified During the Audit* considers what a misstatement is and deals with the auditor's responsibility in relation to misstatements.

It identifies a misstatement as being: A difference between the amount, classification, presentation, or disclosure of a reported financial statement item and the amount, classification, presentation, or disclosure that is required for the item to be in accordance with the applicable financial reporting framework. Misstatements can arise from error or fraud.

It also then defines uncorrected misstatements as: Misstatements that the auditor has accumulated during the audit and that have not been corrected.

There are three categories of misstatements:

(i)   Factual misstatements are misstatements about which there is no doubt.

(ii)   Judgemental misstatements are differences arising from the judgements of management concerning accounting estimates that the auditor considers unreasonable, or the selection or application of accounting policies that the auditor considers inappropriate.

(iii)   Projected misstatements are the auditor's best estimate of misstatements in populations, involving the projection of misstatements identified in audit samples to the entire populations from which the samples were drawn.

The auditor has a responsibility to accumulate misstatements which arise over the course of the audit unless they are very small amounts.

Identified misstatements should be considered during the course of the audit to assess whether the audit strategy and plan should be revised.

The auditor should determine whether uncorrected misstatements are material in aggregate or individually.

All misstatements should be communicated to management on a timely basis and request that they make necessary amendments. If this request is refused then the auditor should consider the potential impact on their audit report.

A written representation should be requested from management to confirm that unadjusted misstatements are immaterial.

(b) **Reliance on the work of an independent valuer**

ISA 500 *Audit Evidence* requires auditors to evaluate the competence, capabilities including expertise and objectivity of a management expert.

This would include consideration of the qualifications of the valuer and assessment of whether they were members of any professional body or industry association.

In addition, the auditor should meet with the expert and discuss with them their relevant expertise; in particular whether they have valued similar properties to Minnie Co in the past. Also consider whether they understand the accounting requirements of IAS 16 *Property, Plant and Equipment* in relation to valuations.

The expert's independence should be ascertained, with potential threats such as undue reliance on Minnie Co or a self-interest threat such as share ownership considered.

The valuation should then be evaluated. The assumptions used should be carefully reviewed and compared to previous revaluations at Minnie Co. These assumptions should be discussed with both management and the valuer to understand where the misstatement has arisen.

In order to correct the misstatement, it might be necessary for the valuer to undertake further work and this should be agreed. Daffy & Co would not be able to state in their audit report that they had relied on an expert for the property valuation.

(c) **(i)** **Depreciation on land and buildings**

Depreciation has been provided on the land element of property, plant and equipment and this is contrary to IAS 16 *Property, Plant and Equipment,* as depreciation should only be charged on buildings.

The error is material as it represents 7% of profit before tax (0.7m/10m) and hence management should remove this from the financial statements.

If management refuses to amend this error then the audit report will need to be modified as management has not complied with IAS 16.

The error is material but not pervasive therefore a qualified opinion would be necessary. The opinion paragraph would be qualified 'except for' – due to material misstatement.

The basis for qualified opinion paragraph would explain the material misstatement in relation to the provision of depreciation on land and the effect on the financial statements.

(ii) **Wages program**

Minnie Co's wages program has been corrupted leading to a loss of payroll data for a period of two months. The auditors should attempt to verify payroll in an alternative manner. If they are unable to do this then payroll for the whole year would not have been verified.

Wages and salaries for the two month period represents 11% of profit before tax (1.1m/10m) and therefore is a material balance for which audit evidence has not been available.

The auditors will need to modify the audit report as they are unable to obtain sufficient appropriate evidence.

The issue is a material, but not pervasive, element of wages and salaries and therefore a qualified opinion will be required.

The opinion paragraph will be qualified 'except for' – due to insufficient appropriate audit evidence.

The basis for qualified opinion paragraph will explain the limitation in relation to the lack of evidence over two months of payroll records.

(iii) **Lawsuit**

The company is being sued by a competitor for breach of copyright. This matter has been correctly disclosed in accordance with IAS 37 *Provisions, Contingent Liabilities and Contingent Assets.*

The lawsuit is for $5m which represents 50% of profit before tax (5·0m/10m) and hence is a material matter. This is an important matter which needs to be brought to the attention of the users.

An emphasis of matter paragraph would need to be included in the audit report, in that the matter is appropriately disclosed but is fundamental to the users' understanding of the financial statements; this will not affect the audit opinion which will be unmodified in relation to this matter.

An emphasis of matter (EOM) paragraph should be included after the opinion paragraph.

The EOM paragraph would explain clearly about the lawsuit and cross references to where in the financial statements the disclosure of this contingent liability can be found.

	ACCA marking scheme		
			Marks
(a)	Up to 1 mark per well explained point		
	Definition of misstatements		
	Definition of uncorrected misstatements		
	Factual misstatements		
	Judgemental misstatements		
	Projected misstatements		
	Auditor should accumulate misstatements		
	Consider if audit strategy/plan should be revised		
	Assess if uncorrected misstatements material		
	Communicate to those charged with governance, request changes		
	If refused then assess impact on audit report		
	Request written representation		
		Max	4
(b)	Up to 1 mark per valid point		
	ISA 500 provides guidance		
	Consider if member of professional body or industry association		
	Assess whether relevant expertise		
	Assess independence		
	Evaluate assumptions		
	Agree any further work required		
	No reference in audit report of Daffy & Co		
		Max	4
(c)	Up to 1 mark per valid point, overall maximum of 4 marks PER ISSUE		
	Discussion of issue		
	Calculation of materiality		
	Type of audit report modification required		
	Impact on audit report		
		Max	12
Total			20

Examiner's comments

Part (a) required an explanation of the term 'misstatement' and a description of the auditor's responsibility in relation to misstatements. This question was unrelated to the scenario, and was not answered well by many candidates. Most candidates were able to gain 1 mark by explaining that a misstatement was an error, however they could not then explain the auditor's responsibility.

ISA 450 *Evaluation of Misstatements Identified During the Audit* provides guidance on this area. This is a relatively new ISA and was issued as part of the clarity project. As this ISA had not yet been tested then this is an area which should have been prioritised by candidates. However, many candidates clearly had not studied this area at all. They therefore provided answers which focused on the auditor's responsibilities to provide an opinion on the truth and fairness of the financial statements or to detect material misstatements. In addition a minority of candidates produced answers which focused on materiality.

Part (b) required a description of the factors that should be considered when placing reliance on the work of the independent valuer. Candidates performed well on this question. Many were able to score over half marks by identifying points such as professional qualifications, experience and independence.

The requirement verb was to 'describe' therefore sufficient detail was required to score the 1 mark available per test and some answers were a little brief. Candidates are reminded to look carefully at the verb at the beginning of the question requirement, as this should help them to understand the level of detail required for their answers.

Part (c) required a discussion of three issues in the scenario as well as a description of the impact on the audit report if these issues remain unresolved. Candidates' performance was unsatisfactory on this question.

Each of the three issues had a maximum of 4 marks available and in order to score well candidates needed to consider the following in their answer:

- A description of the audit issue; such as incorrectly depreciating land, or lack of evidence to support wages or contingent liability disclosure.

- A calculation of whether the issue was material or not, using the financial information provided in the scenario.

- An explanation of the type of audit report required.

- A description of the impact on the audit report.

A significant minority of candidates stated that it was acceptable to depreciate land, and the issue was that it should have been charged for the prior year as well. This demonstrates a fundamental lack of accounting knowledge.

In relation to the materiality calculation, some candidates stated the issue was material but without using the financial information provided. What was required was a calculation, for example, the land depreciation was $0.7m and so represented 7% of profit before tax, and then an explanation of whether this was material or not. The benchmark from ISA 320 *Materiality in Planning and Performing an Audit* of 5% of profit before tax was taken as being material.

With regards to the type of audit report required, many candidates provided a scatter gun approach of suggesting every possible audit report option. Candidates often hedge their bets by saying 'if management will make an amendment then we will give an unmodified opinion, however if they do not make the adjustment then we will give a qualified except for opinion.' Giving every possible audit report option will not allow candidates to score well. Many candidates used terms such as 'except for', 'modified' or 'qualified' but the accompanying sentences demonstrated that candidates did not actually understand what these terms meant. In addition a significant proportion of candidates do not understand when an 'emphasis of matter' paragraph is relevant, and seemed to think that it was an alternative to an 'except for' qualification. Also candidates are reminded that since the clarified ISAs have been issued the old terminology of 'disagreement' is no longer relevant and instead should refer to 'material misstatement'. In relation to the impact on the audit report, many candidates were unable to describe how the opinion paragraph would change and that a basis for qualified opinion paragraph was necessary for issues (i) and (ii). In addition a significant proportion of candidates provided procedures the auditor would undertake in order to understand or resolve the issues. For example, alternative procedures for verifying wages were given, or the steps to take in contacting lawyers in relation to the lawsuit. Whilst valid procedures, they did not score any marks as they were not part of the question requirement. Candidates must answer the question asked and not the one they wish had been asked.

Future candidates are once again reminded that audit reports are the only output of a statutory audit and hence an understanding of how an audit report can be modified and in which circumstances, is considered very important for this exam.

Audit and Assurance

Specimen Exam applicable from September 2016

Paper F8

The Association of Chartered Certificate Accountants

KAPLAN

PUBLISHING

SECTION A – Objective test (OT) questions

The following scenario relates to questions 1–5

You are an audit manager of Buffon & Co, and you have just been assigned the audit of Maldini Co (Maldini). The audit engagement partner who is responsible for the audit of Maldini, a listed company, has been in place for approximately eight years and her son has just been offered a role with Maldini as a sales manager. This role would entitle him to shares in Maldini as part of his remuneration package.

Maldini's board of directors is considering establishing an internal audit function, and the finance director has asked Buffon & Co about the differences in the role of internal audit and external audit. If the internal audit function is established, the directors have suggested that they may wish to outsource this to Buffon & Co.

The finance director has suggested to the board that if Buffon & Co is appointed as internal as well as external auditors, then fees should be renegotiated with at least 20% of all internal and external audit fees being based on the profit after tax of the company as this will align the interests of Buffon & Co and Maldini.

1   From a review of the information above, your audit assistant has highlighted some of the potential risks to independence in respect of the audit of Maldini.

   1   Audit partner has been in the position for eight years.

   2   Maldini has asked for advice regarding role of internal audit.

   3   Maldini has asked Buffon & Co to carry out internal audit work.

   4   Fees will be based on 20% of profit after tax.

   Which of the following options correctly identifies the valid threats to independence and allocates the threat to the appropriate category?

	Self-interest	Self-review	Familiarity
A	1 only	2 and 3	4 only
B	1 only	2 only	4 only
C	2 only	3 and 4	1 only
D	4 only	3 only	1 only

2   In relation to the audit engagement partner holding the role for eight years and her son's offer of employment with Maldini:

   Which of the following safeguards should be implemented in order to comply with ACCA's Code of Ethics and Conduct?

   A   The audit partner should be removed from the audit team

   B   An independent review partner should be appointed

   C   The audit partner should be removed if her son accepts the position

   D   Buffon & Co should resign from the audit

3 In line with ACCA's Code of Ethics and Conduct, which of the following factors must be considered before the internal audit engagement should be accepted?

1 Whether the external audit team have the expertise to carry out the internal audit work.

2 If the assignments will relate to the internal controls over financial reporting.

3 If management will accept responsibility for implementing appropriate recommendations.

4 The probable timescale for the outsourcing of the internal audit function.

A 1, 2 and 3

B 2 and 3 only

C 1 and 4 only

D 1, 3 and 4

4 Following management's request for information regarding the different roles of internal and external audit, you have collated a list of key characteristics.

1 Appointed by audit committee.

2 Reports are publicly available to shareholders.

3 Review efficiency and effectiveness of operations to improve operations.

4 Express an opinion on the truth and fairness of the financial statements.

Which of the following options correctly allocates the above statements to the relevant auditor?

	External	Internal
A	2, 3 and 4	1 only
B	1 and 4	2 and 3
C	2 and 4	1 and 3
D	2 only	1, 3 and 4

5 If the internal and external audit assignments are accepted, what safeguards, if any, are needed in relation to the basis for the fee?

A As long as the total fee received from Maldini is less than 15% of the firm's total fee income, no safeguards are needed.

B The client should be informed that only the internal audit fee can be based on profit after tax.

C The fees should be based on Maldini's profit before tax.

D No safeguards can be applied and this basis for fee determination should be rejected.

The following scenario relates to questions 6–10

Balotelli Beach Hotel Co (Balotelli) operates a number of hotels providing accommodation, leisure facilities and restaurants. You are an audit senior of Mario & Co and are currently conducting the audit of Balotelli for the year ended 31 December 20X4. During the course of the audit a number of events and issues have been brought to your attention:

Non-current assets and depreciation

Balotelli incurred significant capital expenditure during the year updating the leisure facilities at several of the company's hotels. Depreciation is charged monthly on all assets on a straight line basis (SL) and it is company policy to charge a full month's depreciation in the month of acquisition and none in the month of disposal.

6   During the audit of non-current assets, the audit team has obtained the following extract of the non-current assets register detailing some of the new leisure equipment acquired during the year.

Extract from Balotelli's non-current assets register

Date	Description	Original cost	Depreciation policy	Accumulated depreciation	Charge for the year	Carrying value
		$		$	$	$
1 May 20X4	15 treadmills	18,000	36 months SL	0	4,000	14,000
15 May 20X4	20 exercise bikes	17,000	3 years SL	0	5,667	11,333
17 August 20X4	15 rowing machines	9,750	36 months SL	0	2,167	7,583
19 August 20X4	10 cross trainers	11,000	36 months SL	0	1,528	9,472
		55,750		0	13,362	42,388

In order to verify the depreciation expense for the year, you have been asked to perform a proof in total. This will involve developing an expectation of the depreciation expense for the year and comparing this to the actual expense to assess if the client has calculated the depreciation charge for the year correctly.

What is the expected depreciation expense for the above assets for the year ended 31 December 20X4 and the resultant impact on non-current assets?

A   Depreciation should be $10,660, assets are understated

B   Depreciation should be $18,583, assets are understated

C   Depreciation should be $9,111, assets are overstated

D   Depreciation should be $12,549, assets are overstated

7   The audit assistant who has been assigned to help you with the audit work on non-current assets has expressed some uncertainty over why certain audit procedures are carried out and specifically is unsure what procedures relate to the valuation and allocation assertion.

Which of the following audit procedures are appropriate to test the VALUATION assertion for non-current assets?

1   Ensure disposals are correctly accounted for and recalculate gain/loss on disposal.

2   Recalculate the depreciation charge for a sample of assets ensuring that it is being applied consistently and in accordance with IAS 16 *Property, Plant and Equipment*.

3   Review the repairs and maintenance expense accounts for evidence of items of a capital nature.

4   Review board minutes for evidence of disposals during the year and verify that these are appropriately reflected in the non-current assets register.

A   1 and 2

B   1, 3 and 4

C   2, 3 and 4

D   2 and 3 only

Food poisoning

Balotelli's directors received correspondence in November 20X4 from a group of customers who attended a wedding at one of the company's hotels. They have alleged that they suffered severe food poisoning from food eaten at the hotel and are claiming substantial damages. Management has stated that based on discussions with their lawyers, the claim is unlikely to be successful.

8   **In relation to the claim regarding the alleged food poisoning, which of the following audit procedures would provide the auditor with the MOST reliable audit evidence regarding the likely outcome of the litigation?**

A   Request a written representation from management supporting their assertion that the claim will not be successful.

B   Send an enquiry letter to the lawyers of Balotelli to obtain their view as to the probability of the claim being successful.

C   Review the correspondence from the customers claiming food poisoning to assess whether Balotelli has a present obligation as a result of a past event.

D   Review board minutes to understand why the directors believe that the claim will not be successful.

Trade receivables

Balotelli's trade receivables have historically been low as most customers are required to pay in advance or at the time of visiting the hotel. However, during the year a number of companies opened corporate accounts which are payable monthly in arrears. As such, the trade receivables balance has risen significantly and is now a material balance.

9   As trade receivables is a material balance, the audit partner has asked that the audit team carry out a trade receivables circularisation.

Which of the following are benefits of carrying out a trade receivables circularisation?

1   It provides evidence from an independent external source.

2   It provides sufficient appropriate audit evidence over all relevant balance assertions.

3   It improves audit efficiency as all customers are required to respond.

4   It improves the reliability of audit evidence as the process is under the control of the auditor.

A   1 and 2

B   1, 2 and 4

C   2 and 3

D   1 and 4 only

10   The results of the trade receivables circularisation carried out by the audit team on balances as at 31 December 20X4 are detailed below. You have been asked to consider the results and determine if additional audit procedures are required.

Customer	Balance per sales ledger	Balance per customer confirmation	Comment
	$	$	
Willow Co	42,500	42,500	
Cedar Co	35,000	25,000	Invoice raised 28 December
Maple Co	60,000	45,000	Payment made 30 December
Laurel Co	55,000	55,000	A balance of $20,000 is currently being disputed by Laurel Co
Oak Co	15,000		No reply

Which of the following statements in relation to the results of the trade receivables circularisation is TRUE?

A   No further audit procedures need to be carried out in relation to the outstanding balances with Willow Co and Laurel Co.

B   The difference in relation to Cedar Co represents a timing difference and should be agreed to a pre year-end invoice.

C   The difference in relation to Maple Co represents a timing difference and should be agreed to pre year-end bank statements.

D   Due to the non-reply, the balance with Oak Co cannot be verified and a different customer balance should be selected and circularised.

The following scenario relates to questions 11–15

Cannavaro.com is a website design company whose year-end was 31 December 20X4. The audit is almost complete and the financial statements are due to be signed shortly. Profit before tax for the year is $3.8 million and revenue is $11.2 million.

The company has only required an audit for the last two years and the board of directors has asked your firm to provide more detail in relation to the form and content of the auditor's report.

During the audit it has come to light that a key customer, Pirlo Co, with a receivables balance at the year end of $285,000, has just notified Cannavaro.com that they are experiencing cash flow difficulties and so are unable to make any payments for the foreseeable future. The finance director has notified the audit team that he will write this balance off as an irrecoverable debt in the 20X5 financial statements.

11   To explain to the board the content of the audit report, the audit partner has asked you to provide details as to why certain elements are included within an unmodified report.

      Which of the following explains the purpose of the ADDRESSEE element of the unmodified audit report in line with ISA 700 Forming an Opinion and Reporting on Financial Statements?

      A   It demonstrates the point at which sufficient appropriate evidence has been obtained

      B   It clarifies who may rely on the opinion included within the report

      C   It explains the role and remit of the audit

      D   It sets out the location where the auditor practises

12   The audit assistant assigned to the audit of Cannavaro.com wants a better understanding of the effect subsequent events have on the audit and has made the following statements:

      1   All material subsequent events require the numbers in the financial statements to be adjusted.

      2   A non-adjusting event is a subsequent event for which NO amendments to the current year financial statements are required.

      3   The auditor's responsibilities for subsequent events which occur prior to the audit report being signed are different from their responsibilities after the audit report has been issued.

      4   The auditor should request a written representation confirming that all relevant subsequent events have been disclosed.

      Which of the statements above in relation to subsequent events are true?

      A   1 and 3

      B   2, 3 and 4

      C   1, 2 and 4

      D   3 and 4 only

13 The audit engagement partner has asked you to make an initial assessment of the materiality of the issue with the outstanding receivables balance with Pirlo Co and to consider the overall impact on the financial statements.

Which of the following correctly summarises the effect of the outstanding balance with Pirlo Co?

	Material	Financial statement impact
A	No	Revenue is overstated
B	No	Gross profit is understated
C	Yes	Profit is overstated
D	Yes	Going concern principle is in doubt

14 The audit engagement partner requires you to perform additional procedures in order to conclude on the level of any adjustment needed in relation to the outstanding balance with Pirlo Co.

Which TWO of the following audit procedures should be performed to form a conclusion as to whether the financial statements require amendment?

1　Discuss with management the reasons for not amending the financial statements.

2　Review the cash book post year end for receipts from Pirlo Co.

3　Send a request to Pirlo Co to confirm the outstanding balance.

4　Agree the outstanding balance to invoices and sales orders.

A　1 and 2

B　1 and 4

C　2 and 3

D　2 and 4

15 The finance director has asked you to outline the appropriate audit opinions which will be provided depending on whether the company decides to amend or not amend the 20X4 financial statements for the issue identified regarding the recoverability of the balance with Pirlo Co.

Which of the following options correctly summarises the audit opinions which will be issued depending on whether or not the 20X4 financial statements are amended?

	Financial statements amended	Financial statements not amended
A	Unmodified	Unmodified with emphasis of matter
B	Unmodified with emphasis of matter	Qualified 'except for'
C	Unmodified	Adverse
D	Unmodified	Qualified 'except for'

SECTION B

1 MILLA

Milla Cola Co (Milla) manufactures fizzy drinks such as cola and lemonade as well as other soft drinks and its year end is 30 September 20X5. You are an audit manager of Totti & Co and are currently planning the audit of Milla. You attended the planning meeting with the audit engagement partner and finance director last week and the minutes from the meeting are shown below. You are reviewing these as part of the process of preparing the audit strategy document.

Minutes of planning meeting for Milla

Milla's trading results have been strong this year and the company is forecasting revenue of $85 million, which is an increase from the previous year. The company has invested significantly in the cola and fizzy drinks production process at the factory. This resulted in expenditure of $5 million on updating, repairing and replacing a significant amount of the machinery used in the production process.

As the level of production has increased, the company has expanded the number of warehouses it uses to store inventory. It now utilises 15 warehouses; some are owned by Milla and some are rented from third parties. There will be inventory counts taking place at all 15 of these sites at the year end.

A new accounting general ledger has been introduced at the beginning of the year, with the old and new systems being run in parallel for a period of two months. In addition, Milla has incurred expenditure of $4.5 million on developing a new brand of fizzy soft drinks. The company started this process in July 20X4 and is close to launching their new product into the market place.

As a result of the increase in revenue, Milla has recently recruited a new credit controller to chase outstanding receivables. The finance director thinks it is not necessary to continue to maintain an allowance for receivables and so has released the opening allowance of $1.5 million.

The finance director stated that there was a problem in April in the mixing of raw materials within the production process which resulted in a large batch of cola products tasting different. A number of these products were sold; however, due to complaints by customers about the flavour, no further sales of these goods have been made. No adjustment has been made to the valuation of the damaged inventory, which will still be held at cost of $1 million at the year end.

As in previous years, the management of Milla is due to be paid a significant annual bonus based on the value of year-end total assets.

Required:

(a) Explain audit risk and the components of audit risk. **(5 marks)**

(b) Using the minutes provided, identify and describe SEVEN audit risks, and explain the auditor's response to each risk, in planning the audit of Milla Cola Co. **(14 marks)**

(c) Identify the main areas, other than audit risks, which should be included within the audit strategy document for Milla Cola Co; and for each area provide an example relevant to the audit. **(4 marks)**

The finance director has requested that the deadline for the 20X6 audit be shortened by a month and has asked the audit engagement partner to consider if this will be possible. The partner has suggested that in order to meet this new tighter deadline the firm may carry out both an interim and final audit for the audit of Milla to 30 September 20X6.

Required:

(d)   Explain the difference between an interim and a final audit.   **(3 marks)**

(e)   Explain the procedures which are likely to be performed during an interim audit of Milla and the impact which it would have on the final audit.   **(4 marks)**

(Total: 30 marks)

2   BAGGIO

Baggio International Co (Baggio) is a manufacturer of electrical equipment. It has factories across the country and its customer base includes retailers as well as individuals, to whom direct sales are made through their website. The company's year-end is 30 September 20X5. You are an audit supervisor of Suarez & Co and are currently reviewing documentation of Baggio's internal control in preparation for the interim audit.

Baggio's website allows individuals to order goods directly, and full payment is taken in advance. Currently the website is not integrated into the inventory system and inventory levels are not checked at the time when orders are placed. Inventory is valued at the lower of cost and net realisable value.

Goods are despatched via local couriers; however, they do not always record customer signatures as proof that the customer has received the goods. Over the past 12 months there have been customer complaints about the delay between sales orders and receipt of goods. Baggio has investigated these and found that, in each case, the sales order had been entered into the sales system correctly but was not forwarded to the despatch department for fulfilling.

Baggio's retail customers undergo credit checks prior to being accepted and credit limits are set accordingly by sales ledger clerks. These customers place their orders through one of the sales team, who decides on sales discount levels.

Raw materials used in the manufacturing process are purchased from a wide range of suppliers. As a result of staff changes in the purchase ledger department, supplier statement reconciliations are no longer performed. Additionally, changes to supplier details in the purchase ledger master file can be undertaken by purchase ledger clerks as well as supervisors.

In the past six months, Baggio has changed part of its manufacturing process and as a result some new equipment has been purchased, however, there are considerable levels of plant and equipment which are now surplus to requirement. Purchase requisitions for all new equipment have been authorised by production supervisors and little has been done to reduce the surplus of old equipment.

Required:

(a) In respect of the internal control of Baggio International Co:

  (i) Identify and explain SIX deficiencies

  (ii) Recommend a control to address each of these deficiencies; and

  (iii) Describe a test of control Suarez & Co would perform to assess whether each of these controls, if implemented, is operating effectively.

  Note: The total marks will be split equally between each part.   **(18 marks)**

(b) Describe substantive procedures Suarez & Co should perform at the year end to confirm plant and equipment additions.   **(2 marks)**

(Total: 20 marks)

3 VIERI

Vieri Motor Cars Co (Vieri) manufactures a range of motor cars and its year end is 30 June 20X5. You are the audit supervisor of Rossi & Co and are currently preparing the audit programmes for the year-end audit of Vieri. You have had a meeting with your audit manager and he has notified you of the following issues identified during the audit risk assessment process:

Land and buildings

Vieri has a policy of revaluing land and buildings, this is undertaken on a rolling basis over a five-year period. During the year Vieri requested an external independent valuer to revalue a number of properties, including a warehouse purchased in January 20X5. Depreciation is charged on a pro rata basis.

Work in progress

Vieri undertakes continuous production of cars, 24 hours a day, seven days a week. An inventory count is to be undertaken at the year end and Rossi & Co will attend. You are responsible for the audit of work in progress (WIP) and will be part of the team attending the count as well as the final audit. WIP constitutes the partly assembled cars at the year end and this balance is likely to be material. Vieri values WIP according to percentage of completion, and standard costs are then applied to these percentages.

Required:

(a) Explain the factors Rossi & Co should consider when placing reliance on the work of the independent valuer.   **(5 marks)**

(b) Describe the substantive procedures the auditor should perform to obtain sufficient and appropriate audit evidence in relation to:

  (i) The revaluation of land and buildings and the recently purchased warehouse; and   **(6 marks)**

  (ii) The valuation of work in progress.   **(4 marks)**

(c)   During the audit, the team has identified an error in the valuation of work in progress, as a number of the assumptions contain out of date information. The directors of Vieri have indicated that they do not wish to amend the financial statements.

Required:

Explain the steps Rossi & Co should now take and the impact on the audit report in relation to the directors' refusal to amend the financial statements. (5 marks)

(Total: 20 marks)

SECTION A – Answers to Objective Test (OT) questions

1   D

Statement 1 – Partner has been in role for eight years, contravenes ACCA's Code of Ethics and Conduct and represents a familiarity threat.

Statement 3 – Providing internal audit services raises a self-review threat as it is likely that the audit team will be looking to place reliance on the internal control system reviewed by internal audit.

Statement 4 – This represents fees on a contingent basis and raises a self-interest threat as the audit firm's fee will rise if the company's profit after tax increases.

Statement 2 – Is not a threat to independence and therefore D is the correct answer.

2   A

If the engagement partner's son accepts the role and obtains shares in the company, it would constitute a self-interest threat but as the partner has already exceeded the seven-year relationship rule in line with ACCA's Code of Ethics and Conduct, the partner should be rotated off the audit irrespective of the decision made by her son. As Maldini is a listed company, an independent review partner should already be in place. It is unlikely that the firm needs to resign from the audit (due to stated circumstances) as the threats to objectivity can be mitigated.

Therefore option A is correct.

3   B

Statement 1 is inappropriate as the external and internal audit team should be separate and therefore consideration of the skills of the external audit team is not appropriate in the circumstances.

Statement 4 does not apply in that the timescale of the work is not relevant to consider the threats to objectivity.

Statement 2 and 3 are valid considerations – as per ACCA's Code of Ethics and Conduct providing internal audit services can result in the audit firm assuming a management role. To mitigate this, it is appropriate for the firm to assess whether management will take responsibility for implementing recommendations. Further, for a listed company the Code prohibits the provision of internal audit services which review a significant proportion of the internal controls over financial reporting as these may be relied upon by the external audit team and the self-review threat is too great.

Therefore option B is correct.

4   C

Internal audit are appointed by the audit committee (external audit usually by the shareholders) and it is the role of internal audit to review the effectiveness and efficiency of internal controls to improve operations. External audit looks at the operating effectiveness of internal controls on which they may rely for audit evidence and a by-product may be to comment on any deficiencies they have found but this is not a key function of the role.

Therefore statements 1 and 3 relate to internal audit.

The external auditor's report is publicly available to the shareholders of the company (internal audit reports are addressed to management/TCWG) and the external auditor provides an opinion on the truth and fairness of the financial statements.

Therefore statements 2 and 4 relate to external audit.

C is therefore the correct answer.

5   D

The proposal in relation to the fees is a contingent fee basis which is expressly prohibited by ACCA's Code of Ethics and Conduct and therefore the only viable option here is to reject the fee basis – D is therefore correct.

6   A

Depreciation should be calculated as:

Treadmills/exercise bikes = (18,000 + 17,000)/36 × 8 months =	7,778
Rowing machines/cross trainers = (9,750 + 11,000)/36 × 5 months =	2,882
	———
Total	10,660
	———

Therefore the correct answer is A and assets are currently understated as too much depreciation has currently been charged.

Option B is based on depreciation being applied for a full year instead of for the relevant months.

Option C is based on depreciation not being charged in the month of acquisition (i.e. seven and four months).

Option D is based on depreciation for the exercise bikes being divided by the three years instead of allocated on a monthly basis.

7   A

Test 4 is a test for existence and test 3 is for completeness. All other tests are relevant for valuation. Option A is correct.

8   B

While all procedures would be valid in the circumstances, only the written confirmation from the company's lawyers would allow the auditor to obtain an expert, third party confirmation on the likelihood of the case being successful. This would provide the auditor with the most reliable evidence in the circumstances. Therefore B is the correct answer.

9 D

As per ISA 505 External Confirmations, the evidence obtained from the trade receivables circularisation should be reliable as it is from an external source and the risk of management bias and influence is restricted due to the process being under the control of the auditor. Therefore 1 and 4 are benefits and option D is therefore correct.

Customers are not obliged to answer and often circularisations have a very low response rate. A circularisation will not provide evidence over the valuation assertion for receivables and therefore 2 and 3 are drawbacks of a circularisation.

10 B

A is incorrect as the balance with Laurel Co would need to be followed up due to the dispute.

C is incorrect as this represents a payment in transit and the payment would need to be agreed to post year-end bank statements – if the cash was received pre year end this would represent a cut-off issue as this should no longer be included in receivables.

D is incorrect as the sample chosen should be verified even if there is no response. As per ISA 505, the auditor should adopt alternative procedures.

Therefore B is the only statement which is true as this does represent a timing difference (invoice in transit) and should be agreed to a pre year-end invoice.

11 B

Addressee – sets out who the report is addressed to – usually the shareholders – and is there to clarify who can place reliance on the audit opinion. B is therefore the correct option.

12 D

Statement 1 is false as not all subsequent events will require an adjustment to the numbers within the financial statements. IAS 10 Events after the Reporting Period makes a distinction between an adjusting and non-adjusting event. Only material adjusting events would require an amendment to the figures within the financial statements.

Statement 2 is false as while a non-adjusting event would not require a change to the numbers within the financial statements, IAS 10 may require a disclosure to be made. If the non-adjusting event is material, non-disclosure could still result in a modification to the audit report.

Statement 3 is true as the auditor is required to carry out procedures up to the date of the audit report to gain sufficient appropriate audit evidence that all relevant subsequent events have been identified and dealt with appropriately. After the audit report is issued, the auditor does not need to actively look for subsequent events but is only required to respond to subsequent events which they become aware of.

Statement 4 is true as ISA 560 Subsequent Events requires the auditor to obtain written confirmation from management/those charged with governance that all subsequent events have been identified and dealt with in accordance with the appropriate reporting framework.

D is therefore correct.

13   C

The outstanding balance with Pirlo Co is likely to be irrecoverable as the customer is experiencing financial difficulties.

The balance is material at 7.4% of profit before tax and 2.5% of revenue.

Currently profit and assets are overstated by $285,000. Therefore the correct option is C.

14   A

Writing to the customer/agreeing to invoices, while valid procedures during the audit to verify the existence of an outstanding balance, would not allow the auditor to assess the recoverability of the balance which is the key issue in determining whether an adjustment is required. Therefore options 3 and 4 are incorrect.

Post year-end cash testing is the best way for the auditor to assess if the balance is recoverable wholly or in part and therefore the cash book should be reviewed for any receipts which will change the assessment of the debt after the year end. The issue should also be discussed with management to understand their reasons for not wanting to amend the financial statements as this may be due to a change in circumstances.

15   D

The debt with Pirlo Co should be provided for and is material to the financial statements at 7.4% of profit before tax and 2.5% of revenue. This represents a material misstatement which is material but not pervasive. As such, if no adjustment is made the auditor will be required to provide a qualified 'except for' opinion. If the required change is made, then no material misstatement exists and therefore the auditor will be able to issue an unmodified opinion.

SECTION B

1 MILLA

(a) Audit risk and its components

Audit risk is the risk that the auditor expresses an inappropriate audit opinion when the financial statements are materially misstated. Audit risk is a function of two main components being the risks of material misstatement and detection risk. Risk of material misstatement is made up of two components, inherent risk and control risk.

Inherent risk is the susceptibility of an assertion about a class of transaction, account balance or disclosure to a misstatement which could be material, either individually or when aggregated with other misstatements, before consideration of any related controls.

Control risk is the risk that a misstatement which could occur in an assertion about a class of transaction, account balance or disclosure and which could be material, either individually or when aggregated with other misstatements, will not be prevented, or detected and corrected, on a timely basis by the entity's internal control.

Detection risk is the risk that the procedures performed by the auditor to reduce audit risk to an acceptably low level will not detect a misstatement which exists and which could be material, either individually or when aggregated with other misstatements. Detection risk is affected by sampling and non-sampling risk.

(b) Audit risks and responses

Audit risk	Auditor response
Milla has incurred $5m on updating, repairing and replacing a significant amount of the production process machinery. If this expenditure is of a capital nature, it should be capitalised as part of property, plant and equipment (PPE) in line with IAS 16 Property, Plant and Equipment. However, if it relates more to repairs, then it should be expensed to the statement of profit or loss. If the expenditure is not correctly classified, profit and PPE could be under or overstated.	The auditor should review a breakdown of these costs to ascertain the split of capital and revenue expenditure, and further testing should be undertaken to ensure that the classification in the financial statements is correct.

At the year-end there will be inventory counts undertaken in all 15 warehouses. It is unlikely that the auditor will be able to attend all 15 inventory counts and therefore they need to ensure that they obtain sufficient appropriate audit evidence over the inventory counting controls, and completeness and existence of inventory for any warehouses not visited.	The auditor should assess which of the inventory sites they will attend the counts for. This will be any with material inventory or which have a history of significant errors. For those not visited, the auditor will need to review the level of exceptions noted during the count and discuss with management any issues which arose during the count.
Inventory is stored within 15 warehouses; some are owned by Milla and some rented from third parties. Only warehouses owned by Milla should be included within PPE. There is a risk of overstatement of PPE and understatement of rental expenses if Milla has capitalised all 15 warehouses.	The auditor should review supporting documentation for all warehouses included within PPE to confirm ownership by Milla and to ensure non-current assets are not overstated.
A new accounting general ledger system has been introduced at the beginning of the year and the old system was run in parallel for two months. There is a risk of opening balances being misstated and loss of data if they have not been transferred from the old system correctly.	The auditor should undertake detailed testing to confirm that all opening balances have been correctly recorded in the new accounting general ledger system.
In addition, the new accounting general ledger system will require documenting and the controls over this will need to be tested.	They should document and test the new system. They should review any management reports run comparing the old and new system during the parallel run to identify any issues with the processing of accounting information.
Milla has incurred expenditure of $4.5 million on developing a new brand of fizzy drink. This expenditure is research and development under IAS 38 Intangible Assets. The standard requires research costs to be expensed and development costs to be capitalised as an intangible asset. If Milla has incorrectly classified research costs as development expenditure, there is a risk the intangible asset could be overstated and expenses understated.	Obtain a breakdown of the expenditure and undertake testing to determine whether the costs relate to the research or development stage. Discuss the accounting treatment with the finance director and ensure it is in accordance with IAS 38.

The finance director of Milla has decided to release the opening balance of $1.5 million for allowance for receivables as he feels it is unnecessary. There is a risk that receivables will be overvalued, as despite having a credit controller, some balances will be irrecoverable and so will be overstated if not provided against. In addition, due to the damaged inventory there is an increased risk of customers refusing to make payments in full.	Extended post year-end cash receipts testing and a review of the aged receivables ledger to be performed to assess valuation and the need for an allowance for receivables. Discuss with the director the rationale for releasing the $1.5m opening allowance for receivables.
A large batch of cola products has been damaged in the production process and will be in inventory at the year end. No adjustment has been made by management. The valuation of inventory as per IAS 2 Inventories should be at the lower of cost and net realisable value. Hence it is likely that this inventory is overvalued.	Detailed cost and net realisable value testing to be performed to assess how much the inventory requires writing down by.
Due to the damaged cola products, a number of customers have complained. It is likely that for any of the damaged goods sold, Milla will need to refund these customers. Revenue is possibly overstated if the sales returns are not completely and accurately recorded.	Review the breakdown of sales of damaged goods, and ensure that they have been accurately removed from revenue.
The management of Milla receives a significant annual bonus based on the value of year-end total assets. There is a risk that management might feel under pressure to overstate the value of assets through the judgements taken or through the use of releasing provisions.	Throughout the audit, the team will need to be alert to this risk. They will need to maintain professional scepticism and carefully review judgemental decisions and compare treatment against prior years.

(c)   **Audit strategy document**

The audit strategy sets out the scope, timing and direction of the audit and helps the development of the audit plan. It should consider the following main areas:

It should identify the main characteristics of the engagement which define its scope. For Milla it should consider the following:

- Whether the financial information to be audited has been prepared in accordance with IFRS.
- To what extent audit evidence obtained in previous audits for Milla will be utilised.
- Whether computer-assisted audit techniques will be used and the effect of IT on audit procedures.
- The availability of key personnel at Milla.

It should ascertain the reporting objectives of the engagement to plan the timing of the audit and the nature of the communications required, such as:

- The audit timetable for reporting and whether there will be an interim as well as final audit.
- Organisation of meetings with Milla's management to discuss any audit issues arising.
- Location of the 15 inventory counts.
- Any discussions with management regarding the reports to be issued.
- The timings of the audit team meetings and review of work performed.
- If there are any expected communications with third parties.

The strategy should consider the factors which, in the auditor's professional judgement, are significant in directing Milla's audit team's efforts, such as:

- The determination of materiality for the audit.
- The need to maintain a questioning mind and to exercise professional scepticism in gathering and evaluating audit evidence.

It should consider the results of preliminary audit planning activities and, where applicable, whether knowledge gained on other engagements for Milla is relevant, such as:

- Results of previous audits and the results of any tests over the effectiveness of internal controls.
- Evidence of management's commitment to the design, implementation and maintenance of sound internal control.
- Volume of transactions, which may determine whether it is more efficient for the audit team to rely on internal control.
- Significant business developments affecting Milla, such as the change in the accounting system and the significant expenditure on an overhaul of the factory.

The audit strategy should ascertain the nature, timing and extent of resources necessary to perform the audit, such as:

- The selection of the audit team with experience of this type of industry.
- Assignment of audit work to the team members.
- Setting the audit budget.

Tutorial note

The answer is longer than required for four marks but represents a teaching aid.

(d) **Differences between an interim and a final audit**

Interim audit

The interim audit is that part of the audit which takes place before the year end. The auditor uses the interim audit to carry out procedures which would be difficult to perform at the year end because of time pressure. There is no requirement to undertake an interim audit; factors to consider when deciding upon whether to have one include the size and complexity of the company along with the effectiveness of internal controls.

Final audit

The final audit will take place after the year end and concludes with the auditor forming and expressing an opinion on the financial statements for the whole year subject to audit. It is important to note that the final opinion takes account of conclusions formed at both the interim and final audit.

(e) Procedures which could be undertaken during the interim audit include:

- Review and updating of the documentation of accounting systems at Milla.
- Discussions with management on the recent growth and any other changes within the business which have occurred during the year to date at Milla to update the auditor's understanding of the company.
- Assessment of risks which will impact the final audit of Milla.
- Undertake tests of controls on Milla's key transaction cycles of sales, purchases and inventory, and credit control.
- Perform substantive procedures on profit and loss transactions for the year to date and any other completed material transactions.

Impact of interim audit on final

If an interim audit is undertaken at Milla, then it will have an impact on the final audit and the extent of work undertaken after the year end. First, as some testing has already been undertaken, there will be less work to be performed at the final audit, which may result in a shorter audit and audited financial statements possibly being available earlier. The outcome of the controls testing undertaken during the interim audit will impact the level of substantive testing to be undertaken. If the controls tested have proven to be operating effectively, then the auditor may be able to reduce the level of detailed substantive testing required as they will be able to place reliance on the controls. In addition, if substantive procedures were undertaken at the interim audit, then only the period from the interim audit to the year-end will require to be tested.

	Marking scheme		Marks
(a)	**Component of audit risk**		
	Explanation of audit risk		2
	Explanation of components of audit risk: Inherent, control and detection risk		3
(b)	**Audit risks and responses** (only 7 risks required)		
	$5 million expenditure on production process		2
	Inventory counts at 15 warehouses at year end		2
	Treatment of owned v third party warehouses		2
	New general ledger system introduced at the beginning of the year		2
	Release of opening provision for allowance for receivables		2
	Research and development expenditure		2
	Damaged inventory		2
	Sales returns		2
	Management bonus based on asset values		2
		Maximum	14
(c)	**Audit strategy document**		
	Main characteristics of the audit		1
	Reporting objectives of the audit and nature of communications required		1
	Factors which are significant in directing the audit team's efforts		1
	Results of preliminary engagement activities and whether knowledge gained on other engagements is relevant		1
	Nature, timing and extent of resources necessary to perform the audit		1
		Maximum	4
(d)	**Difference between interim and final audit**		
	Interim audit		2
	Final audit		2
		Maximum	3
(e)	**Procedures/impact of interim audit on final audit**		
	Example procedures		3
	Impact on final audit		3
		Maximum	4
Total			**30**

2   BAGGIO

(a)   Baggio International's (Baggio) internal control

Deficiency	Control recommendations	Test of control
Currently the website is not integrated into the inventory system.

This can result in Baggio accepting customer orders when they do not have the goods in inventory. This can cause them to lose sales and customer goodwill | The website should be updated to include an interface into the inventory system; this should check inventory levels and only process orders if adequate inventory is held.

If inventory is out of stock, this should appear on the website with an approximate waiting time. | Test data could be used to attempt to process orders via the website for items which are not currently held in inventory.

The orders should be flagged as being out of stock and indicate an approximate waiting time. |

Deficiency	Control recommendations	Test of control
For goods despatched by local couriers, customer signatures are not always obtained. This can lead to customers falsely claiming that they have not received their goods. Baggio would not be able to prove that they had in fact despatched the goods and may result in goods being despatched twice.	Baggio should remind all local couriers that customer signatures must be obtained as proof of delivery and payment will not be made for any despatches with missing signatures.	Select a sample of despatches by couriers and ask Baggio for proof of delivery by viewing customer signatures.
There have been a number of situations where the sales orders have not been fulfilled in a timely manner. This can lead to a loss of customer goodwill and if it persists will damage the reputation of Baggio as a reliable supplier.	Once goods are despatched, they should be matched to sales orders and flagged as fulfilled. The system should automatically flag any outstanding sales orders past a predetermined period, such as five days. This report should be reviewed by a responsible official.	Review the report of outstanding sales orders. If significant, discuss with a responsible official to understand why there is still a significant time period between sales order and despatch date. Select a sample of sales orders and compare the date of order to the goods despatch date to ascertain whether this is within the acceptable predetermined period.
Customer credit limits are set by sales ledger clerks. Sales ledger clerks are not sufficiently senior and so may set limits too high, leading to irrecoverable debts, or too low, leading to a loss of revenue.	Credit limits should be set by a senior member of the sales ledger department and not by sales ledger clerks. These limits should be regularly reviewed by a responsible official.	For a sample of new customers accepted in the year, review the authorisation of the credit limit, and ensure that this was performed by a responsible official. Enquire of sales ledger clerks as to who can set credit limits.

Deficiency	Control recommendations	Test of control
Sales discounts are set by Baggio's sales team. In order to boost their sales, members of the sales team may set the discounts too high, leading to a loss of revenue.	All members of the sales team should be given authority to grant sales discounts up to a set limit. Any sales discounts above these limits should be authorised by sales area managers or the sales director. Regular review of sales discount levels should be undertaken by the sales director, and this review should be evidenced.	Discuss with members of the sales team the process for setting sales discounts. Review the sales discount report for evidence of review by the sales director.
Supplier statement reconciliations are no longer performed. This may result in errors in the recording of purchases and payables not being identified in a timely manner.	Supplier statement reconciliations should be performed on a monthly basis for all suppliers and these should be reviewed by a responsible official.	Review the file of reconciliations to ensure that they are being performed on a regular basis and that they have been reviewed by a responsible official.
Changes to supplier details in the purchase ledger master file can be undertaken by purchase ledger clerks. This could lead to key supplier data being accidently amended or fictitious suppliers being set up, which can increase the risk of fraud.	Only purchase ledger supervisors should have the authority to make changes to master file data. This should be controlled via passwords. Regular review of any changes to master file data by a responsible official and this review should be evidenced.	Request a purchase ledger clerk to attempt to access the master file and to make an amendment; the system should not allow this. Review a report of master data changes and review the authority of those making amendments.
Baggio has considerable levels of surplus plant and equipment. Surplus unused plant is at risk of theft. In addition, if the surplus plant is not disposed of, then the company could lose sundry income.	Regular review of the plant and equipment on the factory floor by senior factory personnel to identify any old or surplus equipment. As part of the capital expenditure process, there should be a requirement to confirm the treatment of the equipment being replaced.	Observe the review process by senior factory personnel, identifying the treatment of any old equipment. Review processed capital expenditure forms to ascertain if the treatment of replaced equipment is as stated.

Deficiency	Control recommendations	Test of control
Purchase requisitions are authorised by production supervisors. Production supervisors are not sufficiently independent or senior to authorise capital expenditure.	Capital expenditure authorisation levels to be established. Production supervisors should only be able to authorise low value items, any high value items should be authorised by the board.	Review a sample of authorised capital expenditure forms and identify if the correct signatory has authorised them.

(b)   Substantive procedures – additions

- Obtain a breakdown of additions, cast the list and agree to the non-current asset register to confirm completeness of plant and equipment (P&E).

- Select a sample of additions and agree cost to supplier invoice to confirm valuation.

- Verify rights and obligations by agreeing the addition of plant and equipment to a supplier invoice in the name of Baggio.

- Review the list of additions and confirm that they relate to capital expenditure items rather than repairs and maintenance.

- Review board minutes to ensure that significant capital expenditure purchases have been authorised by the board.

- For a sample of additions recorded in P&E, physically verify them on the factory floor to confirm existence.

	Marking scheme	Marks
(a)	**Control deficiencies, recommendations and tests of controls** (only 6 issues required)	
	Website not integrated into inventory system	3
	Customer signatures	3
	Unfulfilled sales orders	3
	Customer credit limits	3
	Sales discounts	3
	Supplier statement reconciliations	3
	Purchase ledger master file	3
	Surplus plant and equipment	3
	Authorisation of capital expenditure	3
	Maximum	**18**
(b)	**Substantive procedures for PPE**	
	Cast list of additions and agree to non-current asset register	1
	Vouch cost to recent supplier invoice	1
	Agree addition to a supplier invoice in the name of Baggio to confirm rights and obligations	1
	Review additions and confirm capital expenditure items rather than repairs and maintenance	1
	Review board minutes to ensure authorised by the board	1
	Physically verify them on the factory floor to confirm existence	1
	Other	
	Maximum	**2**
Total		**20**

3   VIERA

(a)   Reliance on the work of an independent valuer

ISA 500 Audit Evidence requires auditors to evaluate the competence, capabilities including expertise and objectivity of a management expert. This would include consideration of the qualifications of the valuer and assessment of whether they were members of any professional body or industry association.

The expert's independence should be ascertained, with potential threats such as undue reliance on Vieri Motor Cars Co (Vieri) or a self-interest threat such as share ownership considered.

In addition, Rossi & Co should meet with the expert and discuss with them their relevant expertise, in particular whether they have valued similar land and buildings to those of Vieri in the past. Rossi & Co should also consider whether the valuer understands the accounting requirements of IAS 16 Property, Plant and Equipment in relation to valuations.

The valuation should then be evaluated. The assumptions used should be carefully reviewed and compared to previous revaluations at Vieri. These assumptions should be discussed with both management and the valuer to understand the basis of any valuations.

(b)   (i)   Substantive procedures for land and buildings

- Obtain a schedule of land and buildings revalued this year and cast to confirm completeness and accuracy of the revaluation adjustment.

- On a sample basis, agree the revalued amounts to the valuation statement provided by the valuer.

- Agree the revalued amounts for these assets are included correctly in the non-current assets register.

- Recalculate the total revaluation adjustment and agree correctly recorded in the revaluation surplus.

- Agree the initial cost for the warehouse addition to supporting documentation such as invoices to confirm cost.

- Confirm through a review of the title deeds that the warehouse is owned by Vieri.

- Recalculate the depreciation charge for the year to ensure that for assets revalued during the year, the depreciation was based on the correct valuation and for the warehouse addition that the charge was for six months only.

- Review the financial statements disclosures of the revaluation to ensure they comply with IAS 16 Property, Plant and Equipment.

(ii)   Substantive procedures for work in progress (WIP)

- Prior to attending the inventory count, discuss with management how the percentage completions are attributed to the WIP, for example, is this based on motor cars passing certain points in the production process?

- During the count, observe the procedures carried out by Vieri staff in assessing the level of WIP and consider the reasonableness of the assumptions used.

- Agree for a sample that the percentage completions assessed during the count are in accordance with Vieri's policies communicated prior to the count.

- Discuss with management the basis of the standard costs applied to the percentage completion of WIP, and how often these are reviewed and updated.

- Review the level of variances between standard and actual costs and discuss with management how these are treated.

- Obtain a breakdown of the standard costs and agree a sample of these costs to actual invoices or payroll records to assess their reasonableness.

- Cast the schedule of total WIP and agree to the trial balance and financial statements.

- Agree sample of WIP assessed during the count to the WIP schedule, agree percentage completion is correct and recalculate the inventory valuation.

(c) **Audit report**

Discuss with the management of Vieri why they are refusing to make the amendment to WIP.

Assess the materiality of the error; if immaterial, it should be added to the schedule of unadjusted differences. The auditor should then assess whether this error results in the total of unadjusted differences becoming material; if so, this should be discussed with management; if not, there would be no impact on the audit report.

If the error is material and management refuses to amend the financial statements, then the audit report will need to be modified. It is unlikely that any error would be pervasive as although WIP in total is material, it would not have a pervasive effect on the financial statements as a whole. As management has not complied with IAS 2 Inventories and if the error is material but not pervasive, then a qualified opinion would be necessary.

A basis for qualified opinion paragraph would need to be included before the opinion paragraph. This would explain the material misstatement in relation to the valuation of WIP and the effect on the financial statements. The opinion paragraph would be qualified 'except for'.

Marking scheme

			Marks
(a)	**Reliance on independent valuer**		
	ISA 500 requires consideration of competence and capabilities of expert		1
	Consider if member of professional body or industry association		1
	Assess independence		1
	Assess whether relevant expertise of type of properties as Vieri Motor Cars		1
	Evaluate assumptions		1

(b) **(i)** **Substantive procedures for revaluation of land and buildings**

- Cast schedule of land and buildings revalued this year — 1
- Agree the revalued amounts to the valuation statement provided by the valuer — 1
- Agree the revalued amounts included correctly in the non-current assets register — 1
- Recalculate the total revaluation adjustment and agree recorded in the revaluation surplus — 1
- Agree the initial cost for the warehouse to invoices to confirm cost — 1
- Confirm through title deeds that the warehouse is owned by Vieri — 1
- Recalculate the depreciation charge for the year — 1
- Review the financial statements disclosures for compliance with IAS 16 Property, Plant and Equipment — 1
- Other

Maximum 6

(ii) **Substantive procedures for work in progress (WIP)**

- Discuss with management how the percentage completions are attributed to WIP — 1
- Observe the procedures carried out in the count in assessing the level of WIP; consider reasonableness of the assumptions used — 1
- During the count, agree a sample of percentage completions are in accordance with Vieri's policies — 1
- Discuss with management the basis of the standard costs — 1
- Review the level of variances between standard and actual costs — 1
- Obtain a breakdown of the standard costs and agree a sample of these costs to actual invoices — 1
- Cast the schedule of total WIP and agree to the trial balance and financial statements — 1
- Agree sample of WIP assessed during the count to the WIP schedule, agree percentage completion is correct and recalculate the inventory valuation — 1
- Other

Maximum 4

(c)	**Impact on audit report**		
	Discuss with management reasons for non-amendment		1
	Assess materiality		1
	Immaterial – schedule of uncorrected adjustments		1
	Material not pervasive – qualified opinion		1
	Basis for qualified opinion paragraph		1
	Opinion paragraph – qualified 'except for'		1
		Maximum	**5**
Total			**20**